Frontiers of Globalization

FRONTIERS OF GLOBALIZATION: KINSHIP AND FAMILY STRUCTURES IN AFRICA

EDITED BY
Ana Marta González
Laurie DeRose
and Florence Oloo

AFRICA WORLD PRESS
TRENTON | LONDON | CAPE TOWN | NAIROBI | ADDIS ABABA | ASMARA | IBADAN

AFRICA WORLD PRESS
541 West Ingham Avenue | Suite B
Trenton, New Jersey 08638

‹ STI ›

Social Trends Institute
NEW YORK · BARCELONA

Copyright © 2011 Ana Marta González, Laurie DeRose, & Florence Oloo
First Printing 2011

Book and cover design: Saverance Publishing Services
Cover photo courtesy of Toyin Falola

Library of Congress Cataloging-in-Publication Data

Frontiers of globalization : kinship and family structures in Africa / edited by Ana Marta González, Laurie DeRose, and Florence Oloo.
    p. cm.
Includes bibliographical references and index.
ISBN 1-59221-771-0 (cloth : alk. paper) -- ISBN 1-59221-772-9 (pbk. : alk. paper)
1. Families--Africa. 2. Africa--Social conditions--21st century. 3. Globalization--Africa. I. González, Ana Marta, 1969- II. DeRose, Laurie Fields, 1968- III. Oloo, Florence.
HQ691.F76 2010
306.850967--dc22
                    2010038844

Table of Contents

Acknowledgements

The editors would especially like to thank Katherine Semler, Christa Byker, and Lynden Parry for their incredible patience and diligence in both organizing the conference from which these papers spring as well as helping to keep track of the various administrative tasks required for the eventual publication of this volume. We would also like to thank James Brown and Craig Iffland for their assistance in editing. Angela Ajayi and Kassahun Checole of Africa World Press ought to be mentioned for their patience and helpfulness in bringing the manuscript to publication as well as their editorial support. For all those that participated in the 2008 STI Experts Meeting, "Frontiers of Globalization," we extend our utmost gratitude for helping to craft the eventual volume. Most of all we would like to thank Carlos Cavallé and the Social Trends Institute for their institutional and financial support in carrying out the present project.

A Note on the Social Trends Institute

We live in a world subject to rapid transformations. Underlying these broad social changes, however, it is possible to identify specific social and cultural trends, which affect people and institutions alike. The Social Trends Institute (www.socialtrendsinstitute.org) is a non-profit research center that offers institutional and financial support to academics of all fields who seek to make sense of emerging social trends and their effects on human communities.

STI focuses its research on four subject areas: Family, Bioethics, Culture and Lifestyles and Corporate Governance. STI organizes Experts Meetings, which bring together various scholars to present and discuss each other's original research in an academic forum. These meetings are not open to the public and are intended to foster open intellectual dialogue between scholars from all over the world, of various academic backgrounds, disciplines and beliefs. At times, STI helps to publish a collection of the conference papers in a single volume, revised and reviewed in light of the meeting's discussion.

STI's sole aim is to promote research and scholarship of the highest academic standards. In so doing, we hope to make a scholarly contribution towards understanding the varying and complex social trends that are intertwined with the modern world. We are committed, then, to that which makes such scholarship possible: intellectual freedom, openness to a diversity of viewpoints and a shared commitment to serve our common humanity.

Preface

Abena P.A. Busia

FAMILY CHANGE IN AFRICA

We have survived it all;
Wrong definition, self-definition, re-definition,
Crack–up,
Break-up, make up, break-down, re-make,
Translate, re-assemble and re-define again—

stretched and strained.

The original global village transported
We made the modern world
At the moment of our collective un-making;
Fragmented, racinated, detribalized,
Searching another kind of freedom—

stretched and strained.

We search for ties to:
Reassemble definitions and re-define assemblages—
Patrifocal, matrilineal, tribalistic,
Matrifocal, patriarchal, westernized;
None of the above, all of the above—

stretched and strained.

In new urban spaces we re-invent ourselves
And scandalize the neighbors;
In Kaduna and Bamako,
And from Paris to New London
We re-conceive peer-groups, sex roles, community,
And rites now taboo—

stretched and strained.

From shebeens to shanty towns
And High Courts to World Assemblies
We reformulate codes, and reform the Law;
Reconceiving family ties, kinship, community
And those tribes now taboo—

stretched and strained.

What concepts:
Polygynous, polyandrous, poly-amorous,
Just too much sex,
Masculine, feminine, transgender,
Just too many children—

stretched and strained.

Rethink gender, Rethink power,
Consider gender power—
Consider gender, Consider power,
Rethink gender power:
Transnational, intergenerational, globalized—

stretched and strained.

But not Broken.
Stretched and strained but not broken;
Towards a different kind of freedom.

– Accra, August 2009

Introduction

There is no question that globalization has a significant impact on Africa. Yet, the nature of this impact is not homogeneous, not only because globalization is a complex process—involving both structural and cultural changes—but also because of African diversity. Most African nations have high levels of cultural and linguistic diversity that offer them a rich array of possibilities. Nation building has therefore faced the challenges of integrating multicultural traditions with globalization. By choosing to focus on the impact of globalization on African Family Structures, the Social Trends Institute has tried to contribute to the understanding of a crucial aspect of global social change.

Family structures—to use the language of sociologists—or kinship—to use the language of anthropologists—both affect and are affected by changes stimulated by a global economy and the cultural ideals disseminated by global media. Clarifying the way in which these influences work is not an easy task, and yet it is a pre-condition for understanding the direction of social change. This understanding, in turn, is key for the African people to be in a better position to effectively govern themselves amidst the somewhat complex social changes prompted by globalization. It is argued that solutions to problems that currently plague the continent must proceed from the understanding of local capacities such as the role of indigenous knowledge in promoting sustainable development. This can be achieved by integrating indigenous knowledge into the formal education systems. This integration can help address some of the knowledge deficiencies of development that is mainly formulated from a western perspective.

Social change is always Janus-faced. It involves both gains and sacrifices. Governing social change requires one to know what one is renouncing and/or gaining in choosing a certain path. In just over a century, rapid changes and ways of life have been witnessed on a scale unknown in sub-Saharan African. This naturally brought with it unprecedented challenges in adapting to these changes. From this perspective, the present volume is just a modest contribution to the self-reflection necessary to discriminate the positive and the negative aspects of social change. What should count as positive and negative social change, in a given situation, can only be determined by each African community in light of *both* universal moral principles and particular African traditions.

The contributions collected in this volume combine general views of African family structures and specific studies of particular communities or countries. These contributions are founded on a number of different perspectives: law, sociology, anthropology, literature, political science, and demography. The multidisciplinary approach, along with the discussion it stimulates, has proved a useful way to appreciate the complexity of the issue.

In this regard, it is opportune to note that throughout the discussions it became clear that methodological problems very often involve substantive positions. We must not forget the words of Thomas Hobbes "knowledge is power," which stand at the beginning of modern philosophy. The way that modern science has developed has a lot to do with this sentence. In modern science the scientist determines the scope and limits of the object. This means that depending on what you are interested in, the object you frame, you will get one image or another of reality. With these assumptions as a backdrop, it is no surprise that social sciences have often been considered a western way of imposing western interests upon others. Confronted with this critique, a natural reaction has been to give voice to others, and other different ways of approaching reality: hence, for instance, the relevance of art and literature.

Yet, the epistemological challenge is still present. Perhaps, in analyzing the impact of globalization on African family structures this challenge is particularly obvious. As suggested above, a possible way to approach this challenge is by recognizing the plurality of methodologies and the limits and scope of each one of them. While we keep working from our different perspectives, we have to cultivate a philosophical attitude which enables us to relativize our findings and complement them with others, being more inclusive of the experience of others and, at the same time, not absolutizing those experiences. We have to find a way to integrate first person perspective—as recorded by art or literature—and third person perspective, as developed by social science.

Another topic that is implicit in the discussion is the connection between universalism and westernization. This connection is tricky, especially when we come down to the discussion of human rights. Indeed, if we are only to recognize human rights according to cultural criteria of socialization we miss the whole point of human rights: that their very existence depends on nobody defining who is worthy of them. Among human rights we would like to emphasize is the one Hannah Arendt referred to: the human right to be a citizen and therefore to have full civil rights.

While there are different cultural ways of realizing humanity, humanity most certainly involves recognition of universal human rights. It is obvious that this two-fold dimension brings some tensions within every culture. Relativizing human rights as a product of Western civilization would be a poor way to approach non-western cultures. It seems more appropriate to discover the ways in which every culture develops its own articulation of the demands of humanity. Cultural diversity indeed reflects the reasonable ways in which individuals and communities have enshrined basic human goods in their lives. The importance of culture cannot be overstated. It impacts our understanding of others. "In Africa you do not count people." This strikes us as a way of stressing that human beings do not merely have value, but rather dignity–as Kant would put it.

On the other hand, it is true that the development of a civil society, understood as a social space beyond the social bonds of family and kinship, in which modern economic life built on a strong Western competitive individualism is supposed to develop, has not been easy to achieve within the African contexts with its strong tendencies to cooperative communalism. Whether we can speak of an African civil society or not is still an open question. If we can, it is certainly not similar to modern European civil society.

In Africa we discover many unsolved tensions between traditional and modern ways of life. Particularly pressing is the question of whether we are able to protect individual human rights without eroding the traditional African web of relationships modeled on kinship; and also which kind of ethical notions are able to permeate a modern social life without inflicting violence on African culture. Two big issues emerge in this regard. First, the way we approach the distinction between the public and the private spheres, and related to this is whether in order to speak of civil society we need to transfer the weight from kinship to a mononuclear conception of the family. Second, the way we understand the role of religion in civil society.

It seems that we have to work on recognizing the universal elements within particular cultures and institutions and then on how to articulate those universal elements in ways that are respectful of differences. There is no easy way to do this. While we learn to understand the implicit script of every culture, we have to engage in a philosophical reflection on what families are. In absence of that reflection, people in search of certitude switch directly to religion. And religion without rational mediation could be dangerous.

This volume begins with an overview of family change in Africa by Erdmute Alber and Astrid Bochow. They highlight how in Africa, as everywhere, family change includes co-existence of old, persistent family forms together with newly evolved ones. The authors draw parallels between family change in Africa and elsewhere as well as calling attention to distinctly African elements of family change. Most notably, polygyny has been more persistent both officially and unofficially in Africa than elsewhere. The rise of the nuclear family in some (especially urban) parts of Africa has not undermined traditional understandings of children belonging first to their lineages and secondarily to their immediate parents.

An overview of family change on such a vast continent is obviously too large a task for a single chapter. Alber and Bochow limit the scope of their work by first focusing on West Africa and then in a more provocative way by analyzing scholarly discourse on family change to give attention to both the questions and answers that (primarily) outsiders have brought to the study of African families. As such, they walk us through the colonial period with its influences from governments and missionaries, the 1940s and 1950s with a structural functionalist lens, the 1960s from a modernization perspective, the rise of neo-Marxism and gender studies in the 1970s and 1980s, and finally "new kinship" studies in the 1990s that were inspired more by technological change outside of Africa than anything else. Their section describing new kinship studies brings out more than just a new lens for viewing African families, it contains concrete examples of ways that globalization is infiltrating traditional family practices (e.g., money and weapons being incorporated into exchange cycles that include bride price). They then turn from this brief history to a discussion of the family under global influences. Globalization seems to be reaching further into the African continent than earlier changes from the outside did. They highlight how current changes are reaching into the countryside rather than being confined to more "modern" (urban and more educated) segments of society. They also describe constructionist research that focuses on the fluidity and negotiability of kinship —a perspective that would have left earlier studies better informed but that has become indispensable during an era of increasing influence from the outside.

The kinship section of our volume includes two essays: one on kinship in Nigeria by Daniel Jordan Smith and one on change in the lives of children by Erdmute Alber. Smith emphasizes, in contrast to a modernization paradigm, that kinship systems "remain pivotal for how African people navigate the contemporary world." He does not ignore forces that could lead to more homogeneous cultures and societies, but documents how the Igbo-speaking people of southeastern Nigeria are adapting to outside changes using resources from kinship networks. In particular, he describes how kinship networks can increase access to "modern goods," especially education. He maintains that given the difficulties of living up to traditional obligations in a globalizing economy, "kinship is at once people's biggest problem and their most important resource."

The forces of globalization that manifest and impact marriage and family in Smith's Nigerian setting are hardly unique: economic diversification, labor migration, urbanization, education, and religious conversion. While not at all claiming that other African peoples would respond in the same way to these forces, Smith nonetheless builds a convincing case that traditional kinship resources are more likely to be used than abandoned by people and families making their way in an increasingly global world. Similarly, he describes a profound change with the emergence of romantic love as the preferred basis for the conjugal bond, but simultaneously describes how these new marriages are not as independent of kin influences as the new ideal and its surrounding discourse might indicate. Using the same framework, he explains the slow pace of fertility decline among the Igbo. Smith's explanations have some of the same flavor as earlier descriptions of the socio-cultural supports for high fertility in West Africa (e.g., Caldwell and Caldwell 1987), but are nonetheless distinct: he does not simply describe forces of modernization eroding socio-cultural supports for high fertility, but rather a dynamic interaction where the old and the new are both retained to some degree because they are both valuable. His work also contributes to the existing literature in its anthropological detail. As he notes, the ways in which competing pressures unfold in the lives of people undergoing marital and fertility transitions are generally not well documented. Smith's chapter also includes discussion of how these changes are influencing gender dynamics now and might do so in the future. As such, it provides an important complement to the chapters we included in the gender section of our volume.

Erdmute Alber's paper, "Child Trafficking in West Africa?," explores the images of childhood in the anti-child-trafficking campaigns in West Africa—particularly in the Republic of Benin—showing that the definitions of child-trafficking found in those campaigns do not arise from local conceptualizations of the problem, but are rather framed by globally recognized UN conventions. Yet, insofar as the idea of childhood implicit to those conventions is often in contrast to the changing conceptions of childhood found in those countries, the reception by local populations to those conventions can result in the stigmatization of local practices. Alber makes note of one such practice—that of young girls working as housemaids—which expresses both the contrast between local and international understandings of childhood and how the language of international condemnations of child trafficking can serve to stigmatize a widely accepted practice. The importance of this example is heightened when one takes into account that at precisely the same time that the demand for housemaids is increasing, and while the girls employed as housemaids do not see themselves in the least bit as being "trafficked children," the practice is viewed as incompatible with international standards and hence morally dubious. In light of this example, Alber concludes that we should consider replacing such uncritical talk of human trafficking by a serious analysis of the causes of the precarious nature of the African labor market.

The section on institutional change contains three essays that often overlap with other themes, but most notably with the question of gender. Leslie Bank challenges the idea that matrifocal families in South Africa are a pathological response to globalization. Instead, he locates their existence in South Africa's history and their current poverty as a result of structural change. Bank describes matrifocal households as emerging in the 1930s (despite social criticism) and having an upwardly mobile class position during the economic boom years of the 1950s. Apartheid urban planning changed this position dramatically and many of these households were moved into far less desirable locations. Apartheid era laws also shut down many home-based enterprises, thus effectively discriminating against women. Bank argues that these households have recently lost further as thousands of women's jobs have been lost in the textile sector due to global competition. Female-headed households in contemporary South Africa suffer disproportionately from unemployment and poverty. Bank's chapter should be of interest to many with no specific interest in either matrifocality or South Africa because it stands as an excellent example of how to bring literatures on economic change, race, and gender together in order to understand the impact of globalization. Those with an interest in South Africa or in historical gender studies will appreciate Bank's attention to apartheid as a patriarchical and not just a race project.

Paloma Durán describes how the United Nations has sought to protect human rights related to marriage and family, starting with the Universal Declaration of Human Rights of 1948. She explains how this legislation was intended to legally protect the freedom to initiate a life project between two people. We know from Smith's contribution to this volume that this concept of marriage is currently emergent among young Igbos (whereas their parents had considered marriage more of a contract between lineages). Clearly, some of the legislation she covers does not automatically map onto African social reality, but Durán acknowledges this. She also discusses rights of individuals within families, particularly children, the right to family reunification, and the right to consensual marriage. She also reviews activity by the Organization for African Unity and the African Commission on Rights.

Susanna Wing's treatment of family law reform in West Africa provides a more on-the-ground perspective. Wing acknowledges that globalization has created pressure for legal change, but questions whether these changes reach the intended recipients. She describes how difficult it is for individuals in West Africa—particularly women—to access their legal entitlements. Some of the opposition is from conservative religious leaders. Further, it is not surprising to outsiders that many illiterate rural dwellers are not aware of legal rights. What is more surprising is that formal courts sometimes rule in favor of tradition rather than law (e.g., not allowing women to inherit land). These conservative arguments (in favor of tradition) are often framed in terms of cultural survival in the face of Western-imposed values. Wing gives an example from a Senegalese case where technicalities were used by the court to avoid enforcing protective law.

Wing further shows that when legal reform precedes social change, women can be left in precarious situations. For instance, outlawing of polygyny and the levirate can lead to a loss of support for women. Divorced or abandoned women are likely to remarry polygynously for emotional and financial support even where polygyny is not allowed, and these "illegal" marriages lack inheritance rights. Social inequality also easily becomes social stratification through laws such as those in Benin that allow only civil ceremonies to confer rights; illiterate and other isolated women used to be protected by rights conferred in traditional ceremonies. Thus, Wing writes as a supporter of Family Law reform who also understands the difficulties in bringing enabling reform to African women.

The next section on gender includes contributions from both literature and sociology. Abena Busia's chapter puts the question of how globalization affects African women into a longer history of how politics affected the bodies of African women. In particular, she describes the impact of the World Bank's structural adjustment policies on African women in particular as "being structurally adjusted downwards into increasing infrastructural insecurity, spiraling indebtedness and accelerating poverty." She sets the stage for considering current effects of globalization by demonstrating from a wide assortment of literature that aspects of the global economy have always affected African women's lives. She also has an extended section on Chimamanda Ngozi Adichie's award winning novel *Purple Hibiscus*, an intimate family drama that portrays "the interaction between capitalist consumer economies and liberal democratic ideals." Busia's work highlights how socially salient events like counting people can be for

Africans. And while outsiders may lack consciousness of this, Busia illustrates through her literary examples aspects of globalization touching daily lives about which African characters show no consciousness. She creates a richly textured picture of how in overt and subtle ways the global economy shapes African family life.

Victor Seidler's sociological approach considers forces associated with globalization like urbanization that makes breaking with past patriarchal structures easier. He also points to economic disempowerment associated with globalization that motivates men to assert masculinity in traditional ways, including authoritarian headship of families. This theme of men losing authority conferred by economic provision and regaining it by asserting their power over women echoes literature on structural obstacles to controlling the spread of HIV. In both the HIV literature and Seidler's work, economic change is conceptualized as a threat to manhood that needs to be met by better alternatives than the subordination of women. And like in Bank's chapter, Seidler's chapter pays attention to the intersections of race and gender that increase the complexity of pursuing positive change. Africa is the only continent that has urbanized without substantial economic growth, and thus faces different challenges for gender equality.

Seidler is circumspectly optimistic about prospects for change. First, he calls attention to the lack of individualism in traditional African families and the ways men's groups can promote some of the sensibilities this squelches. Further, he seems to argue that modern economies—and in particular urban migration—are undermining the authority of senior men over other men in ways that allow more flexibility. Seidler also consider institutions other than the family where gender is shaped. Interacting with peers committed to gender equality emerges as one of the important ingredients of change and allowing men to be more involved with their children. Despite these proscriptions sounding somewhat Western, Seidler calls for engaging with the diversity of African cultural traditions and their inherent tensions to produce more equal gender relations.

The final chapter in this volume focuses on religion. Laurie DeRose's chapter on religion and HIV risk contains evidence on the effects of world religions (specifically Islam and Christianity). DeRose's chapter reviews both what is known and what is not known about the effects of religion on the probability of being HIV positive, and also on the mostly commonly recognized protective behaviors: abstinence, fidelity, and condom use. Although the literature she reviews identifies some effects of denominational affiliation and devoutness, she also identifies many unanswered questions regarding whether religion is protective (and how it is protective where it is). In particular, her review highlights how few studies have considered religious attributes of communities rather than just individuals. The broader literature on HIV transmission prevention has recognized that interventions need to target more than abstinence, fidelity, and condom use, and DeRose points to particular ways in which the literature on religion and HIV also needs to break out of this simplistic framework.

References

Caldwell, John C., and Pat Caldwell. 1987. The Cultural Context of High Fertility in Sub-Saharan Africa. *Population and Development Review* 13 (3):409-437.

Adichie, Chimamanda Ngozi. *Purple Hibiscus: A Novel.* New York: Harper Perennial, 2003.

Chapter 1

CHANGES IN AFRICAN FAMILIES: A REVIEW OF ANTHROPOLOGICAL AND SOCIOLOGICAL APPROACHES TOWARD FAMILY AND KINSHIP IN AFRICA[1]

Erdmute Alber *and* Astrid Bochow

INTRODUCTION

Family structures in Africa are changing: on the one hand, the two-generation family with fewer members is on the rise in the urban areas,[2] while on the other a new type of urban extended family has emerged. The latter provides accommodation for a large number of village kin out of a variety of motives, and creates a new resource of familial networks. The model of a new extended family also applies to transnational family structures such as closely intertwined households in West Africa and Paris, London or Berlin (Bryceson and Vuorela 2002b). At the same time, we see the continuation of old forms of family organization, such as the persistence of polygyny, which remains important in many regions of Africa, or the insistence that children belong not exclusively to their biological parents, but rather to the extended family. This combination of the development of new and the continuation of old forms of family organization appears in different regional and local variants.

Not only are these empirical findings changing constantly, but the theoretical perspectives anthropologists and sociologists have developed to describe and theorize these changes have also seen constant change. Social science research has taken up the subject of the family in Africa since the 1940s only in part due to the changing realities in African family life. While that research has focused on empirical observations of societal transformations in Africa, it has also focused on questions particular to Europe at different times (for instance questions about woman's equality or global overpopulation). Hence, the scholarly discourses themselves also reflect particular notions about change, continuity and societal transformations.

Our contribution aims to outline this process of changing ideas and images about African kinship and family. Thereby we review the changing anthropological and sociological approaches towards these topics in the twentieth century. In so doing, we intend to demonstrate the entanglement between the theoretical perspectives and hypotheses on the one hand and the empirical findings of these studies on the other. A third, yet often overlooked factor which influences European researcher's perspectives and questions towards African family change are problems and concerns they faced in their own society.

We will present our findings in the form of examples taken from individual texts, focusing on the literature on family change in West Africa, where our own current research is centered. Of course, drawing a history of ideas about and images of family change in Africa by European researchers is always a risky enterprise because while one has to avoid the tendency of oversimplification, one must also avoid becoming lost in particularities. We offer a survey of the research on African families in the twentieth century that structures our article as follows: we begin with early colonialism as characterized by colonial writings about family in Africa which is prior to any empirical social research. This period was followed by the first "golden age" of anthropological research in Africa, the structural-functionalist approach of the forties.

After that, sociological and more urban centered research followed, inspired by modernization theory. In the seventies and eighties, Marxist inspired women's and gender studies followed, being replaced by new kinship research of the nineties and, finally, globalization studies. We end our article with a final section that summarizes central questions and findings and offers an outlook on new avenues for future research.

1900-1940:
COLONIAL WRITINGS ABOUT INDIGENOUS RULES

In the first three decades of the 20th century, colonialism was implemented and consolidated in West Africa. This was not yet the high time of empirical social research in the colonies, but of the documentation of what some colonizers observed in their locations. Even if colonial bureaucracy could in general be well characterized as "autistic and self-centered" (Spittler 1981), there was a need to have some information about local forms of self-organization in order to understand the local rules of chieftaincy succession or marriage. This documentation was required by the colonial administration. The colonial administrators were in a dire need to understand local norms and rules in order to have a framework for indigenous jurisdiction. Thus, in several colonies, data on local customs with focus on family law were collected, for which the "coutumier de Dahomey" in 1933 gives an example (Gouvernement Général de l'Afrique Occidentale Francaise 1933). Some of the local colonial officers also produced texts that described local customs and forms of family organization.

One of the rare "real" ethnographers in charge of the colonial administration was Reverend Robert S. Rattray, who carried out research in Ashanti, today Ghana, during the 1920s and published on Ashanti Law and Constitution (1929/1956) and Ashanti Art and Religion (1927/1979). His detailed account of Ashanti law explores political and kinship rule of the matrilineal Ashanti which for instance governs succession of ministries and inheritance of land. Next to this he also gives a detailed account on funeral (Rattray 1927/1956:147-166), birth (51-68) and puberty rites (69-75). He offers insights into the relationship between mother and child—the child belongs to the matrilineage of the mother—as well as father and child which is tightened through a spiritual bond (Rattray 1929/1956: 8-18). One of his

3

most criticized paragraphs is the one on marriage which lists seven different forms of Akan marriages, among them *mpena awaree*, marriage outside wedlock (26-27). More than half a century later, Jean Allman and Victoria Tashjian (2000) reject Rattray's view on marriage arguing that marriage had been a process in various steps which involves the two families of the married couple. Rattray was blind to these kinds of policies and negotiations. His interest, quite typical for the writings of the ethnographers of his time, did not target the dynamics and social processes in the society he described. Instead, he gathered information by visiting the area and by interviewing some few key informants. His books, however, still serve as a valuable source for contemporary scholars working on the Akan.

In these very first decades of European presence in colonial Africa anthropologists produced the first publications on African family life. Many of the documentations of ethnographic value can be found in the colonial archives in form of reports. Being strongly linked to and often paid by colonial administration, their work was not yet based on field research but on the information key informants gave to them. As they aim to give a solid basis for indigenous colonial jurisprudence, they mainly describe family in Africa as being relatively static. Early colonial time, however, became later a topic in the work of recent social historians as for example by Jean Allman and Victoria Tashjian (2000), Emmanuel Akyeampong (1997) and Jane Guyer (1995). Even if most of the historians have not explicitly treated the subject of the African family, we will summarize some findings of this research.

The study by Allman and Tashjian (2000) mentioned above suggests that changes in marriage and the family under colonial influence occurred only in certain areas. A key socio-economic factor for the change in forms of marriage was the introduction of cocoa cultivation and the entry of peasant households into the cash economy that accompanied it. In the course of this development, women increasingly took on the role of working in their husbands' fields and their ties to the matrilineage became looser. In comparison to wider economic development, the state influenced family formations only secondarily. Thus, the introduction of marriage laws and colonial courts accorded the biological fathers more rights and duties in relation to their children *de jure*, but in practice men generally did not meet their responsibilities so colonial legislation was not actually enforced (Allman and Tashjian 2000:16-18).

The attempts described by Allman and Tashjian (2000: 183-208) of missions to train Ashanti women to be good mothers through special classes provide a vivid illustration of the selective adoption of Western notions of family and gender roles. While the women gladly accepted instruction and hygiene products such as soap and powder, they did not fundamentally change their way of life.

Individual studies indicate that the introduction of colonial law and the influence of the mission churches lead to changes in marriage during the colonial period,[3] but they emphasize at the same time that neither state nor church institutions succeeded in asserting their own notions of the family across the board. During the colonial period, European influence was limited mainly to the colonial centers and the elites, while into the mid-twentieth century broad segments of the African population were well aware of the Europeans and their life-style without fundamentally changing their own family and kinship concepts and practices.

THE GOLDEN FORTIES OF EMPIRICAL ANTHROPOLOGICAL RESEARCH: STRUCTURAL FUNCTIONALIST RESEARCH ON KINSHIP IN AFRICA

The only partial changes in local practices during colonial times are reflected in structural functionalist anthropological kinship research in Africa in the 1940s and 1950s. This was the high time for research in rural areas of West Africa, and the first time that anthropologists realized empirical field research using, at least partly, the methods of participant observation. The structural functionalists regarded kinship, alongside politics and above all religion, as a fundamental organizational form of non-modern societies. This led to the first empirical studies of kinship, upon whose rich material we can still draw today, even if they scarcely addressed societal change, being generally a-historical in structure. The objective of this work was to describe kinship systems in individual societies, which were then classified in a synchronic comparison with other societies and viewed in relation to other arenas of society such as politics or religion. This literature largely ignored the question of whether these kinship systems were actually so static before the changes that occurred in the colonial era (Radcliffe-Brown 1975: 3; Fortes 1957: 1).

In his introduction to the classic collection of essays *African Systems of Kinship and Marriage* (Radcliffe-Brown and Forde 1950), Alfred Radcliffe-Brown describes knowledge of kinship systems as fundamental to an understanding of the social systems of African societies. The chief purpose of kinship was the formal regulation of relations between parents and children (Radcliffe-Brown and Forde 1950: 1). For Radcliffe-Brown, kinship goes beyond the 'ties of blood'. He writes that:

> A system of kinship and marriage can be looked at as an arrangement which enables persons to live together and co-operate with one another. ... [W]e have to consider how it links persons together by convergence of interest and sentiment and how it controls and limits those conflicts that are always possible as the result of divergence of sentiments and interests (1950: 3).

Radcliffe-Brown then goes on to describe the aim of anthropological research in this area as follows:

> This kind of understanding of a kinship system as a working system linking human beings together in an orderly arrangement of interactions, by which particular customs are seen as functioning parts of the social machinery, is what is aimed at in a synchronic analytic study (1950:3).

Kinship, the object of study of this brand of anthropology, was thus regarded as a control system that created binding social relationships between people in everyday co-existence. The focus of attention was on the systematic nature of kinship and the norms and rules that structured everyday practice.[4] Radcliffe-Brown's reference to the importance of kinship in containing conflicts draws attention to a problem with his assumptions: he foresees no difference between everyday practice and social structure, so that for him, everyday practice remains a reproduction of the structure. The assumed convergence between rules and everyday practice is manifested in an account that undervalues conflicts and scarcely addresses behavior that deviates from the rules. This is typical of structural functionalist theory building more generally.

6

The structural functionalists posed fundamental questions about institutions and practices. They described forms of matrilineality and patrilineality and discovered institutions such as niece fostering among the Tallensi (Meyer Fortes 1949) and sororal polygyny or 'leviratic marriage' among the Nuer (Evans-Pritchard 1973). It is to their anthropological circumspection that we owe our detailed knowledge of marriage rules and taboos, inheritance rules and regulations concerning ownership of land and movables and even of the distribution of political power among people connected by descent or marriage.

Because of this anthropological wealth, structural functionalist studies remain important ethnographic sources on family and kinship in Africa in the first half of the twentieth century. Nevertheless, we need to read them critically today and place them within their time. They have also spurred scholars on to conduct *re-studies* such as Sharon Hutchinson's (1996) study inspired by Evans-Pritchard's work on the Nuer.

THE FAMILY IN POST-COLONIALISM: SOCIOLOGICAL RESEARCH ON ELITES IN THE SIXTIES AND SEVENTIES

Sociological studies adopted a new perspective in the 1960s, explicitly turning their attention to those segments of society that had not only come into contact with Europeans, but had also undergone particularly drastic changes. This applies above all to the African elites in the cities and colonial centers. The paradigm of the 'modernization' of African societies was put on the agenda of sociological research on Africa at that time. William Goode's (1964) model, with which sociologists of the family outside Europe are still grappling, may be regarded as exemplary of this perspective. It posits that in the so-called developing countries, the dominant traits of pre-modern families such as multi-generational families sharing a common dwelling, polygamy (or polygyny) and above all a large number of children change with increasing industrialization and modernization. In analogy to European developments in the age of industrialization, Goode sees the extended family being replaced by the nuclear family with a small number of children. This research increasingly came to focus on changes in family forms in modern urban Africa.[5]

This modernization model must be viewed not least as an expression of hope and as a reaction to disproportionate population growth in Africa, which has preoccupied demographers since the end of the Second World War. Thus, following this model, John C. Caldwell predicted that the birth-rate and thus the proportion of children in the population would drop with a growing orientation towards the monogamous model of marriage. In fact, there was some reason to believe that this model would prove accurate. According to Caldwell, the average age at marriage of African elites rose with education and professional qualifications, which shortened their reproductive phase. He also observed a tendency for marriages to become more stable (Caldwell 1969: 10).

The findings of Caldwell's later study on family size in urban Ghana (1977), however, run counter to his assumptions: they show a further growth in the proportion of children in the total population, and thus a tendency for society to become younger. Caldwell explains his findings in terms of the fall in childhood mortality: despite a drop in the birth-rate, because of the lower mortality rate more children than previously survived the first decade of life. As a consequence, the average number of children per couple in the urban milieu remained high, and in some cases even rose (Caldwell 1977: 79). With this line of argument, Caldwell retained the hope that the number of children would fall in the long run, thus verifying his modernization theory model. In West Africa, however, Caldwell's prognosis has proved incorrect thus far.

Caldwell's research also suggests that the urban elite aspires to the European concept of the family. In his questionnaires, Caldwell (1977: 65) characterizes this concept as follows:

> Usually only the husband, wife and their children, who have not yet grown up, live together in a house of their own. Most husbands and wives live together all their lives and never live at any time with another woman or man. Most families have only one, two children. Often the most common type of entertainment is for the whole family to go out in their car taking lunch with them to a beach or a drive in the countryside.

The researchers, and perhaps their interview partners as well, associate the family form of life-long monogamous marriage with two children—in whom and in whose education the family invests a substantial portion of its income—with wealth and comfort, as well as with certain notions of consumption, most notably automobiles and single-family homes. The new forms of family thus represent a particular lifestyle, which is orientated towards Europe. The question of how people would like to live rather than how they in fact can live fails to problematize the relationship between concepts and social practice. Behind this lies the assumption that the preferred models were actually being put into practice in people's lives.

The sociologist Christine Oppong (1981) also studied this new family type among the educated urban elite. Her work addresses the marital problems of higher civil servants, which she attributes mainly to financial support for the couple's children, their education and the organization of the household budget. The shift to new forms of marriage and family was fostered by the husband's sometimes only partial release from agricultural production on the family land and his entry into an economic form in which he earned an individual salary.

The modernization theorists focused on the family and not, as in the case of the structural functionalists, on kinship. For that reason, they were no more interested in studying questions of belonging and exchange between related persons than in the forms and structures of the oft–mentioned so-called traditional extended family.[6] Above all, the aspiration to demonstrate the general developmental of individual segments of the population and to relate them to each other demands methods other than participant observation. Demography used, and still uses, mainly quantitative methods. Instead of attempting a holistic approach, it takes representative *samples* in order to make assertions about the behavior of particular groups. An important trait shared by the studies inspired by modernization theory seems to us typical of the mindset of the period in which they were written: all of the authors mentioned here found in the urban milieu a break with what they called traditional forms of marriage and family, and stressed how different or new the urban ways of life were. They regarded them as the result of a process of removal from the traditions of the rural milieu.

THE REVOLUTIONARY EIGHTIES: MARXIST INSPIRED WOMEN'S AND GENDER STUDIES

The anthropological discussion on family and kinship in Africa has silenced after these major theories. Instead, new insights about family relations have been generated by first women's and later gender studies.[9] Gender studies (as well as women studies) embrace much more topics than the issue of marriage, family and kin relation, but the study of the latter is not thinkable without a consideration of gender roles within these unions. We are far from trying to give a canonical overview of feminist and gender studies; instead we will sketch the major trends of women's and gender studies which has been important for studying family and kinship in Africa.

Women's role and women's concern in Africa became debatable during the 1970s when the women's movement gained ground in Europe and North America. Attention was given to subjects previously neglected or overlooked by 'male bias,' such as female rites of passage as for example the *rite des passage* for females of the Maasai in Tanzania. Even though genital mutilation is part of these rites, Mitzlaff (1994)[7] describes them as institutions in which women in fact appear to be influential rather than oppressed. She further shows the power of women in sexual marital and extra marital relationships which had been overlooked by male researches before her. Despite these examples of an ethnography which attributes much more agency to women, these early feminist scholars tend to view women in Africa merely as victims (Mohanty 1988; Cornwall 2005: 3).

Classifying these early Women's studies two major traditions can be discerned which are still of importance today. The first attributes women's role to economic conditions and had been inspired by Marxist thinking. In his utopia of a better, because economically equal and free society, Friedrich Engels (1892) had, at the beginning of the 20th century, projected ideals of family life into the long forgotten past of the "matriarchy" that in his model of material historicism was the beginning of mankind.[8] This model of the family and its evolution had impacted not only feminist thinking but also brought forward the idea that certain forms of family life are correlated with economic conditions. The idea that family organization and modes of production are linked to each other has influenced research in African societies.[9]

The neo-Marxists anthropologists of the seventies had (re)discovered the household and the household economy as objects of research in order to show the intersection of modes of production and above all the relationship between the allegedly subsistence-oriented peasant economy and the world market. One of the best-known and most influential thinkers is Claude Meillassoux (1981) who sketches a theory of the development of household production that begins with an agrarian, gerontocratic community in the pre-capitalist era[10] which he believes to be observed in African rural society. He criticizes anthropologist's writing for their focus on kinship and suggests looking into the household as a unit of production and living instead. In his model the middle generation carries the burden of reproduction and production in order to provide for the younger generation and the old (Meillassoux 1981: 65-76). In subsistence oriented African societies, he claims, old men are monopolizing the access to means of production and reproduction, namely women. Exploited are young men and especially women who contribute with their labor to the up-keep of old (men) without enjoying a privileged position during their lifetime (Meillassoux 1981: 92-99). The denial of descent as a basic principle of social organization is crucial to Meillassoux's theory, but is interestingly a largely overlooked point of his book. The hypothesis of suppressed women in relation with their economic role, however, has inspired a lot of studies ever since. Whereby these Marxist and neo-Marxist influenced studies had dominated the discourse on gender relation and therefore also on family life in the African context for almost fifteen years (Cornwall 2005: 5),[11] it is striking that today no popular study is associated with this school. It has, however, sharpened the researcher's eye to look into conjugal relations and labor division within marital unions and households.

The fruitfulness of looking into the materiality of family relations is shown by more contemporary studies such as Gracia Clark's study on Ashanti market women in Kumasi. However not directly relating her work to Marxist theory (production plays indeed a minor role in her research) she demonstrates that women may inhabit a strong economic position in Ashanti society. Their economic performance determines their success as wives (1999) and mothers (2000).

The second wave of these early feminist writers stands in the tradition of structural approaches and coins the symbolic representation of women in cosmology and society (e.g. Ardener 1971). Being preoccupied with the suppression of women in the so-called West these early scholars were concerned about 'women's issues,' considering gender asymmetry as a universal fact: "Women may be important, powerful, and influential, but it seems that, relative to men of their age and social status, women everywhere lack generally recognized and culturally valued authority" (Rosaldo 1980: 17). Therefore, articles were largely conceptual and empirical findings were not the main focus of most articles and books during this period.[12] In this debate the subject of 'household' took on a different meaning than the mere economic meaning assigned to it by Meillassoux. Exploring the topic of households, Michelle Rosaldo (1980: 25) succeeded in showing in a comparative study that the members of different societies drew the lines between the public and private spheres in different ways. In so doing, she made it possible to address the house as a social space in new ways, and facilitated a new understanding of public and private.

Not only had later scholars, headed by African feminists, criticized these early feminist writers for perceiving African women as merely victims, but in addition they pointed out to the fact that gender roles[13] and therefore also family constructions were historically more flexible than Western ethnographers had presumed. In her well known book *Male Daughters, Female Husbands* Amadiume (1998) showed that in Igbo societies women could be put in the position of sons in order to inherit land and cattle from their fathers, which usually would only be possible for sons, and rich barren women were able to marry other women in order to get their children as their own. Not only do her historical examples show that gender roles are flexible and less suppressive as Amadiume herself makes clear, but they also carry implications for understanding family life and social structure in Igbo society. The case of gynaegamy shows that same sex (legal) marriages[14] are possible and that the bearing of children is the most important purpose of marriage rather than sexuality as such. It also draws attention to the role wealth plays in African family life since these unions were open only for women of wealth. This means that their masculine status was closely linked to their possession of wealth. The role money plays for the making up of other than conjugal family ties is still one that is empirically under-researched.[15]

As further important insights into family relation in African societies we would like to name new approaches in social history which analyzed changes in men's roles in colonial and postcolonial societies in Africa. To name one of few pioneering scholars in this field (Moodie 1988; Morrell 2001; Miescher and Lindsay 2003; Miescher 2005) is Linda Lindsay's (2003) study on railway workers in Nigeria. She demonstrates how the model of the "husband as breadwinner" had changed the role of men and women in marriage considerably since men sought employment as wage laborers. Whereas before women and men had their own income—men owned crops and had therefore access to larger sums of cash but women who mostly traded were well disposed to a steady income irrespective of the season—women became economically more dependent on men when they left their home and migrated with them. In the 1980s, with the economic decline of the country and decreasing real wages, women's economic position acquired through petty trading became more important for entertaining the household again. By this time however, the masculine ideal had changed already so that women felt obliged to hide their contribution in order not to violate their husband's pride.

Gender studies in Africa opened up new avenues for the study of family as we have shown above. Looking deeper into the latest discussion one can see that access to resources as well as means of production is often seen as manifesting gender relations in the conjugal setting, thus echoing the emphasis on economic power relations by neo Marxist approaches. The question of the materiality of kinship relations is generally treated under aspects of gender roles, but it might as well be assigned to the field of family relations: what role does money play in the formation of family relations? Since wealth may make possible the converting of gender roles, as has been shown by Amadiume's study of gender relation in Igbo society, it might also be a factor in determining kinship belonging. In sum, we see that the contribution of gender studies to kinship and family research lies above all in the discovery of new empirical objects of study. One consequence of turning to gender relations, however, seems to us to be that the subject of the family has largely been treated from the perspective of the division of power between spouses, so that the focus is mainly on horizontal relationships, while vertical ties—such as those between children and parents or even between grandparents and grandchildren—are rarely examined.

'NEW KINSHIP' IN THE 1990s: THE RECENT RENAISSANCE OF KINSHIP RESEARCH

In the 1990s we can note a renaissance in kinship studies in anthropological research. The impulses for this renewal, which concerned not only empirical research but also theoretical discussions and reflections, came less from the "classical" regions of anthropological kinship studies, as Asia or Africa, than from studies of (post)modern societies in Europe and North America.[16] Labeled as "new kinship," the discussions were inspired in part by new medical knowledge and the therapeutic possibilities of new reproductive technologies, as well as by emerging analytical perspectives of forms of non-biological "made" kinship such as adoption, fosterage, or parenting responsibilities taken on by godparents.

As outlined in the introduction of the book *Cultures of Relatedness* (Carsten 2000), new procedures for artificial insemination, genetic testing and surrogate motherhood provided challenges for anthropological kinship research in general but especially for the formation of theories that could accommodate these new "ways" of fostering parenthood. The European "biological" ideas of unambiguous motherhood and fatherhood no longer persisted and thus a redefinition of the relationship between biological (natural) and social kinship became necessary. It had to take account of the fact that, on the one hand, not even biological maternity and paternity was clear-cut anymore, and on the other that a shift had occurred in the metaphoric field from blood kinship to genetic kinship.

"Nature can no longer be taken for granted anymore," writes Janet Carsten (2000: 9), picking up the programmatic title of Marilyn Strathern's book *After Nature* (1992). In this view, kinship is deemed an exclusively social construct, which is expressed in naturalistic or biologistic symbols. These, in turn, point to an understanding of nature in the various societies. When Carsten proposes that we understand kinship as relatedness or belonging, she is suggesting that scholars transfer their attention from formal kinship structures to the sense of belonging and the accompanying forms of exchange and solidarity.[17]

Up until now, such constructionist kinship studies have been rare for Africa. Rita Astuti (2000) however, shows that the Vezo of Madagascar recognize several transformative stages of kinship, which point to different perspectives on society. She describes an old man with substantial knowledge of kin and kinship. He represents a central "knot" that holds together the strands of the infinite casting-net of kinship. This man's knowledge is valued as a resource, since it can prove quite useful, for example when traveling, to be able to locate relatives in new places. At the same time, though, according to Astuti, this knowledge can conflict with the interests of those of marriageable age, who prefer to ignore too detailed a knowledge of kinship because this would narrow the circle of potential spouses. According to the normative concept of the strictly exogamous Vezo, marriage is supposed to create kinship, and this demands that no previous kinship relationship exists between the partners. With this finding Astuti draws attention to the problem that kinship and belonging are defined and evaluated differently according to life stage and individual perspective. In addition, her work points to a methodological problem of structural functionalist theory, namely the question of how a potentially infinite network (or family tree) of kin can be reduced to a concretely defined co-operating group.

Decisive for Astuti's understanding of kinship and more generally that of proponents of *new kinship* is the observation that kinship relationships are negotiable and fluid. In particular, the line between kinship and non-kinship can be drawn situationally and does not depend dogmatically on a person's respective position within the kinship system. After all, even the qualities attributed to the respective relationships are anything but static or self-evident. The interest of researchers is directed at detecting or describing them in concrete empirical contexts and addressing the substances or symbols upon which kinship relationships are based in the societies in question.

Another direction of research within *new kinship* places systems of exchange in the foreground. Exemplary of the research on Africa are Sharon Hutchinson's detailed studies (1996; 2000) of changes in the marriage system and more particularly bride price among the Nuer as a result of the introduction of money economy. With entry into the market economy and later with civil war, money and weapons entered as new elements into an old exchange cycle. As a result, the goods that at first belonged to different spheres altered in value, became mutually convertible, and gave rise to a new cycle of exchange. By analyzing its deep and complex transformations, Hutchinson shows that a traditional value system neither disappears as a result of external structural influences nor loses its significance for everyday action.

Such research addresses not family relationships but changes in marriage payments as well as marriage ceremonies and the institution of matrimony itself. It enquires into the consequences of the introduction of new currency systems for social values (Guyer 1995), and demonstrates that transformations in financial and economic systems are often accompanied by social change. Marriage and bride-price-payments can change in amount and mode of payment when social relationships, marriage, or the roles of wives or the lineage are re-evaluated. Family-relevant themes are thus presented within the context of their dependence on changes in society and values.

A further field of new kinship inspired studies in Africa can be seen in recent studies on fosterage and adoption (Alber 2003, 2004, Notermans 2004). In West Cameroon, Catrien Notermans (2004) showed that women having raised their own children already take one or several of their grandchildren as foster children. By sharing home, bed and food with these foster children they not only find company for their everyday activities but also ensure their status as grandmothers. Some of these women even neglected their own biological children in order to be able to live out their new (and superior) status as grandmothers. Thus, the status of being a grandmother is not determined by the biological facts of one's children having children, but an actively achieved position in the society. Fosterage practices are part of these ongoing negotiations and conflicts about the concrete status of women. Additionally, Notermans shows how the sharing of food and bed contributes once more to transform kinship rules into lived praxis.

What seems central to the constructionist approach is that belonging and relatedness are not merely subject to strict rules, but are also in need of reconstruction and in part also negotiation in everyday life. Relatedness regulates solidarity as well as exchange and assistance. The terms 'belonging' or 'relatedness' point to the links between kinship and other forms of membership (country, religion, status). However, a still missing point and unsolved problem in the recent new kinship debates is that the terminology of relatedness does not allow a clear distinction between kinship and other forms of relatedness, be it friendship, neighborhood or even ethnicity. Thinking about kinship as an imagined and constructed structure of belonging and relatedness between people should, finally, come to a new but clear and analytically value definition between kinship ways of belonging and others.

THE END OF THE TWENTIETH CENTURY: GLOBALIZATION STUDIES

During the past decade, a number of phenomena have been treated under the slogan 'globalization' that arose in connection with the increasing compression and acceleration of communication and transport routes between the world's information and economic centers.[18]

On the whole, few studies have confronted the effects of processes of globalization on kinship and family structures. Particularly interesting for research on the family is the observation that the images conveyed by the mass media have also become accessible on the 'periphery' (Appadurai 1991: 198). Studies that address the question of how flows of migration alter family structures have also proved relevant.[19]

The articles in the above-mentioned essay collection by Bryceson and Vuorela (2002b) borrow conceptually from the constructionist literature on kinship already discussed here, and introduce the term 'relativizing' for the creation of kinship relationships (Bryceson and Vuorela 2002a: 6). They continue to apply Benedict Anderson's (1983) concept of the nation as an 'imagined community' to the family, and point out that the concepts of both the nation and the family refer to naturalist symbols that create membership (Bryceson and Vuorela 2002a: 10). The contributions in their essay collection focus on describing and analyzing the migration situation and the so-called second generation. What they do not illuminate are the effects of transnational relations on local family structures.

In our view, the greatest deficiencies of these essays is that the authors scarcely conceptualize "family," do not develop their questions systematically, and mainly describe relations between parents and children or husbands and wives (Erel 2002; Timera 2002). Other kinship relationships, such as those among siblings, cousins, grandparents and grandchildren, in contrast, are rarely if ever mentioned.[20] The notion of the family harbored by researchers here seems implicitly limited to the nuclear family. They thus ignore not just the concepts of kinship developed in structural functionalist anthropology,[21] but also the family relationships that have increasingly attracted the attention of sociologists in recent years.[22]

A few studies on Africa address the reception of media images of the family and partnership and how they affect local practice. The first of these to become well-known is Lila Abu-Lughod's (1996) essay on the imitation of American television soap operas in Egyptian everyday life, in which the ideal of romantic love is adapted and renegotiated as a partnership model. Young people in (West) African cities confront not just the Western image of the family, however. Brian Larkin (2002), for example, describes the dominance of Indian cinema and popular literature in Kano in northern Nigeria. Here, too, romantic love does not coincide with traditional courtship patterns, which are being renegotiated in confrontation with emerging popular culture trends.

In Lagos, Daniel Smith (2001) has observed that the marriages of the urban elites are often contracted under the guise of romantic love. The success of this new type of partnership appears rather ambivalent, however, for after the wedding the couple's integration into the family gains in importance. Smith explains this in terms of the indispensability of family networks within the political economy of Nigeria. He also notes that a wife's social reputation is still determined by having a large number of children, while it remains a sign of prestige for men to have one or more affairs on the side. As long as the husband does not endanger the family's security or wealth, according to Smith, the only risk he runs is provoking a marital drama. This is a necessary result of an extramarital affair being discovered, but such dramas generally have no formal consequences, since women are pressured by their families not to sue for divorce. In the patrilineal context, divorce means losing the children to the father's family. Smith (2001: 148) concludes that marriages based on love contain a paradox: while romantic love implies the possibility of choice, once the marriage begins, the traditional moral codes that conflict with this ideal regain importance as the couple becomes integrated into the families.

The few studies that explicitly examine global influences on the family and marriage point to new problems arising, for example, from changed patterns of migration. This raises various questions: what shapes do the family structures of transnational families take? How do they construct and constitute mutual belonging? The works by Smith and Larkin mentioned here may remind us at first of studies by modernization theorists. The latter, however, envisioned one model of society towards which all societies were developing at different rates, so that African societies could be measured against this model. Smith and Larkin, in contrast, understand the marriages they study, which are based on the ideal of romantic love, as contemporary ways of life and as the products of societal processes which, with all of their contradictions and ruptures, are not essentially developing in the same direction. Behind this–if not explicitly–may be the assumption that African societies have already become modern, or that different modernities have arisen in Africa.[23]

These more recent works follows the trend toward studying changing social structures mainly in the urban areas. Family change in the countryside, in contrast, is scarcely addressed. Considering the extent of urbanization processes in Africa, this appears unjustified to us. After all, even today, the majority of people in Africa live in rural areas. Because of the broad dissemination of media such as television and radio in the countryside, as well as the fact that state and church-run programs as well as development co-operation projects are also at work in the rural areas, we can assume that processes of family change are transforming forms of social existence in the country as well as the cities. Our own fieldwork in Ghana and Benin confirms this.[24]

This means that nowadays, unlike in the 1960s, ideas such as the equation of social with biological parenthood, romantic love, or the independence of married couples from their families, are known not merely to a small segment of society, but to broad sections of the population. These concepts and discourses also affect social practice.[25] Exactly how this occurs has received little attention from scholars, however.

Even if the topic of family change is occasionally touched upon under the paradigm of globalization, current anthropology does not accord great importance to either the family or family change. Up until now, research not just on family change but also on globalization more generally has failed to grapple in a meaningful way with the question of which global influences affect, or potentially affect, family structures.

SUMMARY AND OUTLOOK

In this article we have shown how the subject of the family and family change in Africa has been addressed by various anthropological and sociological approaches. We hope that we have made clear that the sociological and anthropological view of the family in Africa has clearly been influenced by societal processes in Europe. In retrospect, it becomes apparent that reflections on family life in particular frequently possess a strong normative component. This is true for African societies, as their above-mentioned discourses on family change show, as well as for the people who study them. Thus the desire of the British anthropologists of the 1930s to 1950s to record the rules and legalities of supposedly unchanged societies ethnographically gives us some notion of how these late witnesses to the world order of the waning British Empire saw and experienced life. Their writings may reflect the idea that life, and more particularly everyday life, obeyed fixed laws and rules.

The research conducted by modernization theorists in the 1960s and 1970s was influenced by the Cold War. Believing in the civilizing mission of the West, they were at once inspired by the hope of worldwide modernization and alarmed by population growth. Guided by the paradigm of modernization, sociologists and demographers in particular studied the changes in the families of the African urban elites. When conducting their surveys, the demographers of the 1970s proceeded from the assumption that by studying preferences, they could easily draw conclusions about their application and enforcement. At times, they overlooked the potential tension between concepts and social practices. This tension is gaining renewed relevance for the research on global influences on local practice. The social sciences now face the questions of whether and how the images of foreign ways of life made available by the almost total penetration of the mass media into African societies are changing local social practice.

In the late 1960s and the 1970s, not least in the light of the obvious failure of western policies in the Vietnam War, to name but one important example, doubts arose about the West's self-pronounced civilizing mission. This becomes evident in the thinking of intellectuals influenced by the critique of capitalism and by neo-Marxism, which in Africa, too, enquired into the modes of production and economic mechanisms of capitalism. In the 1980s, at a time when women were championing their political and social rights in Europe and North America, and power relations between the sexes came to occupy the minds of women anthropologists as well, this also raised questions about the lives of women in other societies. The field of gender studies deserves credit for putting topics relevant to the family, such as the division of labor between the sexes and the position of women within marriage on the scholarly agenda. Nowadays 'family' is even primarily associated with the questions posed by gender studies. In comparison, other aspects such as intergenerational relations, child fostering or the care of the elderly appear secondary. Only quite recently have they begun to attract the attention of anthropologists once again.[26] Like gender studies, neo-Marxist analyses have also mainly addressed the integration of families (or of households) into economic, social and political relationships as well as their dependence on these relationships. The observation that family and kinship are embedded in social systems also underlies more recent research in symbolic anthropology,[27] which understands family change as a product of general transformations in society and values.

In the 1990s, new birth and reproductive technologies revived intellectual reflections on the limits to the biological preconditions to kinship. This opened our eyes to the different qualities of kinship relationships, which can be fulfilled in individual ways. We see possible borrowings here from the structural functionalist idea that kinship consists of social relationships that regulate everyday co-existence as reliably as relationships of exchange between related persons. And yet the assumption of the systematic character of kinship, based solely on relationships of descent and alliance, is beginning to waver. Constructionist research, more frequently than structural functionalism, addresses the ruptures and contradictions in norms and behavior. The focus here is on the fluidity and negotiability of kinship.[28]

What the structural functionalist and constructionist approaches share, however, is the assumption of the autonomy of kinship, which they regard as a web of relationships that follows its own logic and laws, which it is up to scholars to uncover. Thus, we are faced with two distinct approaches: one explains forms of family life in terms of their integration and addresses their changes in the context of broader social change while the other has always sought to understand familial ways of life as autonomous. In fact, a look back at the politically inspired hopes of sociologists working within the modernization paradigm or feminist gender studies reminds us of how resistant to change the family can be. We only need to recall the failure of family planning programs and the fact that, despite quotas, women are still far less likely than men to occupy positions of leadership. At the same time, as research on bride price or migrant labor has shown, the various areas of family life are particularly subject to social transformations, which sometimes occur extremely rapidly. The question of the independence and autonomy of familial ways of life on the one hand and their dependence on and integration into processes of social change on the other could thus prove quite fruitful.

Notes

1. This essay is the result of collaborative work on the sub-project 'Westafrikanische Familienstrukturen im Wandel' (Changing Family Structures in West Africa) within the University of Bayreuth's Special Research Area (SFB) 'Lokales Handeln in Afrika im Kontext globaler Veränderungen' (Local Action in Africa in the Context of Global Changes). We would like to thank the University of Bayreuth and the Deutsche Forschungsgemeinschaft for financial support and our colleagues in the SFB for their discussion of our text. We also wish to thank Karola Elwert-Kretschmer and Katja Werthmann for additional suggestions.

2. The urban Baatombu of Benin, whom Erdmute Alber has studied, are an example of this family type.

3. As an example, see Meyer 1999:23, 178–188, 209.

4. Meyer Fortes (1949: 78) writes, similarly: "[W]e are concerned only with structurally significant norms."

5. Apart from African elites, this work also addressed phenomena of migration from the countryside to the city, for instance in the study *African Rural-Urban Migration* (1969) by John C. Caldwell, the best-known sociologist of the West African family.

6. There were, to be sure, occasional modifications to the modernization theory model, for example in studies of industrial workers in Nigeria by sociologists of the family, who noted and stressed the interconnections between rural and urban areas, for example via the financial exchange in familial networks (H. D. Seibel 1967; H. R. Seibel 1969: 53).

7. First published in 1988.

8. In his essay *The Origin of the Family, Private Property and the State* Engels (1986) argued that matriarchy as the primordial state of human society in which any object of value belonged to the whole community. In these societies the mother held the leading position since she was responsible for the reproduction of the group. According to his under-

standing, privatization of property became more prevalent and women lost their rights in the course of history. The peak of this development was the capitalist middle class family in which the husband and father would be engaged into paid labour and the wife and mother would stay at home and watch over the house and the children.

9. As an early adaptation of Engels' model for the African context is to be seen in Baumann's (1928) article in *The Division of Work according to Sex in African Hoe Culture*.

10. With the introduction of capitalist commodity production in capitalism and imperialism—to give a condensed version of his argument—the agrarian household community was integrated into the world market, with various mechanisms regulating the skimming off of added value.

11. In Germany, this approach was taken up by the so called "Bielefeld school," *(Bielefelder Verpflechtungsansatz)*. See Elwert 1983 and Bierschenk 2002.

12. Another edited volume that represents this kind of women's anthropology is Reiter (1975) *Towards Anthropology of Women*.

13. In this respect her argument is very much in line with the by then popular writings of Judith Butler and Michel Foucault who both point to the fact that gender is a social construct that is changing over time and space.

14. Amadiume describes these unions as purely legal and not as sexual ties.

15. Although Mary Douglas (1969) had claimed that wealth and economic growth plays an important role for fostering and up keeping of kin relation in matrilineal societies.

16. Inspiration came from David Schneider's (1968, 1984) reflections on 'American kinship' as well as Marilyn Strathern's (1992) studies of kinship in late twentieth-century England.

17. See Franklin and Ragoné (1998), Greenhalgh (1995).

18. See for example Beck (1999), Castells (1998) and Sassen (1994).

19. Nancy Scheper-Hughes (2002) extends the question concerning the flow of persons and ideas that is altering family structures, and also addresses the issue of the direction of traffic in human organs. She notes that children available for adoption, like organs, move from poorer to richer countries, in contrast to the concepts and laws that regulate family law and the rights of children, which move from the rich to the poor countries.

20. Among the exceptions are Vuorela (2002) and Cole and Durham (2007).

21. This is surprising for a collection of essays in social anthropology.

22. For example, see Lepenies (1997) as well as Kohli and Szydlik (2000) on intergenerational relationships.

23. For example, see Deutsch, Probst and Schmidt (2002).

24. See Alber (2004a, b) and Bochow (2008).

25. Thus Arjun Appadurai (1991: 198) notes that fantasy is now a social practice.

26. See van der Geest (1997), Whyte, Alber and Geißler (2004) and Alber, van der Geest and Whyte (2008).

27. For an example, see Guyer (1995).

28. A theoretical problem arising from the constructionist approach is that of delimiting concepts. If kinship is inferred above all from the emotional content of everyday relationships and no longer primarily defined by descent, we need to ask which relationships belong to kinship and which do not. This can be explained using the example of the nominal aunt: is she considered a relative, thus demonstrating that kinship can be expanded at will? Or does the reference to kinship not instead merely express social closeness to the person in question? The reception of the works of David Schneider draws attention to this problem (Carsten 2000:4–6).

References

Abu-Lugod, Lila. 1995. The object of soap opera: Egyptian television and the cultural politics of modernity. In *Worlds apart: modernity through the prism of the local*, ed. Detlef Miller. London: Routledge.

Aidoo, Ama Ata. 1972. *No sweetness here*. London: Longmans, Green.

Akyeampong, Emmanuel. 1997. Sexuality and prostitution among the Akan of the Gold Coast, c.1650–1950. *Past and Present* 156: 144-173.

Alber, Erdmute. 2003. Denying biological parenthood—Child fosterage in northern Benin. *Ethnos* 68/4: 487-506.

_____. 2004a. Ethnologische Anmerkungen zum Kinderhandel in Benin. In *Arbeit—Konsum—Globalisierung: Festschrift für Gerd Spittler zum 65*, ed. Kurt Beck et al, 145–158. Köln: Rüdiger Köppe Verlag.

_____. 2004b. Grandparents as foster parents: transformations in foster relations between grandparents and grandchildren in Northern Benin. *Africa* 74(1): 28–46.

Alber, Erdmute, Sjaak van der Geest, and Susan R. Whyte, ed. 2007. *Generations: contrasts and connections.* Hamburg: LIT.

Allman, Jean. 1997. Fathering, mothering and making sense of Ntamoba: reflections on the economy of child-rearing in colonial Asante. *Africa* 67(2): 296–321.

Allman, Jean, and Victoria Tashjian. 2000. *'I will not eat stone': a women's history of colonial Asante.* Oxford: James Currey.

Aluko, T. M. 1970. *Chief the honourable minister.* London: Heinemann.

Amaduime, Ifi. 1998. *Male daughters, female husbands. Gender and sex in an African society.* London and New Jersey: Zed Books.

Anderson, Benedict. 1983. *Imagined Communities: reflections on the origin and spread of nationalism.* London: Verso.

Appadurai, Arjun. 1991. Global ethnoscapes: notes and queries for a transnational anthropology. In *Recapturing anthropology: working in the present,* ed. Richard G. Fox, 191-210. Santa Fe: School of American Research Press.

Ardener, Erwin. (1971). *Belief and the problem of women. The interpretation of ritual. Essays in the honor of A. I. Richards.* J. S. L. Fontaine. London.

Astuti, Rita. 2000. Kindreds and descent groups: new perspectives from Madagascar. In *Cultures of relatedness: new approaches to the study of kinship,* ed. Janet Carsten, 90-104. Cambridge: Cambridge University Press.

Beck, Ulrich, ed. 1999. *Was ist Globalisierung.* Frankfurt am Main: Suhrkamp.

Bierschenk, Thomas. 2002. Hans-Dieter Evers und die Bielefelder Schule, Entwicklung und Zusammenarbeit, Jg. 43, H. 10: 273-276

Bochow, Astrid. 2001. "Europe is charming, right?" Vorstellungen über Wandel, Modernität und dem guten Leben in Gesprächen über Europa in Accra. Master's thesis, Freie Universität Berlin.

_____. 2008. Valentine day in Ghana: Youth, sex and fear between the generations. In *Generations in Africa: Contrasts and Connections,* ed. Erdmute Alber, Sjaak van der Geest and Susan Reynolds Whyte, 418-429. Hamburg: LIT.

Bryceson, Deborah, and Ulla Vuorela, ed. 2002a. *The transnational family: new European frontiers and global networks.* Oxford: Berg.

_____. 2002b. Europe's transnational families in the twenty-first century. In *The transnational family: new European frontiers and global networks*, ed. Deborah Bryceson and Ulla Vuorela, 3-31. Oxford: Berg.

Burguiè, André, and François Lebrun. 1996. The one hundred and one families of Europe. In *A History of the Family, vol. 2: The Impact of Modernity*, ed. André Burguière et al., 11-94. Cambridge: Polity Press.

Caldwell, John C. 1969. *African rural-urban migration: the movement to Ghana's towns*. New York: Columbia University Press.

_____. 1977. *Population growth and family change in Africa: the new urban elite*. London: C. Hurst & Co.

Carsten, Janet. 2000a. Introduction: cultures of relatedness. In *Cultures of relatedness: new approaches to the study of kinship*, ed. Janet Carsten, 1-36. Cambridge: Cambridge University Press.

_____, ed. 2000b. *Cultures of relatedness: new approaches to the study of kinship*. Cambridge: Cambridge University Press.

Castells, Manuel. 1998. *The rise of network society*. Malden: Blackwell.

Clark, Garcia. 1999. Negotiating Asante Family Survival in Kumasi, Ghana. *Africa* 69(1): 66-85.

_____. 2000. Mothering, work, and gender in urban Asante ideology and practice. *American Anthropologist* 101(4): 717-729.

Cole, Catherine M., and Deborah Durham, ed. 2007. *Generations and globalization: Youth, age, and family in the new world economy*. Bloomington: Indiana University Press.

Collier, Jane F., and Sylvia Junko Yanagisako, ed. 1987. *Gender and kinship: essays towards a unified analysis*. Stanford: Stanford University Press.

Cornwall, Aandrea. (2005). *Introduction. Readings in gender in Africa*. Bloomington & Indianapolis, Indiana University Press: 1-19.

Deutsch, Jan-Georg, Peter Probst and Heike Schmidt, ed. 2002. *African modernities: entangled meanings in current debate*. Oxford: James Currey.

Douglas, Mary. 1969. Is matrilineaty doomed in Africa?. In *Man in Africa*, Mary Douglas and Phyllis M. Kaberry, ed. 121-135. London: Tavistock Publication.

Eckert, Andreas, and Adam Jones. 2002. Historical writing in everyday life: introduction. *Journal of African Cultural Studies* 15(1): 5–17.

Ekwenski, Cyprian. 1954. *People of the city*. London: Dakers.

_____. 1961. *Jagua Nana*. London: Heinemann.

_____. 1966. *Isaka*. London: Heinemann.

_____. 1967. *Beautiful feathers*. London: Heinemann.

Elwert, Georg. 1983. *Bauern und Staat in Westafrika: Die Verflechtung sozioökonomischer Sektoren am Beispiel Bénin*. Frankfurt am Main: Campus.

Engels, Friedrich. (1892/1986). *The origin of the family, private property and the state*. London, Penguin Books.

Erel, Umut. 2002. Reconceptualising motherhood: experiences of migrant women from Turkey living in Germany. In *The transnational family: new European frontiers and global networks*, ed. Deborah Bryceson and Ulla Vuorela, 127-146.

Evans-Pritchard, Edward E. 1973. *Kinship and marriage among the Nuer*. Oxford: Clarendon Press.

Fortes, Meyer. 1957. *The web of kinship among the Tallensi*. London: Oxford University Press.

Franklin, Sarah, and Helena Ragoné. 1998. *Reproducing reproduction: kinship, power, and technological innovation*. Philadelphia: University of Pennsylvania Press.

Gluckman, Max. 1975. Kinship and marriage among the Lozi of Northern Rhodesia and the Zulu of Natal. In *African systems of kinship and marriage*, ed. Alfred R. Radcliffe-Brown and Daryll Forde, 166-206. London: Oxford University Press.

Goode, William J. 1964. *The family*. New Jersey: Englewood Cliffs.

Gouvernement General De L'Afrique Occidentale Francaise. 1933. Coutumier du Dahomey. Porto-Novo.

Greenhalgh, Susan, ed. 1995. *Situating fertility: anthropology and demographic inquiry*. Cambridge: Cambridge University Press.

Guyer, Jane I., ed. 1995. *Money matters: instability, values and social payments in the modern history of West African Communities*. London: James Currey.

Hutchinson, Sharon E. 1996. *Nuer dilemmas: coping with money, war and the state*. Berkeley and Los Angeles: University of California Press.

_____. 2000. Identity and subsistence: the broadening bases of relatedness among the Nuer of southern Sudan. In *Cultures of relatedness: new Approaches to the Study of Kinship*, ed. Jane Carsten, 55–72. Cambridge: Cambridge University Press.

Ike, Vincent Chukwuemeka. 1965. *Toads for supper*. London: Harvill.

_____. 1970. *The naked gods*. London: Harvill.

Jones, Adam, ed. 2002. *Everyday life in colonial Africa. Journal of African Cultural Studies* 15(1).

Kohli, Martin, and Marc Szydlik, ed. 2000. *Generationen in Familie und Gesellschaft*. Opladen: Leske und Budrich.

Larkin, Brian. 2002. Indian films and Nigerian lovers: media and the creation of parallel modernities. In *The anthropology of globalization: a reader*, ed. Jonathan Xavier Inda and Renato Rosaldo, 350–78. Malden: Blackwell Publishers.

Lenz, Ilse. 1995. Geschlechtssymmetrische Gesellschaften: Neue Ansätze nach der Matriarchatsdebatte. In *Frauenmacht ohne Herrschaft: Geschlechterverhältnisse in nicht patriarchalischen Gesellschaften*, ed. Ute Luig and Ilse Lenz. Berlin: Orlanda Verlag.

Lepenies, Annette, ed. 1997. *Alt und Jung: Das Abenteuer der Generationen*. Basel and Frankfurt am Main: Stroemfeld/Roter Stern.

Lindsay, Lisa A., and Stephan F. Miescher, ed. 2003. *Men and masculinities in modern Africa*. Portsmouth: Heinemann.

Lindsay, Lisa A. 2003. Money, marriage, and masculinity on the colonial Nigerian railway. In *Men and masculinities in modern Africa*, ed. Lisa A. Lindsay and Stephan F. Miescher, 138-156. Portsmouth: Heinemann.

Little, Kenneth. 1975. *African women in towns: an aspect of Africa's social revolution*. Cambridge: Cambridge University Press.

Meillassoux, Claude. 1981. *Maidens, meal and money: capitalism and the domestic economy*, English trans. London: Cambridge University Press.

Meyer, Brigit. 1999. *Translating the devil: religion and modernity among the Ewe in Ghana*. London: Edinburgh University Press.

Miescher, Stephan. F. (2005). *Making men in Ghana*. Bloomington, Indianapolis, Indiana University Press.

Mitzlaff, Ulrike von. 1994. *Maasai-Frauen: life in a patriarchal society: field research among the Parakuyo, Tanzania*. Dar es Salaam: Tanzania Publishing House.

Mohanty, Chandra. T. (1988). "Under Western eyes: feminist scholarship and colonial discourse." *Feminist Review* 30: 61-88.

Moodie, T. Dunbar. 1988. Migrancy and male sexuality on the South African mines. *Journal of Southern African Studies* 14(2): 228-56.

Morrell, Robert., Ed. (2001). *Changing men in Southern Africa*. London, New Jersey, ZED Books LTD.

Newell, Stephanie. 2000. *Ghanaian popular fiction: 'thrilling discoveries of conjugal life' and other tales*. Oxford: James Currey.

Notermans, Catrien. 2004. Sharing home, food, and bed: Paths of grandmotherhood in east Cameroon. *Africa* 74(1): 6-27.

Oppong, Christine. 1981. *Middle class African marriage: a family study of Ghanaian senior civil servants*. London: George Allen & Unwin.

Radcliffe-Brown, Alfred R., and Daryll Forde, ed. 1975. *African systems of kinship and marriage*. London: Oxford University Press.

Radcliffe-Brown, Alfred R. 1975. Introduction. In *African systems of kinship and marriage*, ed. Alfred R. Radcliffe-Brown and Daryll Forde, 1–86.

Rattray, Robert S. 1927/1979. *Religion and Art in Ashanti*. Oxford: Clarendon Press.

_____. 1927/1957. *Ashanti law and constitution*. Oxford: Clarendon Press.

Reiter, Rita., Ed. (1975). *Toward an anthropology of women*. New York, Monthly Review Press.

Rosaldo, Michelle Zimbalist. 1980. Woman, culture and society: a theoretical overview. In *Woman, culture, and society*, ed. Michelle Zimbalist Rosaldo and Louise Lamphere, 17-42. Stanford: Stanford University Press.

Rubadiri, David. 1967. *No bride price*. Nairobi: East African Publishing House.

Sassen, Saskia. 1994. *Cities in a world economy*. Thousand Oaks: Pine Forge Press.

_____. 1996. *Metropolen des Weltmarktes: Die neue Rolle der Global Cities*, German trans. Frankfurt am Main: Campus Verlag.

Scheper-Hughes, Nancy. 2002. The global traffic in human organs. In *The anthropology of globalization: a reader*, ed. Jonathan Xavier Inda and Renato Rosaldo, 270-308. Malden: Blackwell Publishers.

Scneider, David. 1968. *American kinship: a cultural account*. Englewood Cliffs: Prentice-Hall.

_____. 1984. *A critique of the study of kinship*. Ann Arbor: University of Michigan Press.

Seibel, H. Dieter. 1967. Struktureller und funktionaler Wandel der Familie in Afrika. *Afrika heute* 5(67): 1–8.

Seibel, Helga Renate. 1969. *Die Afrikanerin in Beruf und Familie. Eine Untersuchung bei nigerianischen Industriearbeiterinnen.* Freiburg: Arnold-Bergstraesser-Institut.

Smith, Daniel Jordan. 2001. Romance, parenthood, and gender in a modern African society. *Ethnology* 40(2): 129–151.

Strathern, Marilyn. 1992. *After nature: English kinship in the late twentieth century.* Cambridge: Cambridge University Press.

Timera, Mahamet. 2002. Righteous or rebellious? Social trajectory of Sahelian youth in France. In *The transnational family: new European frontiers and global networks*, ed. Deborah Bryceson and Ulla Vuorela, 147-154. Oxford: Berg.

Van der Geest, Sjaak. 1997. Money and respect: the changing value of old age in rural Ghana. *Africa* 64(7): 534-601.

Vuorela, Ulla. 2002. Transnational families: imagined and real communities. In *The transnational family: new European frontiers and global networks*, ed. Deborah Bryceson and Ulla Vuorela, 63-82. Oxford: Berg.

Whyte, Susan R., Erdumte Alber, and Wenzel Geißler. 2004. Lifetimes intertwined: African grandparents and grandchildren. *Africa* 74(1): 1-5.

Chapter 2

STRETCHED AND STRAINED BUT NOT BROKEN: KINSHIP IN CONTEMPORARY NIGERIA

Daniel Jordan Smith

INTRODUCTION

Understanding the effects of globalization on family structure in
Africa can benefit from building on investigations of demographic
change in the context of "modernization." The standard story about
how families evolve in response to modernization circulates widely and
has achieved the status of conventional wisdom, influencing scholarship as well as popular perceptions. It suggests that with industrialization, urbanization, and rising levels of formal education, societies
experience a transition from arranged to choice marriage, lower fertility, a shift to an increasingly nuclear family structure, a transformation
in the relationship between generations away from gerontocracy and
toward a privileging of youth and investments in children, and a level-
ing of gender inequality. This story reflects European experience and
there is much that is true, in broad strokes, about the transitions that
are described in this generalized accounting of European demographic
history. But of course scholars of demography in Europe have shown

that even there many aspects of the story unfold differently (Coale and Watkins 1986). Conventional accounts obscure not only considerable diversity but also significant theoretical questions and insights that emerge in more nuanced analyses (Kertzer and Brettell 1987; Kertzer and Hogan 1989; Schneider and Schneider 1996).

For people who work in Africa, the most troubling legacy of the modernization paradigm is its Eurocentric unilinealism, marked by the presumption that the European trajectory is the normal and superior path for any "advancing" society. While scholars of social and demographic change in Africa can certainly learn from comparisons with Europe and other regions, and while it is an equal fallacy to assume African exceptionalism, understanding the relationship in Africa between social change and demography in general and globalization and family structure in particular requires close attention to African history, political economy, social organization, and culture. African demographic adaptations to globalization need not mirror European experience. It is odd to expect that they would. Not only is it likely that African families will change in ways different from the European experience, it is also likely that an African path to success—measured in today's world by various indicators of "development"—need not follow the European model. Indeed, scholars must be prepared to uncover and understand a range of diverse trajectories of social and demographic change within Africa. Further, the focus on Africa as a whole can be a misleading prism that obscures tremendous intra-continental heterogeneity.

Ever since anthropologists began studying African family structure during the colonial period, scholars have recognized the centrality of kinship in African family systems, not only as an organizing principle for domestic and family life, but as a central mechanism for economic subsistence, governance, and social order (Radcliffe-Brown and Forde 1950). The idea that in traditional Africa economic success and political influence were achieved through "wealth in people" is widely accepted (Miers and Kopytoff 1977; Miller 1988; Guyer 1993, 1995). Political and social order depended significantly on a patron-client system. An expansive conception of kinship was typically a primary mechanism whereby patrons recruited clients and vice-versa. In addition, the idiom of kinship shaped a moral economy that asserted and protected the reciprocal obligations of patrons and clients (Barnes 1986; Oliver de Sardan 1999).

In this chapter I address the question of the effects of globalization and related social changes on the institution of kinship, using the case of the Igbo-speaking people of southeastern Nigeria to explore broader questions about the way in which traditional structures of kinship are both threatened by ongoing changes and central to how people are adapting to these changes. While some have suggested or feared that globalization leads to an increasing homogenization of cultures and societies, I argue that rather than being obliterated by globalization, African kinship systems remain pivotal for how African people navigate the contemporary world.

Using ethnographic examples from Nigeria, focusing particularly on the intersections between broader social and economic transformations and the demographic processes of marriage and fertility, I examine how ties of kinship are stretched and strained in current circumstances. In the context of increasing globalization, rapid urbanization, and the expansion of capitalist economic organization and consumption, the traditional moral bonds and social obligations of kinship can be experienced as burdensome. Much of the social and demographic behavior of Igbos in Nigeria, and arguably of Africans in many societies, can best be interpreted as an effort to manage, distance, and even sometimes break the yoke of the extended family and community of origin. Yet these ties remain crucial for how people—even educated urban migrants who are by conventional measures the most "modern" of Africans—strategize in and traverse through the rapidly changing social and economic situations presented in contemporary society. Attending to and analyzing how kinship is at once people's biggest problem and their most important resource, and connecting this reality to demographic behavior, offers important insights into the dynamic relationship between family structure and social change.

THE RESEARCH SETTING

Igbos are the third largest of Nigeria's nearly 250 ethnic groups, numbering approximately 15-20 million. I have lived and worked periodically in Igbo-speaking southeastern Nigeria beginning in 1989. Since 1995 I have conducted anthropological research in the semi-rural—but increasingly peri-urban—community of Ubakala, located just six miles from Umuahia, a town that became the a state capital when Abia State was created in 1991. Data for this chapter have been collected while undertaking a variety of research projects carried out over the past thirteen years, during which I have lived in Ubakala for more than three years.[1] Research methods to collect the data I incorporate here included participant observation, semi-structured interviewing, extended case studies, village household surveys of women of reproductive age and their husbands, large sample surveys of secondary school and university students, and multiple interviews with adolescent and young adult rural-urban migrants.

Over the years, I have spent extended time doing participant observation, and it is, I think, the source of the most interesting and valuable data. Participant observation has meant attending all manner of local social events and ceremonies—marriage rites, burials, chieftaincy installation ceremonies, family meetings, gatherings to resolve local disputes, child naming ceremonies, and so on. But perhaps more important, it has entailed accompanying and spending time with people as they went about their everyday lives—farming, fetching water, cooking, trading in the market, drinking palm wine or beer, going to church, and traveling to town. It has also meant listening to, and often participating in, the conversations, negotiations, and gossip that unfolded in all of these different settings and contexts. Much of what I know about Igbo kinship, marriage, family, and fertility comes from observation and participation in the kinds of informal conversations and exchanges that can best be achieved through extended fieldwork.

MODERN MARRIAGE
AND CONTEMPORARY KINSHIP[2]

Over the past several decades, Igbo society has changed dramatically. Intertwining factors that have contributed to the transformation of marriage include: economic diversification and labor migration, urbanization, education, and religious conversion—changes all related to globalization. Contemporary economic strategies hinge on rural-urban migration and a strong emphasis on the importance of education for children (Uchendu 1965a; Chukwuezi 2001). Schools are only one arena where young Nigerians are creating and absorbing new values regarding sex, gender, marriage, and family. Modern media—especially music, videos films, television, cell phones, and the internet—provide many young Nigerians with daily opportunities to observe, contemplate, and grapple with alternative futures, albeit futures often not realistically within their grasp (Haynes 2000; Smith 2006b). Life in Nigerian cities connects young people to social networks that create peer pressure to conform to modern identities forged in relationship to images, fashions, and aspirations circulating in global media (Smith 2000, 2004a). Increasingly popular Pentecostal and evangelical churches create bonds between young converts through which they feel part of a worldwide movement (Marshall-Fratani 1998). All of these changes have been complemented by ideological and moral discourses that also affect the institution of marriage.

On its face, marriage in southeastern Nigeria seems to be changing in ways that make it increasingly similar to marriage in Western societies. Describing the differences between her marriage and her parents' marriage, a 30-year-old woman in Ubakala married for three years said: "My father had three wives and 14 children. Often it was every woman for herself. My husband and I have a partnership. We decide things. There is love between us." The modern marriages of young couples in southeastern Nigeria are clearly different from their parents' relationships. The vast majority of young people choose their own spouses—the notion of "arranged" marriage is anathema to most youth and the conjugal relationship is increasingly privileged relative to other kinship ties.

Perhaps the most concise way to contrast modern Igbo marriages with the past is to note that young couples see their marriages as life-project in which they as a couple are the primary actors, whereas their parents' marriages were more obviously embedded in the structures of the extended family. The differences are most pronounced in narratives about courtship, in the way husbands and wives describe how they resolve marital quarrels, in how they make decisions about and contribute to their children's education, and, in some cases, in the allusions to Christianity as the basis for conjugal dynamics. In each of these arenas people in more modern marriages tend to emphasize the primacy of the individual couple, often in conscious opposition to the constraints imposed by ties to kin and community. For example, a 43-year-old teacher in Ubakala reported: "For me and my wife our marriage is our business, whereas in my parents' time everything was scrutinized by the extended family. If they had any little problem everyone might become involved. We try to keep things within the married house. If we have any problem we handle it ourselves and maybe pray over it, but we don't go running to the elders broadcasting our problems here and there."

It is important not to exaggerate these trends. Even in the most modern marriages, ties to kin and community remain important, and the project of marriage and child-rearing remains a social project, strongly embedded the relationships and values of the extended family system. Indeed, the continued importance of ties to family and community and ongoing concerns about the collective expectations of wider social networks permeate the stories of modern courtship, marital disputes, and child-rearing that also indicate change. The choice of a future spouse based on love is, in almost all cases, still subjected to the advice and consent of families. Describing the process after he informed his family of his intention to marry his wife, a 32-year-old barber in Ubakala recounted: "My people did investigations. They sent a delegation to her village to find out about the family. In our place we always like to know the character of the family from which we marry." His parents assented to the marriage, but he acknowledged that their objections would have led him to rethink his choice.

ROMANTIC LOVE, CHANGING MARRIAGE, AND THE ENDURING INFLUENCE OF KIN

Evidence from Nigeria (Obiechina 1973; Okonjo 1992) and across Africa (Mair 1969; Little 1979; van der Vliet 1991) indicates that Africans are increasingly likely to select marriage partners based, at least in part, on whether they are "in love." The emergence of romantic love as a criteria in mate selection and the increasing importance of conjugality (by which I mean here a couple's *personal* relationship to each other) in marriage relationships should not be interpreted to mean that romantic love itself has only recently emerged in Africa. When I asked elderly Igbos about their betrothals, about their marriages, and about love, I was told numerous personal stories and popular fables that indicated a long tradition of romantic love. A number of men and women confessed that they would have married a person other than their spouse had they been allowed to "follow the heart." Scholars have documented the existence of romantic love in Africa long before it became a widely accepted criterion for marriage (Bell 1995; Plotnicov 1995; Riesman 1971, 1973). Uchendu (1965b) confirms the existence of passionate love in his study of concubinage in traditional Igbo society. Interestingly, both men and women were accorded significant institutionalized extramarital sexual freedom and a related proverb survives to the present: *uto ka na iko* ("sweetness" is deepest among lovers). As Obiechina notes: "The question is not whether love and sexual attraction as normal human traits exist within Western and African societies, but how they are woven into the fabric of life" (1973: 34).

Exactly when Africans in general and Igbos in particular began to conceptualize marriage choices in more individualistic terms, privileging romantic love as a criterion in the selection of a spouse, is hard to pinpoint. In some parts of Igboland and in many parts of West Africa the social acceptance of individual choice in mate selection is still just beginning. Certainly these changes occurred first in urban areas among relatively educated and elite populations (Marris 1962; Little and Price 1973). Obiechina's (1973) study of Onitsha pamphlet literature indicates that popular Nigerian literature about love, romance, and "modern" marriage began to emerge just after World War II. Historical accounts suggest that elements of modern marriage began even earlier in the twentieth century (Mann 1985). By the 1970s, a number of monographs about modern marriage in West Africa had been produced (e.g., Oppong 1974; Harrell-Bond 1975). In contemporary Igboland, the majority of young people choose their own spouses and the expectation to do so is almost universal among those still in school.

Anthropologists have long portrayed changes in the criteria and process of mate selection as reflective of profound transformations in the social organization of African societies (Krige 1936; Mair 1969). In particular, individual choice in the selection of marriage partners and the emergence of conjugality as an important dimension of marriage dynamics have been depicted as being associated with the breakdown of collective, kinship-oriented systems of production and reproduction (Marris 1962; Mair 1969). As early as 1953, in an introduction to a classic study of African marriage and family life, Phillips writes:

> In attempting an analysis of modern trends, mention should perhaps first be made of the diminishing importance of the collective or group aspect of marriage. Emphasis is shifting to the individual aspect of marriage

as a relationship between two persons.... The traditional function of the marriage relationship as a continuing bond between two kinship groups...is being lost to view.... The developments referred to above are attributable to a combination of factors, which cannot be examined in detail here but which may broadly be comprehended under the term 'culture contact' (1969 [1953]: xii-xiii).

Demographers have also focused on changing patterns of marriage and family organization as key processes in social transformation. Demographers have sought to explain and predict declines (and the lack thereof) in African fertility based on changes (or not) in the structure of family organization (e.g., Goode 1963; Caldwell 1982). Characterizing the overall thrust of theorizing about fertility patterns in developing countries, Lesthaeghe writes that it is:

the concept of Westernization, that is, the penetration of Western ideals about the conjugal family which provide a direction for family change in the Third World. The shift towards nuclear residence patterns for households, and especially toward European-like conjugal marriage, is seen as taking place either because corporate kinship systems or extended families are too rigid and curtail individual freedom, or because their economic basis is gradually being withdrawn (1989: 6).

Both the early anthropological literature (Krige 1936; Phillips 1969 [1953]) and the demographic literature (Goode 1963) focused attention on the penetration of Western ideas and patterns of family organization. But Lesthaeghe rightly cautions that Africans are not simply adapting and reproducing Western family structures, rather "African populations are currently producing their own versions of new systems that are still far from crystallized" (1989: 11).

As indicated above, a good deal of the early evidence for the rise of romantic love and the transformation of marriage into a more conjugal relationship in Africa focused on urban populations, particularly the urban elite (Krige 1936; Oppong 1974). A number of interesting analyses of the transformation of marriage drew on evidence from popular media and literature such as letters to editors and advice columns in popular African magazines (Jahoda 1959; Little 1979). The content of these popular literatures suggests, and the analysts concur, that major changes have been taking place for several decades in the social construction of African marriage. But as the words of many of the letter writers indicate, Africans are not simply abandoning "traditional" practices in favor of "modern" ones. Rather, they are creating their own systems of marriage and family organization that use resources of the past *and* the present, negotiating the tensions that emerge, and drawing on both "traditional" and "modern" moralities as they see fit (van der Vliet 1991). Processes of social reproduction and social transformation are mutually implicated (Grosz-Ngate 1988; Bourdieu 1977; Giddens 1979; 1984), such that "modern" African marriages are both "new" *and* embedded in longstanding social and cultural systems.

The relative influence of the "old" and the "new" varies at different points in the life course. In processes of mate selection and in the unfolding of marriage relationships in contemporary Igbo society, I found striking contrasts between the dynamics of courtship and marriage. Courtship most often privileged the nature of a couple's personal relationship and was negotiated based on interpersonal intimacy and expressions of love. In contrast, couples' relationships after marriage were more attuned to and influenced by continuing ties and obligations to extended family and community, privileging fertility and the social roles of mother and father. While modern courtship fostered a more egalitarian gender dynamic, modern marriage reinforced a more patriarchal hierarchy. Neither men nor women are passive actors in these processes. They deploy strategies from "traditional" and "modern" value systems to achieve their goals and negotiate their positions within relationships (van der Vliet 1991).

"Traditional" Igbo Marriages

Igbos are generally patrilineal (meaning that people trace their ancestry through the male line and inheritance is passed from fathers to sons) and marriage is lineage exogamous (meaning that one cannot marry from within one's extended lineage). Traditionally, marriages occurred between close neighboring peoples, creating alliances across nearby communities. In the past, Igbo marriages were mostly arranged between families. Among the elder generation—those above seventy years old or so—stories of mate selection typically include a memory of the time that one's father or mother pointed out a young woman or man and said "that will be your spouse." Even in the days when arranged marriages were taken for granted, this was a frightening and awesome moment. Almost every old person I asked—male and female—could narrate in great detail the moment they found out about their betrothal. Elder Igbos say that both men and women have always had the right to refuse marriage partners, but social pressure to conform to community and family expectations made it difficult to opt out. Memories of girls who ran away to avoid a particular marriage, or men who defied their parents and married the woman of their choice demonstrate that a tension between arranged marriage and personal preferences has always existed. Popular fables and myths often recount men and women who acted out of love and defied family and community demands. In some stories the protagonists end up as heroes or heroines; in many others their defiance serves to explain their ill fate.

These stories, both those that are true and those that are apocryphal, show that the idea of love predates the growing acceptance that marriage should be based on love. But they also demonstrate the power of cultural norms that insist marriage is very much the business of kin groups and communities, and not simply a private affair between consenting individuals. "Traditional" Igbo marriage ceremonies—called *igba nkwu* ceremonies—involve hundreds of people from and associated with the lineages of the man and woman who are getting married. Extended negotiations over bridewealth, a host of obligatory exchanges, and the tremendous amount of cooperation between the two kin groups that must occur to perform the ceremony successfully instill the respect and mutual obligations that characterize affinal relations in Igboland.[3] For those who attend an *igba nkwu* ceremony, and certainly for the couple getting married, there can be no doubt that many people are invested in the marriage.

CONTEMPORARY IGBO MARRIAGES

Today the vast majority of young couples initiate their own marriages. Few marriages are strictly arranged. But the process of actually getting married still includes the extended families and communities of both the man and the woman. The performance of the *igba nkwu* ceremony without the consent and assistance of kinfolk is impossible. Even among the most "modern" Igbos of the younger generation, one is not considered *really* married without the *igba nkwu* ceremony—despite the fact that it is possible to marry *legally* in the church or a court.

Although the current generation claims to and, in most senses, certainly does choose its own marriage partners, it is very difficult for Igbos to marry someone to whom their families object. The criteria for approval entail class and ethnic dimensions. It is unusual and difficult to marry a non-Igbo. It happens, but it remains rare.[4] Even in the Igbo diaspora, most people come home to find a mate. Marrying below one's social class is also difficult, but more common. Men find it easier than women to marry "beneath them" because a couple's social class depends mainly on the position of the husband.

But the most interesting and conflict-producing restriction in spousal selection has to do with "place of origin" within Igbo society itself. As I mentioned above, traditionally, Igbo people observed specific rules of lineage or village exogamy, but married from among close-by neighboring communities with whom they have longstanding ties. Affinal relationships create and solidify social networks that are useful politically and economically. Historically, such alliances helped maintain peace between potentially warring communities, created allies in the event of warfare, and facilitated trade networks and relationships upon which the Igbo economy depended. Presently, these relationships are no less important— as the means of access to the resources of the nation-state and the Nigerian economy (Bayart 1993; Chukwuezi 2001; Smith 1999, 2007a).

The fear of marrying from strange or distant Igbo communities stems from a practical concern that effective reciprocal relationships cannot be adequately cultivated. The woman's family cannot easily monitor the marriage, will not be as familiar with and involved in the lives of the children produced, and may not, therefore, benefit as those children become important resources in the wider world. The husband's family will not be able to depend on their affines to contribute support for the children, and will find it difficult to appeal to affines for help in stabilizing the marriage or assisting in family problems.

In today's more fluid and urbanized Nigeria, many young Igbos from distant communities and clans meet in towns while they attend school, work, or seek business opportunities. Sexual and romantic relationships often evolve into marriage proposals. Igbo couples from communities separated by tens and sometimes hundreds of miles decide they want to get married. Their families often find these proposed unions problematic. When two people from distant Igbo communities decide to marry, their respective families often try to talk them out of it. All of the intra-Igbo stereotypes are deployed to convince the couple of the inauspicious nature of the marriage. "*Ngwa* people are cannibals;" "*Aro* people are arrogant and selfish;" "*Mbaise* people are criminals;" "*Wawa* people are primitive".... *Ngwa, Aro, Mbaise,* and *Wawa* are the names of Igbo sub-groups. For every Igbo sub-group that one is not supposed to marry there is a stereotype that will be invoked to show why marrying such people is dangerous or dirty. The marshaling of prejudices and stereotypes is meant to persuade young people to marry from communities with whom they can more assuredly have effective affinal relations.

It is my sense that it is more often the woman's people than the man's people who reject a potential marriage with a partner from a distant place—because they have more to lose given that the woman (and any children she produces) will reside in her husband's place. To discourage a marriage, the young man and/or his delegation can be repeatedly put off as they come to negotiate the bridewealth with their potential affines. The woman's people are typically polite, but always find one excuse or another to slow and frustrate the negotiations. Sometimes the man will give up, or the woman will withdraw from the arrangement, telling her suitor she is no longer interested.

But families and communities do not always win these battles. A young couple that remains insistent about getting married can often outlast their elders. Most young people still marry from close to home. But the number of marriages that cross traditional intra-Igbo cultural divides is growing, and the acceptability of such marriages is increasing. In part this is because Igbo people are recognizing the potential benefits of taking advantage of affinal ties that reach across wider distances in Nigerian society. However, it is also a capitulation to the changing conception of what a marriage should be—the change grounded, to some extent, in the increasing acceptance of conjugality, intimacy, and "love" as the basis for marriage.

CHANGING MARRIAGE, CHANGING GENDER

The gender dynamics that characterize contemporary sexual and marital relationships in southeastern Nigeria mark significant changes from the past, as well as interesting continuities. The whole arena of courtship and premarital sexuality is a relatively recent phenomenon, at least in its currently prevalent form. In traditional Igbo society, female chastity before marriage was highly valued, and opportunities for young women to experience sexual intercourse before marriage were severely limited by the early age at marriage (Uchendu 1965a; Okonjo 1992). The same social transformations that have led to later age at marriage for women—i.e., formal schooling, urban migration and employment, and aspirations for upward social mobility—have also contributed to the proliferation and acceptance of premarital sexuality. Uchendu notes that:

> increasing acculturation, the long period of schooling, the separation of girls from their mothers, the rejection of traditional sanctions by educated girls and boys, and the rising age at marriage have made the girl who is a virgin at marriage into a social curiosity (1965a: 189).

While many Igbo parents and elders still say that young women should stay virgins until marriage, almost no one expects this to be the case and young women do not harm their chances for attracting a mate by engaging in premarital sexual relations. In fact, as Little (1979) and Harrell-Bond (1975) observed in Sierra Leone, young women may risk losing potential suitors if they try to remain chaste. As one of Harrell-Bond's informants noted: "in order to get a good husband, you have to be good, but you also have to be careful not to be too good" (1975: 158).

The general acceptability of premarital sexual relations must be understood in the context of the changing relationship between sexuality and procreation. As Krige concluded several decades ago: "The key to the attitude of Africans towards this subject is that the religious values associated with sex are concentrated on procreation and not on sexual activity as such" (1936: 3). Because young Igbo women are able to engage in premarital sexual relations without necessarily having a child, families and communities are not overly concerned about young women's chastity per se. Not surprisingly, a premarital pregnancy brings much greater concern, and young Igbo women commonly resort to unsafe illegal abortions to terminate unwanted premarital pregnancies (Oriuwa 1999; Smith 2000). The fact that premarital sexual relationships and processes of courtship are negotiated between individual men and women, based largely on the quality of their personal relationship, affords women considerable power. While family approval for a marriage is still important, and issues of compatible social status are still implicit, a man who expects to woo a woman into marriage must be ready to perform as a romantic lover. He must win her heart, not just pay her brideprice.

But after marriage, gender dynamics seem to revert to a more patriarchal pattern. In this context, it is worth asking whether Igbo men are as committed as Igbo women to the idea of romantic love as the basis for marriage. Certainly young Igbo women were well aware that Igbo men try to manipulate women's affections in order to get sex, and some married women I spoke to who were unhappy with their philandering husbands wondered out loud whether their husbands had ever really loved them. Such sentiments were echoed by the South African women that van der Vliet studied. One of them is quoted:

> When he wants to marry you he tells you all sorts of lies. 'You'll be my equal, I'll be faithful to you' and all that, and you think, 'This is the man I must marry!' The minute you put the rings on—hunh!—the trouble starts.... What you are expected to do when you are a woman is to be a housewife and give birth to children. In fact, that's the main thing when they marry, they always think about how this woman will give birth to many children for the sake of our family name and to increase the whole clan (1991: 236).

While one could argue that Igbo men profess love to their desired spouses in order to secure their consent in marriage, and that they enter marriage with a nod and wink, knowing that they will eventually expect women to submit to more traditional and unequal gender roles, I think the explanation is more complicated. Changes in gender dynamics that occur after marriage must be understood in the context of the life course, taking into consideration the continuing centrality of parenthood, fertility, and kinship ties in Igbo social organization. Despite longstanding predictions that the strength of corporate kin-groups in Africa will wane with the establishment of "Western" forms marriage and household organization (Phillips 1969 [1953]; Goode 1963), in Igbo society, as in much of Africa, the importance of kinship and allegiance to "place of origin" remains powerful (Gugler and

Geschiere 1998; Gugler 2002; Smith 1999, 2004b; Chukwuezi 2001). Parenthood and relatively high fertility are essential to the social reproduction of corporate kin-groups, and considerable social pressure is exerted on people to marry, produce children, and fulfill their obligations to their extended families and communities.

A powerful confluence of social and demographic changes in sub-Saharan Africa has contributed to changing the dynamics of courtship and marriage. Increasing education, urban migration and employment, the influence of widely circulating ideas about love and romance, and the related rise in the age of marriage have created a process of courtship that privileges individual choice and interpersonal emotions. In the Igbo case, this new pattern of courtship seems to provide women with relative equality in the arena of sexuality and mate selection. But the consequences for women in marriage are quite different, and arguably less equal than in "traditional" Igbo society. Because fertility and parenthood remain the paramount values associated with family, married women are socially evaluated primarily in their role as mothers. A number of scholars have noted that transformations to modern marriage may have a deleterious effect on women's status (Little 1979; Hollos 1991). Most of these studies emphasize the increased economic dependence associated with women's transition from productive farmers and traders to "housewives." Though many women try to negotiate a more companionate and gender-equal marriage relationship drawing on "modern" cultural scripts for marriage, the enduring social importance of parenthood provides men powerful leverage in negotiating power within marriage based on more "traditional" scripts (van der Vliet 1991).

Social actors inevitably work to manipulate social resources—including concepts like "traditional" and "modern"—to achieve their goals. Processes of social and demographic transformation proceed partly under the influence of these actors and partly beyond their control. Changes in the construction of marriage and the nature of courtship in Igbo society can only be understood in the context of the complex melding of historical patterns of social organization and new practices and ideas introduced over time. The outcome for institutions, and for individuals, is not completely predictable, and certainly African societies do not simply mimic and adopt whole cloth ideas introduced from elsewhere. The enduring importance of kinship in Igboland, and in Africa more generally, is rooted in the reality of African political economies, as well as in their associated moralities. Increasingly prevalent ideals about love and romance and about the value of individual autonomy and choice must respond and adjust to the continuing reliance on corporate groups based on family and community. In addition, the effects of these changes and adjustments may be distributed differently over the life course, such that in Nigeria Igbo women appear to much freer in the premarital sexual lives than in their marriages, where they are subject to collective surveillance and male-dominated interpretations of gender expectations.

Of course it is possible to imagine that ongoing social changes will strengthen women's position in the household and weaken the influence of extended families. Increasing female education and employment, urban migration, more exposure to "Western" images of marriage, and the growing popularity of "born again" Christian churches that emphasize marital fidelity all could contribute to further transformations in gender roles. But as long as parenthood remains the primary value associated with marriage, and kinship ties remain so important for securing social resources, I suspect that in this patrilineal society courtship and marriage will continue to produce dramatically different gender dynamics.

"LAGGING" FERTILITY TRANSITION: CHILDBEARING AND KINSHIP[5]

Striking in these unfolding processes is the continued social importance of fertility and parenthood. While most conceptualizations of the relationship between changes in the structure of marriage and the value of fertility have made fertility the dependent variable, the evidence from my research suggests that the direction of influence may run the other way as well. Even as mate selection, marriage, and family structure seem to be changing in ways that are typically described as "Western" or "modern," the extent of those changes and the gender dynamics that emerge are highly sensitive to the continuing value of parenthood and fertility. In this section I argue and try to explain why the persistent value of fertility is itself a product of continuities in the importance of corporate kinship groups, even in modern African contexts (Lesthaeghe 1989; Gugler and Geschiere 1998; Smith 1999).

While much of the existing literature in anthropology and demography charts a complex array of economic, social, and cultural forces that both drive and constrain fertility transition in Africa, the way in which competing pressures unfold in the lives of people in the midst of these transitions is not well documented. Nigerians experience fertility transition paradoxically, simultaneously acknowledging the potential benefits of smaller numbers of children while lamenting the pressures to curtail fertility. I argue that these contradictions are best explained by examining the intertwining of kinship and patron-clientism, and specifically by understanding how processes of kin-based patronage are being undermined, but also reconfigured, in response to rapid social change.

The experience of fertility transition as contradiction is manifest in the ways that Nigerians express understandings of the social processes that shape their fertility behavior. People perceive pressures to limit fertility as related to economic hardship, but also link having fewer children to economic development and progress. The seeming paradox that fertility transition is driven by perceptions of hardship yet is also part of a process of economic development is recognized in demography (van de Walle and Foster 1990; Caldwell, Oruboloye, and Caldwell 1992:229, 233, 236-237), but has not been adequately addressed ethnographically. Perhaps needless to say, people who are actually having children do not conceptualize what they are doing in the language or formulas of demography. From an anthropological point of view, important questions are: (1) how do people participating in Nigeria's fertility transition perceive what they are doing, and (2) what can be learned from approaching fertility transition from this perspective?

Of course, people's feelings about and interpretations regarding their fertility and the state of their society's political economy are not necessarily the best (and certainly not the only) criteria to evaluate what is happening. Clearly, as some of the evidence below will suggest, rising expectations about things like education, living standards, and relative individual independence from kin and community networks change the criteria for what counts as hardship. But the experiences and understandings of the people who actually populate and produce the demographic trends we try to understand are surely an important form of data, and they open up some interesting theoretical questions about the social context of fertility transition.

The main theoretical argument advanced in this section is that the fertility behavior of Nigerians must be understood in the context of the ways that children, parenthood, family, and kinship are inextricably intertwined with how Nigerians navigate a political economy organized around patron-clientism. Patron-client social networks are an essential, indeed, in current circumstances, virtually irreplaceable, resource for advancing individual and collective interests in Nigerian society (Joseph 1987; Chabal and Daloz 1999; Smith 2001a, 2007a). Further, kinship continues to be the most reliable and trustworthy basis for creating and navigating patron-client networks, and having children is the mechanism for the biological and social reproduction of kinship networks.

Without a doubt, important social transformations, such as the movement towards a less agriculturally based economy, formal education, urbanization, and exposure to globally circulating ideas about individuality, marriage and family, are reconfiguring the political economic and cultural forces that shape demographic processes. Some of these changes pose threats to and create resentments over structures of patron-clientism. But these changes do not happen with unilineal momentum. Even as Nigerians increasingly value educational investment in children, as they resent some of the inequalities associated with patronage and resist some of the pressures to share resources with extended family, and as they develop ideals of marriage and family formation that conflict with the traditional models, they face simultaneous pressures to stay connected to and invested in their larger kin groups and communities of origin (Berry 1985; Trager 2001; Gugler 2002; Renne 2003; Smith 2004b). Further, they maintain continued desires for relatively large families. It is these paradoxes and the social organizational realities that underlie them that require better understanding and that I try to address below.

HAVING PEOPLE: KINSHIP AND PATRONAGE

Before presenting ethnographic examples that illustrate the contradictory pressures that Nigerians experience as part of the process of fertility transition, it is important to lay out briefly a theoretical overview of the political economic and social organizational dynamics that underlie the ways my interlocutors understand community, family, and

48

childbearing in contemporary Nigeria. As indicated above, central to the social organizational structure of Igbo society, and to the structure of Nigeria more generally, is the tremendous importance of kinship, and particularly the extent to which people perceive that survival and success in their political economic context depend upon what Nigerians commonly call "having people" (Smith 1999, 2007a; Renne 2003).

To understand how people experience fertility transition as contradiction, it is necessary to explain how processes of social transformation simultaneously undermine some of the ways that Nigerians traditionally relied on "having people," and yet also produce new contexts where reliance on social networks rooted in kinship and community of origin are essential for access to social resources, even when those resources are modern ones like education, urban employment, or business opportunities (Joseph 1987; Berry 1989; Smith 2001a).

Integral to the ways that Nigerians experience and interpret these transformations is the fact that social networks, including kinship networks, are often highly hierarchical, such that navigating Nigeria's political economy depends upon social ties of patron-clientism (Barnes 1986; Joseph 1987; Chabal and Daloz 1999). A strong morality of reciprocity is crosscut by the realities of inequality. Animating the contradictions Nigerians face with regard to fertility are three intertwining aspects of kinship in contemporary Nigeria: (1) the continuing importance of kin-based social networks for access to social resources (Berry 1989; Smith 2001a); (2) the changing (and more inequitable) face of kin and community structures (Trager 2001; Renne 2003); and (3) the growing resentment people feel about the exacerbation of inequalities that characterize networks of kinship and patronage (Watts 1992; Bastian 1993; Nwankwo 1999; Smith 2001c).

In many ways, the current situation in Nigeria builds on longer-term processes. Africanist scholars have long noted that an individual's status and security depends greatly on his ability to control dependents (Goody 1971; Guyer 1993, 1995). Miers and Kopytoff (1977) coined the phrase "wealth in people," arguing that everyone in traditional Africa was bound in a system of rights and obligations. As d'Azevedo (1962) explained about the Gola in Liberia, every adult is a patron to lesser people and a client to a more powerful person. Berry (1985) and Bledsoe (1980) both highlight the overlapping nature of the reciprocal obligations of kinship and the dynamics of patron-clientism. Bledsoe

49

argues specifically that "kinspeople do enter into relations that are best described as patron-client relations" (1980:58). Berry's account of class formation in southwestern Nigeria emphasizes the continued importance of kinship, even as access to the institutions of the state becomes essential for doing business successfully. In my own research, it became clear that Igbos gain access to the resources of the state and the wider economy through social networks of reciprocity and obligation that have their roots in the family, the lineage, and the local community.

Indeed, Igbos have many proverbs that emphasize the importance of "having people," including *"onye were madu were ike"* and *"onye were madu were aku,"* which translate literally into "somebody who has people has power" and "somebody who has people has wealth." Such proverbs were doubtless coined in an era when economic well being was grounded in a household or lineage system of production, tied principally to agriculture, and where political security depended upon the capacity to mobilize followers in local disputes and regional warfare. While a number of demographers have pointed out the durability of certain features of African social organization, and the potential of these features to perpetuate relatively high fertility (Caldwell and Caldwell 1987; Lesthaeghe 1989), much less attention has been paid in demographic accounts to how a "wealth in people" model is being transformed to suit current conditions. The enduring salience of these "wealth in people" proverbs in contemporary Nigeria reflects the continued importance of "having people" in a different kind of political economic context, offering clues to the sociological underpinnings of the present demographic situation.

In the remainder of the section, I expand on the issues that have been raised thus far, using examples collected from interviews, participant observation, and case studies of particular families. I begin by looking at how my informants describe and understand the pressures to have fewer children, expressed most clearly in narratives about a poor economy, insecurity, and hardship, but also in almost ubiquitous stories of the importance and burdens of "training" (educating) children. Manifest in many of these accounts are indications of the ways that the changing structure of communities and families, including the increasing inequality that characterizes kinship relations, are intertwined with people's decisions about fertility.

Examples of the forces and scenarios that lead people to consider limiting their fertility are followed by two cases that illustrate the continuing pressures to have relatively large families. These cases demonstrate the importance of "having people" for succeeding in contemporary Nigerian society and the continued influence that one's kin and community have on how couples think about their fertility options. Individual fertility decisions and the aggregate processes of fertility transition are profoundly intertwined with broader transformations in the political economy and with changes in patterns of social organization from the most micro to the most macro-sociological levels. Rather than being perceived by the participants as inexorable progress, such changes are experienced in terms of contradictions, economic hardship, and personal struggle.

THE BURDENS OF HAVING PEOPLE
AND LOWER FERTILITY

I began my research in 1995 with the aim of trying to investigate the apparent paradox of persistent high fertility in an African population that appeared to be highly "modern" and seemingly most likely to lead Nigeria's fertility transition. Given the high fertility in the region, I was somewhat surprised when I found in my interviews that Igbo people talked constantly about the pressures to have fewer children. The majority of married men and women still in their childbearing years recognized and articulated the need to plan and limit the number of children they would have. Virtually all of the university and secondary students I interviewed talked this way as well. Even a significant number of older people, who had finished with their own childbearing and who were participants in an era of very high fertility, expressed the view that their children should have fewer offspring. Most striking in all of the interviews was the recurrent and dominant view that the main reasons to limit fertility were a bad economy, hard times, and the burdens and expenses of trying to "train" children. I argue that these narratives of hardship show another side of social and demographic change, different from the dominant popular Western tropes that depict fertility transition as part of a grand process of "progress," "modernization," "globalization," and "development."

51

Married Igbo men and women in the midst of their childbearing years commonly voiced the need to plan their families in the language of economic struggle. The words of Chioma, a 27-year-old mother of three in Ubakala with a primary school education and a small commercial stall she runs with her husband in the local market, were typical of scores responses to questions about the motives for limiting fertility: "My husband and I cannot have more than four children. The situation in Nigeria now is bad. Life is hard. It is not possible to support many children." Kalu, a 42-year-old farmer with five children and a still fecund 35-year-old wife said: "I have told my wife to do family planning. We cannot support any more children. Even these ones will be difficult to train. Times are rough. A man cannot have so many children like before." Da Ihuoma, a 52-year-old woman who had eight births and has six living children said about her first daughter, Adanma, who was recently married: "I advised her to do family planning. She should not have more than four or five children. Nigeria is not like before. Everything is costly now. It is better to have a few children and train them well." These quotations are but a few of the countless narratives I collected in which people described the pressures to limit fertility in the language of a changing economy marked by struggle and hardship.

The idea that it is economic hardship that necessitates family planning is reflected in and reinforced by some of the media messages produced and disseminated by the government and international donors. Numerous posters and radio and television advertisements in Nigeria promote family planning. They frequently depict large families as associated with poverty and small families as associated with wealth. I remember one TV spot that ran regularly in the 1990s that showed a haggard man trying to transport his poorly dressed wife and several ragged children on a bicycle. In the commercial, the bicycle crashes and the lesson promoted by the narrator is the need for family planning. Such images both mirror and bolster the popular conception that economic hard times are the primary motive to curtail fertility.

Of course implicit in the TV advertisement, and, indeed, in the narratives of some of my informants, is the idea that planned, smaller families are a symbol of and a means to a more prosperous and modern lifestyle. Many informants who described economic hardship as a motive for limiting fertility simultaneously articulated the importance of educating children. Indeed, some people talked about fertility plans primarily in the language of training children, with the benefits of education as important as the costs. This is compatible with some of the more established theories about the mechanisms that underlie fertility transition (Caldwell 1982). Chinwe, a 32-year-old mother of three said: "My husband and I have agreed to have only four children so that we can train them well. It is better to have a few children who are educated than many who are not. That way they can find good jobs." Renne (2003) found similar views linking the value of education with the need for family planning, but also with allusions to economic hardship, among Yoruba-speaking informants in her study of fertility and development in a rural southwestern Nigerian town. An older uneducated woman Renne interviewed said: "In the past, people used to give birth to about seven or eight children. But the question that worries me is what will they eat? Can we have children without giving them an education? This won't be appropriate" (Renne 2003:11). The idea that family planning is linked to promises of progress and development is certainly promoted by the government and by collaborating international donors, and many Nigerians conceptualize the benefits of smaller families in these terms, even as they also articulate the pressure to have fewer children in a language of hardship and struggle.

Reflected in these statements about the burdens of providing for and educating children is an awareness that Nigeria has changed. The most explicit articulations of these changes use a vocabulary of economic hardship and personal struggle. But the forces that propel family planning and fertility decline are also linked to ongoing changes in the structure of families, the scope of kinship obligations, and the character of patron-client relations. People's sense of the increasing burden of raising children is explained not only by the growing importance of education and the experience of hardship in Nigeria's changing economy, but also by the fact that people feel less able to rely on wide networks of kin and relationships of patron-clientism for help with their children's upbringing and their immediate family's welfare. Amos, a forty-six-year-old father of five, expressed sentiments I heard from growing numbers of parents: "Who else will train my children? Five children are the most I can manage to train. Even this number is a struggle. I cannot look to anyone else to train my children for me. It is my responsibility." Fertility transition, then, is both a product of and window onto fundamental changes in social organization and in the meanings that people attribute to different kinds of relationships.

In Igbo society, discontent over expectations about appropriate sharing and reciprocity certainly preceded the social transformations associated with fertility decline. The fact that kinship relationships have always had a patron-client dimension meant that some level of dissatisfaction over inequality was inevitable. But in contemporary Nigeria the increasing inequality that characterizes patron-client relations and the trend for people to try to narrow the scope of their kinship obligations, both of which are exacerbated by high rates of rural-urban migration, produce a situation where most Nigerians are regularly and profoundly concerned about these issues (Bastian 1993; Renne 2003). As clients, virtually everyone laments the failures of their kin and patrons to offer levels of assistance they would like to receive.

Conversely, as patrons, nearly everyone laments the burdens imposed by kin and other clients who expect assistance. And, as mentioned above, given that in Nigeria everyone is a patron to a lesser person and a client to a more powerful person, contradictions abound. With regard to children and their training, these issues arise most readily in problems of providing for children's education, and in the related phenomenon of child fostering. To the extent that these concerns propel fertility transition, it is because people feel that, as parents, they are, increasingly, the only ones who can be counted on to train their own children. Compared to Western societies, Igbo parents still rely heavily on extended families in undertaking the enterprise of child rearing. Nonetheless, the perception that training children costs more and that the burden for training children falls ever more narrowly on parents is a significant part of people's experience of the pressures to limit fertility.

THE BENEFITS OF HAVING PEOPLE AND HIGHER FERTILITY

Though surveys, in-depth interviews, and participant observation demonstrate that Igbo people are experiencing strong pressures to limit fertility, just as striking are the continued desires and pressures to have relatively large numbers of children. Almost none of the married people in my various samples indicated a desired fertility of less than four children, and even among secondary school and university students, the vast majority desired "four," "four or five," or "at least four" children. People both desire to have at least four children and feel strong social pressure to do so. In this section I present two brief case studies, one that illustrates the pressures to have at least four children and another that shows the continued salience of a "wealth in people" model for how Igbos think about their society, even when people's goals and pursuits are decidedly modern. In Nigeria, as fertility decline takes shape, "having people" remains a dominant value and a rational strategy, producing the contradictions that characterize people's experience of demographic transition.

The Long Reach of "Home People"

Based on the literature on migration, urbanization, and fertility, one would expect that Ubakala natives who have migrated and settled in urban areas will have somewhat lower fertility than their rural kin (Lee 1992; Brockerhoff and Yang 1994; Brockerhoff 1998). However, in the Igbo context (and, arguably, in many African societies), rural and urban fertility are not independent processes. The contradictory pressures to limit fertility and to have relatively large families extend across rural-urban boundaries. This is the case for several reasons. First, the vast majority of Igbo migrants maintain strong ties to their communities of origin, both through continued visits and presence at "home" and because most Igbos participate in associations and networks of "home people" that are established in cities of destination (Smock 1971; Chukwuezi 2001; Gugler 2002). Second, most adults at home in the village are themselves one-time migrants, making the definition of who is a migrant and who is not, or who is "rural" and who is "urban," complicated and ever-changing. As the case below illustrates, even those rural-urban migrants who appear to be most likely to lead the fertility transition are subject to pressures to continue to have relatively large families.

Chima and Oluchi Njoku reside in Kano, the largest city in northern Nigeria, with a population of several million people. They have lived there since before they married—almost fifteen years. Chima sells motorcycle spare parts in one of Kano's sprawling markets. Oluchi teaches in a government primary school. At the time I met them Chima was 36 years old, Oluchi was 32. They had three children, two sons and a daughter, ranging in age from eleven to five. Both Chima and Oluchi hail from Ubakala, though from different villages. They did not know each other in Ubakala; they met in Kano through mutual friends who were also from Ubakala. When they decided to marry, Chima went home to initiate marriage negotiations with Oluchi's family. They completed their traditional *igba nkwo* wedding ceremony in Ubakala about twelve years ago.

Many rural-urban migrants marry from their place of origin and almost all perform the traditional *igba nkwo* ceremony, indicating the continued salience of ties to kin and community of origin. But Chima and Oluchi were also very urban and modern by many standards. They had a modern courtship, including sex before marriage. They saw themselves as "in-love" when they decided to marry. They had hoped to perform a Christian wedding ceremony, in addition to the traditional rituals, but could not afford it. Their marriage is fairly solidly companionate. They share one household budget, sleep together in one room every night, and discuss many family decisions jointly—especially regarding their children. Each of these aspects represents a change from patterns dominant in their parents' generation. At the time I began interviewing them, Oluchi had used an IUD for about four years. At first Chima objected vehemently, saying that it was a sign of promiscuity—and that they were not finished having children. But Oluchi prevailed, mostly because Chima agreed that they could not afford to have more kids yet—especially since Chima's youngest brother was living with them in Kano and Chima was sponsoring him in secondary school. Their own children were advancing in school as well. Providing a good education for their children was Chima's and Oluchi's most important ambition.

Chima and Oluchi typically go home to Ubakala a couple of times a year. Kano is a long and, by local standards, expensive 15-hour bus ride from Ubakala. On trips "home" sometimes Chima and Oluchi travel together; more often they go individually, so that someone can maintain household and work responsibilities in Kano. They remain closely tied to their natal community. In addition to their regular visits home, they also receive guests from home in their Kano flat. Besides the movement back and forth between Kano and Ubakala, there is a substantial community of "home people" in Kano. Ubakala migrants in the city regularly get together—formally to take decisions about Kano migrants' contributions to community projects and life course rituals at home in Ubakala, informally to exchange news and gossip and utilize each other as messengers and resources.

Even in Kano, Chima and Oluchi remain subject to the gaze of their community. Among the aspects of their lives most surveilled is their fertility. At the time I began to get to know them some of their relatives back home were concerned that there had been no children since the third, some five years earlier. Those concerns filtered back and forth between Kano and Ubakala, and were sometimes voiced to Chima and Oluchi by a subtle reference or even a bold question. Eventually "the village" came to their door in the form of Chima's mother. Chima said:

> One evening my mother arrived from the village unexpect-
> edly. We were afraid that something bad had happened at
> home—that someone had died. But my mother assured us
> there was no emergency at home. The next morning she
> revealed that "the problem" which brought her to Kano
> was here. When I said I did not know what she meant,
> she said she and others were troubled that nothing had
> happened for five years. She had come to recommend we
> return home to visit a diviner. When I told her we were
> intentionally not having children and that Oluchi was
> using an IUD my mother was shocked. She condemned
> the practice and blamed Oluchi. How could we stop after
> only three kids, she asked? What was Oluchi after?

Implied in Chima's mother's words and tone was an accusation that Oluchi was responsible for the situation, and not just because she was using an IUD, but perhaps because her own ambitions were interfering with her "duty" to produce enough children. Indeed, it became clear through further discussions that Chima's mother might have even been implying that Oluchi was using some kind of witchcraft or magical medicine to avoid more pregnancies. Oluchi was troubled by her mother-in-law's accusations—even though they were only voiced to her by insinuation. And she lamented the long reach of her extended family. She said:

> In our culture your marriage and your children are not
> simply your business. They are the business of the whole
> extended family and the whole village. Don't you see how

my mother-in-law came all the way here to complain about me? My husband has not said so, but I know he will soon demand another child.

When I asked whether she wanted another, Oluchi said she was not sure. Both Oluchi and Chima had told me before Chima's mother's visit that they might still have more children, but clearly the old woman's visit increased the family pressure. While Chima's mother's visit and interference may appear familiar in Western eyes as a cross-cultural version of a dominant or nagging mother-in-law, in the Igbo case Chima's mother represents a much wider collective interest in a couple's fertility. She gave concrete voice to a concern about Chima's and Oluchi's fertility that manifest itself in local gossip, rumor, and speculation, some of which I heard myself in both Ubakala and Kano.

As mentioned above, Chima and Oluchi thought they might have another child even before Chima's mother's visit. They shared the common belief that a couple should have at least four children. But as urban dwellers they were in a position where they felt pressures to limit fertility most strongly, and they had the knowledge, access, and experience with contraceptives to limit their children to less than four had they decided to. In the end, they had a fourth child less than 18 months after this incident. Despite her earlier statement, Oluchi ultimately described the decision to have a fourth child as a mutual decision with her husband. No matter how one accounts for the decision, the visit of Chima's mother clearly symbolized and gave voice to continued collective expectations about the importance of relatively high fertility.

KINSHIP, PATRONAGE, AND ACCESS TO EDUCATION

The reasons that Igbos continue to value and have relatively large numbers of children are multiple and complex. In interviews, when asked why they wanted "at least four" children, people voiced a number of rationales, including: the love of children; the need to have at least one son; the potential risk of mortality; the importance of having children to perpetuate one's name, lineage, legacy, and community; the benefits of having enough children to assure a diverse set of life trajectories for one's offspring, with the hope that at least some would pay off; and the need to have children who would help provide assistance in old age. To various degrees, each of these responses represents issues that have been well documented in the demographic literature, both with regard to how they serve as props for high fertility and in terms of how changes in these spheres help explain fertility decline (van de Walle and Foster 1990). But very striking in both the interviews and observations of people's daily lives was the continued importance of "having people" as the mechanism through which individuals, families, and communities get access to social resources in Nigeria's patron-client oriented political economy. The continued importance of "having people" contributes strongly to a social context where relatively high fertility remains valued, rational, and collectively promoted.

The case described below is one of many examples of the way in which my informants relied on networks of patronage, rooted in a moral economy tied to kinship, in order to get access to social resources, even those resources most associated with modernization, development, and fertility transition itself. An example related to education is significant because it demonstrates the paradoxes of Nigeria's fertility transition most clearly. Education is one of the most common and powerful variables used by demographers to explain fertility decline (Cleland and Rodriguez 1988; van de Walle and Foster 1990). Further, as the evidence presented above clearly shows, the importance and costs of education are closely associated in the minds of Igbo people with the pressures to lower fertility. Yet, as the case below illustrates, where access to resources continues to depend on networks of patronage that are best navigated through kinship ties, a "wealth in people" model of how the world works is preserved, but in a context where pressures to limit fertility are also powerful, creating the contradictions that characterize Igbos' reproductive lives. The following account of one young girl's route to secondary school is typical of how Igbos must negotiate and manage their networks of social relationship—especially networks of kinship—in order to access opportunities for modern education.

Samuel and Nneoma were nearby neighbors in Ubakala during my fieldwork. They were typical Ubakala residents in that they combined multiple economic endeavors in order to make a living. They both farmed, but in addition, Nneoma sold drinks from a small shop in the market and Samuel utilized his carpentry skills to find occasional work on local construction projects. Samuel and Nneoma had four children, two boys and two girls, who ranged from ages three to ten when I arrived for fieldwork in 1995. As neighbors and informants they were quite familiar with my research, and they knew that in 1996 I was conducting interviews in all the local secondary schools. When their eldest daughter, Ezimma, completed primary school, Samuel and Nneoma had aspirations that she would be admitted to a selective federal government secondary school.

Ezimma scored adequately on her secondary school admissions test, but not well enough to gain entrance to prestigious federal school her parents wanted (federal government secondary schools are generally considered superior to state government schools in Nigeria). Because of the friendship I had with Samuel and Nneoma, they approached me for help. They thought I might have some influence with the principal at the federal school to help Ezimma get admission despite her scores. They also knew my niece had entered the federal school that year, and they assumed (wrongly) that I had been instrumental in her admission. In the event, I did approach the principal about Ezimma, but I was told her score was simply too low. The principal said Ezimma would not qualify for the best local state school, much less the federal school.

I know for a fact that in Nigeria many students get admission to secondary schools and universities, even when they are not officially qualified, based on the influence of their parents or other patrons. I have observed and been told about numerous such cases. Indeed, despite the fact that I turned out to be an ineffectual patron for Ezimma, her eventual admission to her second choice, the best local state secondary school, for which she was also officially unqualified, was made possible through the intervention of a more effective patron. Nneoma's brother-in-law did what I could not. He was connected politically to an important local politician and managed to persuade the influential politician to request a favor from the school's principal. Ezimma's admission to the better school was only possible because of Nneoma's sister's husband's connection.

Though such examples abound in Nigeria, it is important to note that people are generally careful to circumvent state/bureaucratic rules primarily among those they know and trust, partly out of fear that rules can be used against them. Instances of so-called corruption are far more likely when they are undertaken as the fulfillment of expectations and obligations to one's personal network of social relations—especially kinship and affinal relations (Smith 2001a, 2007a). While cases of outright bribery do occur, most people would agree that to accept money from a stranger to facilitate admission of a child who is not qualified based on her exam result is wrong: the rules of the state apply in such an impersonal case. To help your relative get admission when her scores were below the cut-off is expected and morally justified: the rules of kinship, community and reciprocity apply when the stakes are personal and familial.

The story of Ezimma's admission to secondary school is typical of parents' experiences. Igbos routinely rely on their kinship networks to facilitate educational goals. A child's transition from primary to secondary school and from secondary school to university (a rarer and more costly event) is widely recognized as a time when one must mobilize networks of social support. When I lectured at a Nigerian university I regularly witnessed professors deluged with requests from their kin and townsmen for help with discretionary admission. One of my close friends sat on the prestigious fifteen-member university council. Each council member was given five discretionary admissions places—no questions asked. This was considered one of the biggest perks of the office.

The widespread acceptance of formal education as a key credential in contemporary Nigeria has created for parents costs and burdens that seem to fit with conventional demographic models of fertility transition. But the Nigerian situation adds a contradictory twist. In Nigeria, access to secondary and higher education frequently depends on one's social connections. Ironically, the rise of education as a marker of modernization, while creating pressures that promote fertility decline, simultaneously solidifies Igbo notions that you can only make it in the world by "having people." The transformations that make education such an important value and that create burdens on parents that pressure them to limit fertility also reinforce the importance families, kinship, and "wealth in people."

CONCLUSION

Nearly twenty years ago, Ron Lesthaeghe summarized the continuing power of allegiance to corporate kin-groups in sub-Saharan Africa and explained its importance in perpetuating the value of fertility:

reproductive regimes of sub-Saharan Africa are still strongly attached to forms of social control prevailing in societies that capitalize on corporate allegiance.... Change has not been lacking though. The privatization of land ownership, the growth of the wage sector, urbanization or external cultural influences, all have altered the landscape. But, even when it comes to the appropriation of a plot or to securing a job in the wage sector, the reliance on corporate kinship groups or other particularistic networks reemerges with full force. Life is not easy, both in urban and rural environments, and support from others is always wanted. Also the imponderbilia of political life associated with the difficult process of nation building and the extra stress produced by the current economic crisis accentuate the importance of reliance upon and allegiance to trustworthy solidarity networks. In short, survival depends on... "investment in identity." The complement of such an investment is of course the enhancement of moral patronage and social control exerted by the protecting agencies.... the utility of children, and especially their security function, is likely to remain high for decades to come and, as a consequence, any future fertility decline is likely to lose momentum at average parities around four or five (1989: 498-500).

Further back, Jahoda noted that, "feelings of respect and dependence towards the family of origin have not weakened in proportion to the acceptance of new norms in other spheres" (1959:188-89). Their conclusions remain valid today, even as Nigeria experiences many changes associated with globalization. Kinship ties remain strong for practical and strategic social and economic reasons, as well as because of deeply entrenched sentiments.

The idea that kinship-based patronage systems remain important, even as African societies "modernize" by many different measures (e.g., literacy, urbanization, democratization, and consumption), has received substantial attention in the social sciences, especially with regard to issues of politics and the state (Joseph 1987; Bayart 1993; Chabal and Daloz 1999; Smith 2001a, 2007a), but remains relatively unexamined in the literature on African marriage and fertility transition. Arguably, most demographic accounts of African family structure that pay attention to "wealth in people" as part of the relevant political economic, social, and cultural context have adopted a somewhat static approach that equates kinship-based patron-clientism with tradition and resistance to change. The findings here are different. Ethnographic evidence from Igbo-speaking southeastern Nigeria suggests that social transitions propelling changes in marriage and fertility are powerfully underway. But rather than a "wealth in people" system serving as resistance to such changes, it is adapting to them, albeit in ways that create contradictory pressures in people's family and reproductive lives.

Igbo people in Nigeria are conflicted about the breadth of their obligations to extended family and community of origin. They resent and try to narrow their kinship obligations; yet they also realize that they cannot succeed in contemporary Nigeria if they jettison family and community ties (Berry 1989; Smith 2001a, 2007; Renne 2003). The enduring importance but also the paradoxes that characterize kin and community ties in the context of contemporary social change have been well demonstrated in many African contexts (Geschiere and Gugler 1998; Gugler 2002). The continued practical advantages of "having people" in order to deliver modern social resources help explain why marriage continues to be embedded in kinship and relatively high fertility remains valued. Yet these same social forces are reconfiguring the structure of family and community life, putting strains on kin relationships and contributing to economic pressures that push people to reduce the number of children they have. The social changes taking place in Nigeria, exemplified most powerfully in increasing levels of education and high rates of rural-urban migration, are both exacerbating inequality and constricting the networks of kin and community compatriots that people can depend on. Kinship has become people's biggest problem even as it remains their most important resource.

Notes

1.   I am grateful for research support provided by the National Institutes of Health (3 P30 HD28251-10S1 and 1 R01 41724-01A1), the National Science Foundation (BCS-0075764), the Wenner-Gren Foundation for Anthropological Research (6636), and Brown University.

2. The findings from this section draw from and build upon previously published articles, including Smith 2000, Smith 2001a, Smith 2001b, Smith 2006a, and Smith 2007b.

3. While high levels of kin and community involvement contribute to Igbo people's characterization (in English) of the *igba nkwu* ceremony as a "traditional wedding," in fact many aspects of the ceremony are thoroughly modern, including taking photographs, making videotapes, and expectations for conspicuous consumption.

4. Isiugo-Abanihe (1994) argues that high bridewealth in Igboland compared to other ethnic groups in Nigeria is driving many Igbos to marry outside their group. While inter-ethnic marriages are certainly more common than a generation or two ago, it was my observation that they are still rare. There was not one man living in the village where I interviewed 153 married couples, for example, who had a non-Igbo wife. Admittedly such couples might be more likely to reside in urban areas, but I submit that the phenomenon remains unusual.

5. Findings from this section draw heavily on Smith 1999 and Smith 2004c.

References

Barnes, Sandra. 1986. *Patrons and Power: Creating a Political Community in Metropolitan Lagos*. Bloomington: Indiana University Press.

Bastian, Misty. 1993. "'Bloodhounds who have no friends': Witchcraft and locality in the Nigerian popular press," in *Modernity and Its Malcontents: Ritual and Power in Postcolonial Africa*, Jean Comaroff and John Comaroff (eds.). Chicago: University of Chicago Press, pp. 129-166.

Bayart, J. F. 1993. *The State in Africa: The Politics of the Belly*. London: Longman.

Bell, J. 1995. "Notions of romantic love among the Taita of Kenya," in *Romantic Passion: A Universal Experience?*, ed. W. Jankowiak, pp. 152-65. New York: Columbia University Press.

Berry, Sara. 1985. *Fathers Work for Their Sons: Accumulation, Mobility and Class Formation in an Extended Yoruba Community*. Berkeley: University of California Press.

_____. 1989. "Social institutions and access to resources." *Africa* 59: 41-55.

Bledsoe, Caroline. 1980. *Women and Marriage in Kpelle Society*. Stanford: Stanford University Press.

Brockerhoff, Martin. 1998. "Migration and the fertility transition in African cities," in *Migration, Urbanization, and Development: New Directions and Issues,* R. E. Bilsborrow (ed.). Norwell, MA: Kluwer Academic Publishers, pp. 357-392.

Brockerhoff, Martin and X. Yang. 1994. "Impact of migration on fertility in sub-Saharan Africa." *Social Biology* 41(1-2): 19-43.

Bourdieu, P. 1977. *Outline of a Theory of Practice.* Cambridge: Cambridge University Press.

Caldwell, John. 1982. *Theory of Fertility Decline.* New York: Academic Press.

Caldwell, John and Pat Caldwell. 1987. "The cultural context of high fertility in sub-Saharan Africa." *Population and Development Review* 13(3): 409-437.

Caldwell, John, I.O. Oruboloye, and Pat Caldwell. 1992. "Fertility decline in Africa: A new type of transition?" *Population and Development Review* 18(2): 211-242.

Chabal, Patrick and Jean-Pascal Daloz. 1999. *Africa Works: Disorder as Political Instrument.* Oxford: James Currey for the International African Institute.

Chukwuezi, Barth. 2001. "Through thick and thin: Igbo rural-urban circularity, identity and investment." *Journal of Contemporary African Studies* 19(1): 55-66.

Cleland, John and German Rodriquez. 1988. "The effect of parental education on marital fertility in developing countries." *Population Studies* 42(3): 419-442.

Coale, Ainsley and Watkins, Susan, ed. 1986. *The Decline of Fertility in Europe.* Princeton: Princeton University Press.

d'Azevedo, Warren. 1962. "Common principles and variant kinship structures among the Gola of western Liberia." *American Anthropologist* 64(3): 504-520.

Geschiere Peter and Josef Gugler. 1998. "The urban-rural connection: Changing issues of belonging and identification." *Africa* 68(3): 309-319.

Giddens, Anthony. 1979. *Central Problems in Social Theory: Action, Structure and Contradiction in Social Analysis.* Berkeley: University of California Press.

_____. 1984. *The Constitution of Society: Outline of the Theory of Structuration.* Cambridge: Polity Press.

Goode, W. 1963. *World Revolution and Family Patterns.* New York: Free Press

Goody, Jack. 1971. "Class and marriage in Africa and Eurasia." *American Journal of Sociology* 76: 585-603.

Grosz-Ngate, Maria. 1988. "Monetization of bridewealth and the abandonment of 'kin roads' to marriage in Sana, Mali." *American Ethnologist* 15(3):501-14.

Gugler, Josef. 2002. "The son of a hawk does not remain abroad: The urban-rural connection in Africa." *African Studies Review* 45(1): 21-41.

Guyer, Jane. 1993. "Wealth in people and self realization in Equatorial Africa," *Man* 28(2): 243-265.

_____. 1995. "Wealth in people, wealth in knowledge—Introduction," *Journal of Africa History* 36(1): 91-120.

Harrell-Bond, Barbara. 1975. *Modern Marriage in Sierra Leone: A Study of the Professional Group*. Paris: Mouton.

Haynes, Jonathan. 2000. *Nigerian Video Films*. Athens: Ohio University Center for International Studies.

Hollos, Marida. 1991. "Migration, Education, and the Status of Women in Southern Nigeria." *American Anthropologist* 93(4)852-70.

Isiugo-Abanihe, U. 1994. "Consequences of bridewealth changes of nuptuality patterns among the Ibo of Nigeria," in *Nuptuality in Sub-Saharan Africa: Contemporary Anthropological and Demographic Perspectives*, ed. C. Bledsoe and G. Pison, pp. 74-91. Oxford: Clarendon Press.

Jahoda, G. 1959. "Love, marriage and social change: Letters to the advice column of a West African newspaper." *Africa* 29:177-90.

Joseph, Richard. 1987. *Democracy and Prebendal Politics in Nigeria*. Cambridge: Cambridge University Press.

Kertzer, David and Brettell, Caroline. 1987. "Advances in Italian and Iberian family history." *Journal of Family History* 12:87-120.

Kertzer, David and Hogan, Dennis. 1989. *Family, Political Economy and Demographic Change: The Transformation of Life in Casalecchio, Italy, 1861-1921*. Madison, WI: University of Wisconsin Press.

Krige, E. J. 1936. "Changing conditions in marital relations and parental duties among urbanized natives." *Africa* 9(3):1-23.

Lee, B.S. 1992. "The influence of rural-urban migration on migrants' fertility behavior in Cameroon." *International Migration Review* 26(4): 1416-47.

Lesthaeghe, Ron (ed.). 1989. *Reproduction and Social Organization in Sub-Saharan Africa.* Berkeley: University of California Press.

Little, Kenneth. 1979. "Women's strategies in modern marriage in Anglophone West Africa: An ideological and sociological appraisal," in *Cross-Cultural Perspectives on Mate Selection and Marriage,* ed. G. Kurian, pp. 202-17. Westport, CT; Greenwood Press.

Little, Kenneth and A. Price. 1973. "Some trends in modern marriage among West Africans," in *Africa and Change,* ed. C. Turnball, pp. 185-207. New York: Knopf.

Mair, Lucy. 1969. *African Marriage and Social Change.* London: Frank Cass and Co.

Mann, Kristin. 1985. *Marrying Well: Marriage Status and Social Change among the Educated Elite in Colonial Lagos.* Cambridge: Cambridge University Press.

Marris, Peter. 1962. *Family and Social Change in an African City.* Evanston, IL: Northwestern University Press.

Marshall-Fratani, Ruth. 1998. "Mediating the global and the local in Nigerian Pentecostalism." *Journal of Religion in Africa* 38 (3):278-313.

Miers, Suzanne and Kopytoff, Igor (ed.). 1977. *Slavery in Africa: Historical and Anthropological Perspectives.* Madison: University of Wisconsin Press.

Miller, Joseph. 1988. *Way of Death: Merchant Capitalism and the Angolan Slave Trade 1730-1830.* Madison, WI: University of Wisconsin Press.

Nwankwo, Arthur. 1999. *Nigeria: The Stolen Billions.* Enugu: Nigeria: Fourth Dimension Publishing.

Obiechina, Emmanuel. 1973. *An African Popular Literature: A Study of Onitsha Market Pamphlets.* Cambridge: University Press.

Okonjo, K. 1992. "Aspects of continuity and change in mate-selection among the Igbo West of the River Niger." *Journal of Comparative Family Studies* 13(3):339-60.

Olivier de Sardan, Jean-Pierre. 1999. "A moral economy of corruption in Africa?" *The Journal of Modern African Studies* 37 (1):25-52.

Oppong, Christine. 1974. *Marriage among a Matrilineal Elite.* Cambridge: Cambridge University Press.

Oriuwa, Chibuzo. 1999. "Adolescent abortion among non-school girls in southeastern Nigeria." Paper presented at the annual meeting of the

Population Association of America, New York, New York, March 24-28, 1999.

Phillips, A. 1969 [1953]. "Introduction," in *Family and Social Change in an African City*, pp. vii-xiv. Evanston, IL: Northwestern University Press.

Plotnicov, Leonard. 1995. "Love, lust and found in Nigeria," in *Romantic Passion: A Universal Experience?*, ed. W. Jankowiak, pp. 128-140. New York: Columbia University Press.

Radcliffe-Brown, Alfred and Forde, Daryll, ed. 1950. *African Systems of Kinship and Marriage*. London: Oxford University Press.

Riesman, Paul. 1971. "Defying official morality: The example of man's quest for woman among the Fulani." *Cahiers d'Etudes Africaines* 44:602-03.

_____. 1973. "Love Fulani style." *Society* (Jan/Feb):27-35.

Renne, Elisha. 2003. *Population and Progress in a Yoruba Town*. Edinburgh: Edinburgh University Press for the International African Institute.

Schneider, Jane and Schneider, Peter. 1996. *Festival of the Poor: Fertility Decline and the Ideology of Class in Sicily, 1860-1980*. Tucson: University of Arizona Press.

Smith, Daniel Jordan. 1999. *Having People: Fertility, Family and Modernity in Igbo-speaking Nigeria*. Ph.D. dissertation, Department of Anthropology, Emory University.

_____. 2000. "'These girls today *na war-o*': Premarital sexuality and modern identity in southeastern Nigeria." *Africa Today* 47 (3-4):98-120.

_____. 2001a. "Kinship and corruption in Nigeria." *Ethnos* 66 (3):344-364.

_____. 2001b. "Romance, parenthood and gender in a modern African society." *Ethnology* 40 (2):129-151.

_____. 2001c. "Ritual killing, '419' and fast wealth: Inequality and the popular imagination in southeastern Nigeria." *American Ethnologist* 28(4):803-826.

_____. 2004a. "Youth, sin and sex in Nigeria: Christianity and HIV-related beliefs and behavior among rural-urban migrants." *Culture, Health & Sexuality* 6(5):425-437.

_____. 2004b. "Burials and belonging in Nigeria: Rural-urban relations and social inequality in a contemporary African ritual." *American Anthropologist* 106 (3):569-579.

_____. 2004c. "Contradictions in Nigeria's fertility transition: The burdens and benefits of having people." *Population and Development Review* 30 (2):221-238.

_____. 2006a. "Love and the risk of HIV: Courtship, marriage and infidelity in southeastern Nigeria," in *Modern Loves: The Anthropology of Romantic Courtship and Companionate Marriage*, Jennifer Hirsch and Holly Wardlow, eds. Ann Arbor: University of Michigan Press, pp.137-153.

_____. 2006b. "Cell phones, social inequality, and contemporary culture in southeastern Nigeria." *Canadian Journal of African Studies* 40(3):496-523.

_____. 2007a. *A Culture of Corruption: Everyday Deception and Popular Discontent in Nigeria.* Princeton, NJ: Princeton University Press.

_____. 2007b. "Modern marriage, men's extramarital sex, and HIV risk in Nigeria." *American Journal of Public Health* 97(6):997-1005.

Smock, Audrey. 1971. *Ibo Politics: The Role of Ethnic Unions in Eastern Nigeria.* Cambridge: Harvard University Press.

Trager, Lillian. 2001. *Yoruba Hometowns: Community, Identity and Development in Nigeria.* Boulder, CO: Lynne Rienner.

Uchendu, Victor. 1965a. *The Igbo of Southeastern Nigeria.* Fort Worth, TX: Holt, Reinhart and Winston.

_____. 1965b. "Concubinage among the Ngwa Igbo of southern Nigeria." *Africa* 35(2):187-97.

van de Walle, Etienne and Andrew Foster. 1990. "Fertility decline in Africa: Assessment and prospects," *World Bank Technical Paper* no. 125, Africa Technical Department Series. Washington: D.C.: The World Bank.

van der Vliet, V. 1991. "Traditional husbands, modern wives?: Constructing marriages in a South African township." *African Studies* 50(1-2):219-41.

Watts, Michael. 1992. "The shock of modernity: Petroleum, protest and fast capitalism in an industrializing society," in *Reworking Modernity: Capitalisms and Symbolic Discontent*, A. Pred and M. Watts (eds.). New Brunswick, NJ: Rutgers University Press, pp. 21-63.

Chapter 3

CHILD TRAFFICKING IN WEST AFRICA?

Erdmute Alber

INTRODUCTION

If we are to believe media and press reports, the websites of international aid organizations, or the former general secretary of the
United Nations, Kofi Annan,[1] slavery and trafficking in human beings
in the twenty-first century is not restricted to isolated cases, but is on
the increase. In December 2000 a protocol was signed to what is known
as the United Nations "Palermo Convention" against international
organized crime. In this protocol, which by now has been ratified by
more than 150 countries, the signatories agree to prevent, suppress and
punish trafficking in persons, especially women and children (United
Nations 2004: 41-52).

This ratification process was preceded in the 1990s by political
discussions in countries both in the North and in the South, mainly
initiated by human rights organizations and various social institutions
and aid agencies. In these discussions, the terms slavery and human trafficking were revived and applied to the present-day situation: the phenomena which have been referred to since then as human trafficking

or slavery are mainly so-called forms of "new slavery," social constellations in which human beings experience new forms of dependency and become victims of extreme exploitation or sexual abuse (Weissbrodt 2002; Anti-Slavery International 2005; Sommerset 2004; Thimmel 2006; UNICEF 2005; Stefanovic 2004).

Since this time, large international aid agencies such as Terre des Hommes, UNICEF, Save the Children or Anti-Slavery International, have started various campaigns to combat what they refer to as human trafficking all over the world. There are even universities that offer courses and certificates in human trafficking.[2] Yet, although these campaigns are very visible on the websites of the aid agencies and in press reports or international documentations, there have been very few empirical and detailed studies in the social sciences of the social phenomena referred to as human trafficking or slavery, and little critical examination of these new discourses in an empirical context. It would be important to carry out a broad critical investigation into the new use of the terms human and child trafficking and the phenomena they refer to.

The few existing studies in this field include the recently published book *Sex at the Margins* by Laura Agustin (Agustin 2007). She investigates female migrants who work as prostitutes and who are frequently described as victims of human trafficking. Agustin proposes the provocative thesis that if immigrant prostitutes in Europe suffer from exploitation, a negative image and restricted rights, this is not due to human trafficking so much as to the work of social activists and aid agencies. She claims that by labeling them as victims of human trafficking, the agencies have brought about their marginalization. Agustin argues that since the 1990s an image of trafficking in persons, in this case women, has been created by aid agencies, politicians and the media, which presents these women exclusively as victims and thus fails to take into account their worldview and their intentions.

According to Agustin, it is important to understand the complex biographies of these women, who cannot be reduced simply to victims. One of the book's core arguments is that as a rule they were fully aware of the kind of work that awaited them when they left home, in most cases of their own free will, in order to earn money in Europe. They never refer to themselves as trafficked women, even if they gain their employment through professional brokers (male of female) who keep a part of their earnings.

The moral emphasis in Agustin's study is remarkable, for it represents a radical break with the common, normative judgments of the aid agencies, against which the critique in this book is mainly directed. This break effectively draws attention to the fact that the normative connotations of the terms we use to describe social actions evoke images and historical associations that influence our perception of social phenomena, and at the same time make normative judgments of other people's actions. When we speak of trafficking in persons, we inevitably associate the actions of people today with historical forms of slavery. Agustin's book questions whether and to what extent this is justified.

In this article I discuss a modern phenomenon that is considered as a form of human trafficking, although it is empirically very different from the prostitution of female immigrants in Western Europe, namely child trafficking in West Africa, which is described by aid agencies as an increasing and urgent problem. This phenomenon is fundamentally different from the prostitution of women to the extent that sexual activities are not a central feature associated with what is seen as the trade object, although they may play a secondary role. Children are interesting because of their labor power; in concrete terms, they perform agricultural or domestic work and they are placed with employers by paid brokers. Despite this difference, institutions such as Anti-Slavery International or Terre des Hommes frequently link together migrant prostitution in Europe and brokered child labor in West Africa, referring to them as women and child trafficking. This fixed terminology and parallel categorization has a basis in the above-mentioned protocol to the United Nations Palermo Convention.

Just as Agustin used the example of prostitutes, I would like to take the example of child trafficking in West Africa in order to question the indiscriminate and global application of the term human trafficking. I will proceed in two steps. First I will look at a number of texts produced within the framework of anti-child-trafficking campaigns, examining the images of childhood on which they are based and asking what exactly is understood by child trafficking. In a second step, I will present the views and the possible options of those persons who, according to these accounts, are affected by child trafficking. In a concluding section, I will bring these two approaches together. The discussion is based on my own field research carried out in the Republic of Benin.[3]

ANTI-CHILD-TRAFFICKING CAMPAIGNS IN WEST AFRICA

Since the end of the 1990s a large number of non-governmental organizations and aid agencies in the Republic of Benin have been active in the field of public relations and organized campaigns against child trafficking. Signs have been put up along the roadside warning against child-trafficking and asking the public to report offenders. Such warnings can also be seen in many public buildings in Benin, both in local languages and in French, which is the official language. The cartoon poster shown below, for instance, was displayed in the Ministry for Family Affairs.

FIG. 1: CARTOON POSTER

(Photo: Dr. Jeannett Martin)

Advertising spots on TV and radio also transmit the message that children in Benin should not grow up outside their families, and contain urgent warnings against child traffickers. Many conferences and educational seminars have been organized on this subject in the past decade, frequently in conjunction with the Ministries of Justice and Family Affairs, and international organizations.

The sign language of the cartoon figures on the posters or of the wording on the signs is reminiscent of other educational campaigns in West Africa, for instance those intended to educate people about AIDS. In this case, too, signs were erected along the roadside, and there were comics and TV spots. This similarity in the formal repertoire points to the initiators of the campaigns: the condemnation of child trafficking is organized by national and international NGOs, and financed with international development funds.

It is striking that none of the phenomena against which the campaigns are directed are new: children growing up in households other than that of their biological parents, using brokers to place children with employers instead of sending them to school, or sending children to work in neighboring countries. It is well documented that children in West Africa, including Benin, frequently grow up in a household other than that of their biological parents (Page 1989, Bledsoe 1990, Alber 2003). Child labor and illiteracy are common,[4] while the practice of boys traveling as migrant workers to plantations in Ghana or Nigeria has been well known and widespread in Benin/Dahomey since the colonial period. Thus, it is not the phenomena as such that are new, but rather the fact that they, or certain forms of them, have become the object of educational campaigns which label them as "child trafficking."

Symptomatic of this new name, which implies a new evaluation, is the brochure published in 2002 by the Ministry of Family and Social Affairs (République du Bénin, Ministère de la Famille, de la Protection Sociale et de la Solidarité 2002), containing a small compendium of laws. It was distributed to judges, public prosecutors, children's rights organizations and government institutions, and contained extracts from the Benin family law code concerning the freedom to cross the national borders with children, and in particular the rule that children not traveling with their own parents must carry with them their parents' written permission and officially certified papers.

The extracts from the laws all date from the period between 1965 and 1990, and at no point do they contain the term child trafficking. And yet the compendium produced in 2002 is entitled "Recueil de Textes de Loi sur le Trafic des Enfants" (Compendium of Laws Concerning Child Trafficking). The term "child trafficking" (*trafic des enfants*) was thus introduced into the juristic discourse for the first time at the turn of the millennium, and prescribed by the Ministry of Family Affairs as a new name for old practices, for which legal regulations already existed.

The publication of the compendium of laws on the *trafic des enfants* shows that at the turn of the millennium child trafficking became a key term expressing a social reality that must be condemned. The term was introduced at the end of the 1990s and increasingly used after the signing of the Palermo Convention and its protocols. In addition to these instruments, the UN Convention on the Rights of the Child of 1989 and the African Charter on the Rights and Welfare of the Child of 1990 had already focused attention on the issue of childhood in Africa. Projects aimed at improving the situation of children in Benin have been fashionable since the 1990s. They were introduced not as a reaction to dramatic changes that affected children's lives, in other words as a reaction to local changes, but because the topic of childhood and children's' rights had become an important issue in international development programs. In the early 1990s the term "child trafficking" (*trafic des enfants*) did not occur in public debates in Benin, and was inexistent in respect of local practices such as sending girls to work as housemaids.

From the second half of the 1990s onwards, UN organizations such as UNICEF and other international organizations such as OXFAM, Terre des Hommes or Save the Children, set up programs to combat child trafficking. They provided funds for local projects, thus encouraging the formation of local NGOs for children's rights. In addition to educational campaigns, their activities include social projects and preventive measures, such as getting girls into school, legal support for working children, or social centers where children can find help.

The condemnation of child trafficking was also expressed in the local languages, having recourse to existing words in these languages. The best known is the word *vidomegon* in Fongbe. Literally *vidomegon* means "child placed with someone" and originally it was a neutral term used to refer to children who do not live with their biological parents, in other words foster children or apprentices. When warnings are given in Benin today on radio and television or in leaflets against letting children grow up as *vidomegon*, this is a new use of the word. Today *vidomegon* is almost exclusively used to refer to exploited housemaids (for UNICEF for instance, see: http://www.unicef.org/protection/benin_53710.html). In a dictionary published in 2000, under the entry "domestique" (domestic servant) can be found the special entry "petite servante" (under-age housemaid) with *vidomegon* as the translation (Rassinoux 2000: 116).

In my opinion, the rapid growth in Benin of a discourse on child trafficking (in French *trafic des enfants* and in the local language *vidomegon*, which is today generally used to refer not to a foster child but to a young housemaid or trafficked child) is due primarily not to an increase in such practices but to an enormous broadening of the use of the term. Not least this is due to the international attention drawn to the phenomenon of human trafficking by the protocol to the Palermo Convention. In the protocol this broadening makes the definition of trafficking in persons somewhat vague:

(a) "Trafficking in persons" shall mean the recruitment, transportation, transfer, harboring or receipt of persons, by means of the threat or use of force or other forms of coercion, of abduction, of fraud, of deception, of the abuse of power or of a position of vulnerability or of the giving or receiving of payments or benefits to achieve the consent of a person having control over another person, for the purpose of exploitation. Exploitation shall include, at a minimum, the exploitation of the prostitution of others or other forms of sexual exploitation, forced labor or services, slavery or practices similar to slavery, servitude or the removal of organs;

(b) The consent of a victim of trafficking in persons to the intended exploitation set forth in subparagraph (a) of this article shall be irrelevant where any of the means set forth in subparagraph (a) have been used;

(c) The recruitment, transportation, transfer, harboring or receipt of a child for the purpose of exploitation shall be considered

"trafficking in persons" even if this does not involve any of the
means set forth in subparagraph (a) of this article;

d) "Child" shall mean any person under eighteen years of age.

(United Nations 2004: 42f.)

This definition of trafficking in persons is too broad in three respects.
First, the nature of the transfer is rather indeterminate, ranging from
recruitment to transport and shipping of persons. Secondly, this transfer of persons must be associated in some way with pressure or force,
including the exploitation of a position of power or the special vulnerability of children. Then exploitation comes as the third feature. In
the case of children, their agreement plays no role in any assessment of
the situation, and children, according to the definition, are all persons
under eighteen years of age.

On the one hand, this vagueness makes it possible to include
exploitation of very different kinds under the heading of human trafficking, so that threatened violence is sufficient, without any need for
actual violence. On the other hand, a pedantic interpretation of this
definition would mean that practically any movement of children
could be seen as human trafficking, for children are always dependent on adults in some way or another. And finally, no distinction is
made between children and adolescents, so that strictly speaking even
apprenticeship agreements with minors that contain an obligation to
work could be called child trafficking. Naturally no one has made such a
broad interpretation of the term child trafficking. Nevertheless it must
be said that the definition is so vague as to require local interpretations
of child trafficking that will help to distinguish it from all those forms
of work performed by children and of the exercise of power over them
which should not be referred to as child trafficking. In West Africa at
the present time, there are essentially two kinds of child labor that are
labeled as child trafficking. On the one hand this is the recruitment of
girls as housemaids and hawkers by more or less professional brokers,
who place them in households where they also have to live. The other
kind is agricultural work performed by boys who are recruited by
brokers. Brokers in Benin place children with employers both in the
Republic of Benin itself and in other West African countries, especially
Nigeria and the Ivory Coast, but also the Republic of Gabon.

The educational campaigns against child trafficking all operate with similar images of childhood that appear in various documents, which we will now consider. They use two images of childhood, one that serves to describe the actual situation as a result of child trafficking, and one to describe the desired target of a better childhood. In the first of these, children are presented essentially as the exploited and generally defenseless victims of adults who think only of their own profit, especially child traffickers, but sometimes also of their ignorant or profit-oriented parents. This image of the child as victim is visualized in the above poster. The father and the child trafficker embody the profit-oriented adults, and the child is their victim. On the left we see the child trafficker telling the child that he will take it to the town, where it will be able to earn a lot of money. The father is pushing the child towards the trafficker. He says "Take my child and his bundle, I wish you a good journey. In the town you will earn a lot of money." The child is crying and does not want to go, but is being pushed. At the right-hand side of the picture, another child is seen carrying a schoolbag, free and unmolested, while other children are playing football.

This image of children as victims is found consistently, not only in educational texts and pictures but also in all studies on this topic. Even an otherwise very discriminating study such as the contract study carried out by Inga Nagel in 2000 for Terre des Hommes uses the image of children as victims. Nagel writes:

> More and more children have become victims of a network that spreads over the whole of West Africa, consisting of recruiters, brokers and transporters, who carry on a lively cross-border trade with considerable profit. The children are often obliged to labor for many years without pay at the cost of their physical and psychological development. (...) Many never return, because they do not survive the journey across the open sea, die of untreated diseases or as a result of violent treatment, or they may even be killed for occult purposes. Others return with severe psychological problems, having irretrievably lost contact with their own culture, forgotten the name of their home village, and unable to speak their mother tongue. (Nagel 2000: 11)

Nagel explains why it is impossible to hold personal interviews with such children as a result of their status as victims. She writes:

> Firstly, the 'returnees' are widely scattered in the hinterland
> (of Mali or Benin), and secondly they are not particularly
> keen on being reminded of their fate. As a rule they regard
> their adventures as a traumatic experience, a personal
> failure, the end of a long-cherished dream. (Nagel 2000: 5)

The image of a children as victims is maintained because there is no exchange of experiences between returning children or adolescents and those who are leaving home for the first time. There is also no mention of other local channels of knowledge transmission, such as communication between the various groups involved in child trafficking.[5]

In the study by Nagel, as well as in other studies, the fact that the children are treated as trade objects is simply postulated. Thus, there is no questioning of whether it is justified to reduce the children's role exclusively to that of victims in all cases involving brokers. And finally, local conceptions of childhood are rarely investigated, for instance whether the persons affected are actually considered as children, what this means, and whether it is not customary on the local level to distinguish between children and adolescents, the latter being expected to perform various kinds of work. As already laid down in the UN Convention on the Rights of the Child and confirmed in the protocol to the Palermo Convention, children are defined as any person under eighteen years of age.

The second conception of childhood can be expressed as a Western-style protected *Lernkindheit* or "learning childhood."[6] In public discourses of condemnation it represents the normative target, an implementation of the requirements set out in the conventions on children's rights. This childhood has four characteristics. The first is that children have a special need for protection, which must be respected by the lawmakers and by adults in general. This is reflected in the roadside signs shown in Figure 1: all *citoyens* und *citoyennes*, responsible and vigilant citizens, are required to report child traffickers.

The protected "learning childhood" is visualized even more clearly in the cartoon. Here it is the woman on the right who is the child protector. She cries "Assez!" ("Enough!") and thus protects the child at the last minute before it is taken away. She also verbalizes the other main features of a Western-style protected "learning childhood," namely the requirement that children should grow up under the care of their parents or their relatives, who should send them to school and not expect them to work. The women says: "Enough! Don't expose the children to sexual abuse and child labor. They all have the right to grow up in their families and to receive a good education!"

The intensity of the various anti-child-trafficking campaigns has left its mark on Benin society. Thus, practically everyone in Benin today is familiar with the concept of *trafic des enfants* and can say what it means. When asked, they will readily tell stories about the abuse of housemaids, of course always in other families, not their own. One concrete and visible effect of the anti-child-trafficking campaigns is that today it is rare to find housemaids below the age of puberty in private households. In the early 1990s this was still common; at that time I often heard urban women praising the advantages of very young girls as household helps, claiming that they were not only easier to train and more obedient, but also not yet of an age to be interested in boys. What has not changed since then, however, is the high demand for housemaids. If anything, this has increased, due to expansion of the urban middle classes and continuous growth of the population.

HOUSEMAIDS FROM NORTHERN BENIN: ACTION STRATEGIES AND CHILDHOOD IMAGES

In existing studies, two groups are always mentioned as being affected by child trafficking: on the one hand under-age housemaids recruited by brokers, and on the other boys who work for farmers. Minors from the Republic of Benin work in both of these areas, within Benin and in other countries. Boys from Benin frequently go to work on farms in Nigeria; today there is less labor migration to Ghana and the Ivory Coast, which were the preferred destinations during the colonial period. In northern Benin there is a continuous national movement of migrant laborers from the Département of Atakora to Borgu, a center of cotton farming.[7]

In Benin, girls also work on both the national and the international labor markets. Many of them, including young women of legal age, seek work in Gabon, but also in Nigeria, Ghana and the Ivory Coast. I am not aware of any reliable quantitative figures in respect of this phenomenon, although some studies give estimated figures.

The recruitment of children by brokers is widespread in Benin, but takes certain forms in certain regions. One of these is the Atakora region in the northwest of the country. From this area come most of the housemaids who are recruited to work in Parakou, the biggest town in northern Benin. The following discussion is based on this example. My research was carried out both in Parakou itself, and in the home villages of the girls in Ouake. I present here the biography of one girl, Angelique Soni, as representative of many others.[8]

> Angelique Soni is a young Lokpa girl, about fourteen years old. At the time I talked to her she was working as a housemaid in the household of a Beninese social scientist in the town of Parakou. She was born and grew up in Yibessi, a small village in the Atakora mountains in northwestern Benin. Her two sisters also worked as maids until they got married; her brother took over their parents' farm.
>
> Angelique moved to the town three years ago. Her elder sister, who was living at that time in Niamey, the capital of Niger, found a job there for her. After seven months she left Niamey because her sister moved to Kandi. There she found employment as a housemaid again. She ran away from this household because she was frequently beaten and badly treated, and she went to join her other sister in Parakou. This sister found a new job as housemaid for her; but she ran away from this household, too, not only because she was beaten by her employer, the lady of the house, but also because the husband made advances to her.
>
> Obviously indignant that her younger sister had run away for the second time, the older sister engaged a broker who placed her in the household in which she was working at the time of our interview. According to Angelique, at this time there were about twenty girls working in Parakou and in Cotonou after being placed in households by this broker.
>
> The household of Angelique's employers consists of three persons, a young family with a small child, both parents working as academics in Parakou. Angelique sleeps on a mat in the guest room of her employers. During the day this mat is rolled up and tidied away; she keeps her clothes and private possessions in a plastic bag next to the mat. While the mother is out of the house, she looks after

the small child, cooks, cleans, does the washing, performs messages and goes shopping in the market; in other words, she does almost all of the housework.

FIG. 2: *ANGELIQUE'S MAT*

(photo: Erdmute Alber)

Her monthly wage is given to the broker, but she goes with her employer when the money is given to him. He passes it on to her sister, who uses it to buy items of household equipment for Angelique's trousseau. She wants to continue working as a maid for another year, and hopes that the trousseau will then be complete, as well as enough capital to set up a stall selling sorghum beer. Her fiancé, a young man from her home village, works as an apprentice in Parakou. Originally she had asked him to find her a job as a housemaid in Cotonou, but he refused.

In this household, too, she had a conflict with her employer, for which reason she is secretly looking for another job. Her employer had sent her to buy beer and Fanta. But the family's usual shop was closed, and so she had to go to a nearby beer parlor, which charged higher prices. Her employer did not believe her and deducted the difference from her monthly wage. When Angelique told her sister about this, her sister said that she had already run away twice, and that she would not help her again. So at the time of our interviews Angelique was looking for a new employer secretly with the help of her friends. She is convinced that it is better to find a job on your own and not through a broker, because there is more likelihood that you will be able to keep your money.

She meets her friends at the market when she goes shopping for the family. From here she also phones her fiancé occasionally from the public phone box. She says she does not want to meet him as long as she is working for the family, in order not to annoy her employer. Angelique formerly worked for 5000 FCFA per month (about 8 Euros). Now she earns 8000 francs (about 13 Euros), in addition to board and lodging.

Angelique's story is typical. In addition to other ethnic groups from the Atakora region, the Lokpa are today the main suppliers for the housemaid market in Parakou, the biggest town in the north of Benin. Lokpa girls also go to work in other towns, for instance in Djougou, Dassa, Abomey, Cotonou or Niamey, and Abidjan in the Ivory Coast. While Lokpa boys sought employment as temporary agricultural workers even in the time before Dahomey/Benin attained independence, the employment of young girls as housemaids developed only from the 1970s onwards. Today it involves nearly all Lokpa girls.

The second thing that is typical in Angelique's story is that she is working in order to acquire a trousseau. Young Lokpa servant girls in the town have two aims: firstly, the acquisition of a large and impressive trousseau, consisting of fabrics, clothes and, most important, a fine set of household equipment; with this they can return to their villages and get married. And secondly, many girls aim to set up a small business. In this case they use the money they earn either to pay for a training or for capital investments. Angelique, for instance, was saving so that she could set up a stall selling sorghum beer.

The third typical feature in Angelique's story is the social relationship with the broker. She found work at first through her sisters, and later through a broker approached by her sister. In most of the cases I investigated, a social relationship existed between the brokers and the families of the girls. Quite often brokers are relatives, but they can also be persons who are resident and well known in the region. This means that the parties are ensured a minimum of social control, for instance in the conflict-prone matter of the payment of wages.

Fourthly, it is typical for girls to change their place of employment frequently. The most common reasons are sexual harassment by the husband, disputes over wages and accusations of theft. The stories told by the housemaids are relatively stereotyped: the employers accuse them of theft or of embezzling money or food, and then deduct the money from their already very low wages. Also typical is Angelique's story that she first found work through members of her family and a professional broker, but has recently tried to emancipate herself. One housemaid told me that it was normal to receive almost no money in the first year, since the brokers took it all. As a rule, only those who understand how the system works manage to get more money for themselves. This becomes easier as the housemaid gets older, and acquires more experience in dealing with employers and brokers. Angelique's manner of saving is also noteworthy in this connection. The money she earns is not saved and she does not keep it herself, but it is used to buy items for her trousseau which are kept at her sister's.

For Angelique's mother, such a biography would have been unthinkable. Up to the 1970s, Lokpa children were betrothed when they were small. Girls were married soon after reaching puberty, while boys commonly went away as migrant workers. In the 1970s, the first Lokpa girls left their villages to work as housemaids. This gradually became the dominant pattern, so that today, with the exception of those attending school, all girls go away.

These changes were triggered by the introduction of money transfers into the process of marriage. In former times, neither dowry nor bridewealth were customary among the Lokpa. However, the bridegroom and his family performed bride service in the fields of the bride's parents for a number of years until the young bride took up residence in the household of her in-laws. Through the availability of money from the migrant labor of the young men, and as a result of their increased absence, bride service was gradually replaced by the payment of bridewealth. Today, bride service is no longer customary, except for a few symbolic actions performed by the bridegroom.

Parallel to this process, the practice of girls entering marriage with a trousseau or dowry, which had long been customary in neighboring groups, was gradually introduced.[9] The dowry—consisting mainly of household equipment—is not provided by the Lokpa parents, so that the girls have to pay for it themselves with the money they earn as migrant workers. The custom of sending girls to work as housemaids in turn brought about a further change, namely a decline in the practice of betrothing small children. The Lokpa gradually gave up this practice after conflicts increased over girls who, despite payment of the bridewealth, found new marriage partners in the town, or who became pregnant while working as housemaids.

Taken overall, monetarization of the transfers connected with marriage thus led to many changes in the social structure of the Lokpa, including the practice of girls going to work as housemaids. The changes affected not only traditional practices but also conceptions of childhood and normative expectations. Today, Lokpa girls aged around fourteen are considered old enough to leave their parents' home and go to work in a strange place. They are no longer, as in the past, expected to marry at this age. This change in the conception of marriage means that girls have an adolescence, a new period "between childhood and marriage," which corresponds to the extension of childhood proposed by Philippe Ariés (1978). While in Ariés this extension of childhood is a *Lernkindheit* or "learning childhood," or rather a "learning adolescence," we are talking in this case about a "working adolescence"—as was common in Europe in the 18th and 19th centuries.

The emergence of a period of adolescence as something new in the life of girls, which is completely ignored in anti-child-trafficking discourses, can be observed in many parts of Africa and is the subject of a number of recent publications. Usually it is associated with modernization processes, or even, as in Jean and John Comaroff (2005), with the emergence of an "African modernity." While in those studies known to me there is seldom any distinction made between the adolescence of girls and the adolescence of boys, the thesis of the emergence of a period of adolescence appears to me to apply primarily to girls. I cannot go into this in depth here; I can only note that Lokpa boys, like many other boys in Africa, have always had a special period of "adolescence" within the framework of their elaborate age class system. For the Republic of Benin in general, I would argue that the most important subject of discussion in the ubiquitous and manifold normative discourses on "adolescence" should be the development of normative standards for the life of girls whose marriageable age has been raised. It is, however, important not to romanticize the emergence of adolescence in Africa, as is often implicitly the case. Abbink (2005) has already warned against such romanticization.

In the local conceptions of Lokpa girls and their families, it is true that working as a housemaid is associated with the notion of "modernity." One local term for going to work as a housemaid can be translated as "opening the eyes," another as "going on a search," and a third as "going on an adventure." In addition to the intention of earning money, the girls are driven by a desire to see the world and in particular the big towns.

Despite many complaints about working conditions, most girls go of their own free will to work as maids and are aware of what awaits them in the town. It is the easiest way for them to earn large sums of money. During the interviews, some girls did say they were worried about the dangers, but the mothers to whom I spoke were very much more worried about the risks to which girls are exposed in the towns and foreign places where they work. However, these mothers were also very firm about the fact that it is impossible today to talk a girl out of going to work as a maid, for this would mean foregoing a trousseau.

The only alternative to working as a maid is going to school. One mother told me how angry she was when her second daughter, whose schooling she had struggled to finance for several years, one day left school and went away to work. Since many parents are not willing to let their daughters go away to work, it has become common for girls, as well as boys, to leave home secretly. This is what Angelique did. She secretly asked her elder sister to find her a job as a housemaid. She followed her without taking leave of her parents.

CONCLUSIONS

In the foregoing sections, I have discussed two different perspectives of child trafficking in West Africa. On the one hand I examined the images of childhood in the anti-child-trafficking campaigns. I showed that the emergence of the campaigns can be explained not by local processes so much as by the globally recognized UN conventions and their protocols. These contain a very vague definition of human trafficking, which can mean different things depending on local circumstances. In Benin, and in West Africa in general, the local appropriation of this global discourse consists in the belief that the use of brokers to find employers for housemaids and to find work for boys in agriculture is automatically a form of child trafficking. However, this specific appropriation did not have its roots within the country, but was introduced for instance by NGO activists, experts, journalists or development workers. To do this is relatively easy in a country like Benin, where the national budget and the job market for academics depend essentially on development aid funds, and where there is little questioning of current topics and fashions in development discourses. This explains the power of the condemnation discourse. It represents the government's "official" position on the subject of child trafficking, but in the mouth of local government representatives it sometimes sounds like lip service.

The phenomenon of girls going to work as housemaids can itself be seen as the product of local reactions to global influences. These are processes of monetarization and urbanization, and as a consequence an increased demand for housemaids and for dowries consisting of imported foreign goods as a central component of marriage. Thus, although girls going to work as housemaids and discourses condemning child-trafficking can both be read as expressions of globalization processes, they nonetheless developed independently and to this day have nothing to do with each other. This is true despite the fact that the condemnation discourse is directed at the employment of Lokpa girls as housemaids and is aimed at putting an end to this very practice.

That they have nothing to do with each other became very clear to me on one occasion when I spoke to the mayor of a Lokpa village who eagerly condemned child trafficking. Towards the end of our conversation, however, it turned out that he sometimes makes arrangements himself for young girls in his family to go and work in households in Cotonou. He did not see any connection between the two topics.

From my discussion of these two phenomena, one might be tempted to conclude that worldviews and conceptions of childhood, as expressed in the discourse of condemnation, are not as important as economic processes, for instance the demand for children as workers in urban households. One could therefore conclude that spreading normative appeals is not helpful in establishing legal standards such as the protection of children.

However, the case of the Lokpa girls demonstrates something else, namely the importance of normative conceptions for action. The development of the practice among Lokpa girls of going to work as housemaids was not possible without affecting local conceptions of childhood, and in particular the introduction of a period of adolescence for girls. Only after the view had become established that not only boys but girls, too, have a period of adolescence between childhood and marriage, did it become legitimate for Lokpa girls to go out into the world in large numbers, in order to "look for money" or "open their eyes." The fact that to this day many girls do not inform their parents that they are leaving is evidence of serious negotiation processes between parents and children in respect of normal behavior, and of a standardized "exit option" for girls.

These negotiation processes, together with the difficult situation on the local labor market, which offers practically no alternatives for untrained girls who want to earn money, are the determining factors that shape the adolescence of a Lokpa girl. That these people do not refer to the standard ideas of childhood expressed in the condemnation discourse is due to the fact that such conceptions are so far from their own local conceptions that many girls are far from thinking that "child trafficking" could refer to their own work. They do not see themselves as trafficked goods; rather, many of them have had to beg their parents to allow them to go and work in the town, or have defied them by leaving home secretly.

Thus, while the anti-child-trafficking campaigns are intended to promote a universal conception of childhood, the debates in Benin today on what constitutes a "proper" childhood are increasing rather than lessening. Not only in connection with the Lokpa, the question of how childhood and adolescence should be spent, who should decide where children live and for whom they should work, is a topic of incessant debates in which the actors refer to both "old" and "new" conceptions of childhood, legal discourses, laws, and a large number of local legal norms.

A confrontation of the anti-child-trafficking campaigns with the views and free actions of adolescent girls who do not see themselves as trafficked children, suggests that we should be careful to keep a critical distance in the matter of human and child trafficking. Girls go to work as housemaids against a background of precarious labor markets that are governed by the laws of supply and demand, and not because they are forced to go through their special status as children deprived of their rights. It would therefore be quite inappropriate to attribute to these supposedly trafficked persons a special status of unfreedom, and this is not supported by the definition of human trafficking in the protocol to the UN convention. Rather, it could be said that the housemaids are free, not only to accept these badly paid jobs but also to be discharged at any time. One facet of this freedom is the frequency with which the girls change their place of employment, one of the few strategies available to them for escaping from bad working conditions.

It is not necessarily whitewashing the situation of the housemaids when one argues that the category of human trafficking does not apply to them in so far as the girls do not enter their employment under force or threat or as captives, but of their own free will and in full aware-ness of the precarious nature of the labor market which gives them very little choice. Criticizing these forms of employment, with their growing wage differentials and underlying structures—not least, those of internationally linked economies—and analyzing the causes, would in my opinion be more helpful than any normative and uncritical talk of human trafficking by profit-seeking and greedy African brokers. This once again makes Africa itself responsible for its poverty and under-development, while African children are the innocent and defenseless victims.

Notes

1. See United Nations (2004).

2. See, for instance, the "Human Trafficking" course offered by the Insti-tute for the Study of International Migration at Georgetown University, Washington, D.C., described on the Internet at http://www12.george-town.edu/scs/ccpe/ccpe_cert_int_migration_studies.html.

3. Since 1992, I have made a total of 17 field trips to the Republic of Benin. I have studied the topic of childhood systematically since 1998.

4. On the history of schooling in Dahomey/Benin, see Asiwaju (1975).

5. An exceptional case is constituted by those children who are cared for by development projects and whose biographies and experiences can be read on websites and in brochures. Here it is the projects that encourage the children to speak and that are able, through their knowledge of child traf-

ficking, to break the "vicious circle" that is spoken of in many accounts. This legitimizes the work of the institutions that combat child trafficking

6. See Honig 1999: 85 ff. He traces the development of "modern childhood" alongside the development of the modern state, the separation of production and reproduction, privatization of the family and the generalization of institutions of learning for children. Honig speaks of *Erziehungskindheit* or "instruction childhood," but I prefer the term *Lernkindheit* or "learning childhood," since instruction is only one part of learning.

7. For an overview of agrarian labor migration in northern Benin, see Doevenspeck (2005).

8. The interview took place at Angelique's place of work with the approval of her employer, but without this lady being present. The names have been anonymized. I visited Angelique three times altogether.

9. The introduction and immense increase in the size of the trousseau or dowry appears to be general all over West Africa. For more, see Masquelier (2004).

References

Abbink, Jon. 2005. "Being young in Africa: the politics of despair and renewal." In *Vanguard or Vandals: Youth, Politics, and Conflict in Africa*, ed. Jon Abbink and Ineke van Kessel, 1-36. Leiden: Brill.

Agustin, Laura. 2007. *Sex at the Margins: Migration, Labour Markets and the Rescue Industry*. London and New York: Zed Books.

Anti-Slavery International. 2005. Protocol for identification and assistance of trafficked persons and training kit. London: Anti-Slavery International. http://www.antislavery.org/includes/documents/cm_docs/2009/p/protocoltraffickedpersonskit2005.pdf.

Ariés, Philip. 1978. *Geschichte der Kindheit*. München: DTV Wissenschaft.

Asiwaju, A. I. 1975. The colonial education heritage and the problem of nation-building in Dahomey. *Bulleitin de l'I.F.A.N.* 37: 340-357.

Bledsoe, Caroline. 1990. No success without struggle: Social mobility and hardship for foster children in Sierre Leone. *Man* 25: 70-89.

Doevenspeck, Martin. 2005. *Migration im ländlichen Benin: Sozialgeographische Untersuchungen an einer afrikanischen Frontier*. Saarbrücken: Verlag für Entwicklungspolitik.

Hardung, Christine. 2006. *Arbeit, Sklaverei und Erinnerung: Gruppen unfreier Herkunft unter den Fulbe Nordbenins*. Siegener Beiträge zur Soziologie Band 6. Köln: Rüdiger Köppe Verlag.

Masquelier, Adeleide. 2004. How is a Girl to Marry without a Bed? Weddings, Wealth and Women's Value in an Islamic Town of Niger. In *Situating Globality: African Agency in the Appropriation of Global Culture*, ed. Wim van Binsbergen and Rijk van Dijk, 220-256. Leiden: Brill.

Page, Hillary. 1989. Childrearing versus Childbearing: Coresidence of Mother and Child in Sub-Saharan Africa. In *Reproduction and Social Organisation in Sub-Saharan Africa*, ed. Ron J. Lesthaeghe, 401-441. Berkeley, Los Angeles and London: California Press.

Rassinoux, J. 2002. *Dictionnaire Francais-Fon*. Paris: Société des Missions Africaines.

République du Bénin, ministère de la famille, de la protection sociale et de la solidarité. 2002. *Recueil de textes de loi sur le trafic des enfants*. Cotonou.

Sommerset, Carron. 2004. Cause for concern? London social services and child trafficking. London: ECPAT UK. http://www.antislavery.org/includes/documents/cm_docs/2009/c/cause_for_concern.pdf.

Thimmel, Stefan. 2006. Ansätze und Methoden der Kinder und Jugendförderung in der deutschen Entwicklungszusammenarbeit. Eschborn: Gesellschaft für technische Zusammenarbeit. http://www.gtz.de/de/dokumente/de-MH_Kapitel_Literatur-Links_2006.pdf.

UNICEF. 2005. Trafficking in Human beings, especially women and children, in Africa. New York: United Nations Children's Fund. http://www.unicef.org.uk/publications/pdf/trafficking_inn.pdf.

United Nations. 2004. United Nations Convention against transnational organized crime and the protocols thereto. New York: United Nations. http://www.unodc.org/documents/treaties/UNTOC/Publications/TOC%20Convention/TOCebook-e.pdf.

Van Reisen, Mirjam, and Stefanovic, Ana. 2004. Lost kids, lost futures: The European Union's response to child trafficking. Geneva: International Federation Terre des Hommes. http://www.unicef.org.uk/publications/pdf/trafficking_inn.pdf.

Weissbrodt, David and Anti-Slavery International. 2002. Abolishing Slavery and its Contemporary Forms. New York and Geneva: Office of the United Nations High Commissioner for Human Rights. http://www.ohchr.org/Documents/Publications/slaveryen.pdf.

Chapter 4

An Approach to the Concept of Family in the African Union

Paloma Durán y Lalaguna

I will divide this chapter into two parts. In the first, I will try to cover the concept and idea of family used within the framework of the United Nations organization. In the second, I will try to cover the manner in which this work has been conducted within the organization of the African Union. In both cases, I will use the conceptual tools to which I refer in the following introductory section.

Conceptual Assumptions

Perhaps one of the most debated questions of the past decade concerns the definition of what is understood as the family. In theory, it could be said that no one doubts its necessity. Let's begin with Europe. The latest research conducted by Eurostat to discover the principle concerns among European citizens confirms that the family is considered essential in the European understanding of life. Here, it is important not to omit the fact that, in every European country as well as other geographical areas, the reading of what a family is depends on the legislation in effect.

In the case of the protection of life, for example, as there is no European community legislation on this, specific programs to support families can be found, as is the case in Germany. Spain places heterosexual marriage and unions between homosexuals within the same legal framework. Other legislations debate the proper definition of marriage as a contract between two persons and its possible expansion to other individuals via the signing of private documents, as is the case in the Netherlands.

Having stated this, I would like to underscore the fact that there is no one exclusive definition of what the family is. However, at the same time, all societies recognize its necessity as a basic institution for the development of a human being. Having failed to find a singular meaning for the term "family," I have taken the liberty to attempt to systematize the possible rights at stake in the family environment in order to profile the way in which the protection of this institution would have to be regulated.

First, I look at the formulated right to marry and create a family. This right, included in the Universal Declaration of Human Rights of 1948, has been repeatedly included in almost all human rights instruments and is intended to legally protect a basic element: the freedom to initiate a life project between two people and include in that project any children and/or dependents.

Second, I consider the equality of rights among the various members of the family. This could be considered an obvious element in the sense that these rights are individually recognized. In international forums, the prevailing doctrinal tide has supported the idea that the ownership of rights is universal, and the subtle differences therein can be introduced in the way those rights are executed. In any case, what is true is that these rights are not collective. If they were—as was initially planned in the case of third generation rights or in instances such as the right to develop or the right to peace—we would be talking about universal aspirations, the commitment for which can be assumed politically. But there are no instances or legal tools to demand their protection or guarantee. We should add to this the risk posed by using this terminology, given that it could lead to diluting the strength of the rights if they are formulated without content and specific guarantees. As such, I would like to underscore the idea that equality of rights comes not only from the fact that one belongs to a given family but also from a derivation of recognizable rights that concern any and all human beings.

Third, I look at the right to enter into marriage freely, voluntarily and with a minimum age, all of which hinges on the aforementioned points regarding free choice and equality.

Fourth, I consider the rights of children in terms of their parents and vice-versa. Having children is still not recognized as a right and actually appears not to be one, although in some countries this point is being questioned implicitly through the use of artificial reproduction techniques. However, the right for parents to plan their family and organize their own life project while respecting the basic welfare of the people whom this might affect should be recognized. In the case of childhood, it is recognized that children have the right to their parents' care. This, for example, is how we explain protective legislation regarding childhood as well as the criteria for avoiding the separation of siblings in cases of separation and divorce, etc.

Finally, it is important to bear in mind the right to family reunification currently under discussion as a result of the migratory phenomenon in Europe. This right is protected in many European legal systems, especially in Spain.

All of the above-mentioned rights are based upon a clear notion: children are normally born into an environment where there is an attempt to ensure the free development of their personality and their consolidation as people. That objective is the responsibility of the parents, or in certain cases, their guardians. If this environment does not exist, the institutions play a subsidiary role in an attempt to fill the gaps in a child's development generated by the nonexistence of the family. Proof of this can be seen in the institutional interventions in adoption processes or, in some cases, reception or refuge processes according to the current legislation in each different country.

I underscore that no definition of what a family is has been offered with these rights, but at least we have a few assumptions through which general consensus has been reached and for which there exists legislation within the international community. I will refer now to the work conducted by the United Nations concerning these assumptions.

UNITED NATIONS WORK
ON THE SUBJECT OF FAMILY

As is the case in almost all considerations of the work conducted by the most noteworthy international organization, the United Nations, I feel it is important to differentiate between that which is achieved in the political realm and that which is achieved in the legal realm. In both cases, the direct repercussions pertain to the family, but the recognition of rights does not have the same incidence as when a public policy or program exists. Therefore, I am going to consider first the legal instruments and then the political work involved.

The Legal Instruments

As I noted previously, the point of departure is the Universal Declaration of Human Rights, approved in 1948. It is well known that the Declaration was prepared by the Human Rights Commission, which was created in 1946 after the establishment of the United Nations Organization through the signing of the San Francisco Letter of 1945.

The Declaration includes a list of rights and liberties that have been used as the backbone of many constitutional texts. The political nature of the Declaration was put to the acid test, as it was approved through a resolution of the United Nations General Assembly and there was no consensus concerning the text, approved with eight abstentions. In any case, the moral force of the Declaration cannot be denied, and it continues in effect throughout the world of universal constitutionalism.

Article 16 of the Declaration recognizes the individual right to enter into marriage freely and voluntarily, and it expressly dedicates a paragraph to the family. Concretely, article 16.3 states that, "the family is the natural and fundamental basis of society and, therefore, has the right to protection by society and state." It is worth noting that the first paragraph of this same article affirms the right to marry and create a family both for men and for women. The paragraph textually affirms that "men and women of adult age have the right to marry and create a family regardless of race, nationality or religion." Though the profile of the family whose protection is referred to in article 16 could be interpreted within the field of heterosexual relationships and not homosexual ones, I would prefer not to enter into this question. Furthermore, there have been authors who have defended that the plural case with which the paragraph is begun would give way to a broader interpretation of the text. This interpretation would give space for arguments of homosexual couples, even though these arguments would lose effectiveness if the Declaration text were placed in connection with the subsequent legal instruments.

The legal weakness of the Declaration was saved in a way by the approval of the 1966 International Pacts that gave legal reinforcement to the Declaration upon being approved as International Agreements with all the consequences that this has in the realm of international law. Specifically, article 10, paragraph 1 of the Economic, Social and Cultural Rights Pact reiterates that, "the broadest possible protection and assistance should be conceded to the family, which is the natural and fundamental basis of society, especially for its constitution and as long as it is responsible for the care and education of the children under its charge. Marriage should be entered into with the free consent of the future partners." The wording goes on to end with a paragraph dedicated to protecting mothers with respect to childbirth and another directed at protecting childhood.

Specific protection of the family is later highlighted in article 11 of the same Pact, which recognizes the right to an adequate level of living for an individual and his or her family and demands that States approve the appropriate measures for ensuring this. Similarly, article 23.1 of the Pact on Civil and Political Rights affirms that, "the family is the natural and fundamental element of society and has the right to protection by society and the State." Furthermore, paragraph 2 of the same article underscores "the right of a man and a woman to enter into marriage and create a family if each is of the legal age to do so." Here, in light of the use of the singular case to refer to the man and the woman, one could dilute the argument used to interpret article 16 of the Declaration in support of homosexual unions.

I do not wish to open a debate on this question, but I would like to add a brief commentary. I understand that United Nations texts cannot be contorted to justify an approach to life that was not institutionally recognized in any legislation in 1948. In this sense, it doesn't seem too farfetched to argue that the United Nations texts recognize the protection of the family based on the idea of marriage as a contract between man and woman.

It is another thing entirely if we must analyze the possible sources of rights recognition for homosexual individuals who opt for a common life project and, as a consequence, assume a series of patrimonial rights. In this case, though, we would not be talking about a man/woman contract that carries the legal denomination of "marriage" but rather a different man/man or woman/woman relationship that demands a different legal response. This contractual difference is important in terms of the analysis we are proposing.

The references to family, in the proposed terms, are reiterated in other United Nations legal instruments and are also explicit in the Agreement on Consent to Marry of 1962, the Agreement on Children's Rights of 1989, the Agreement on Protection of Rights for Emigrant Workers and Their Families of 1990, and the Agreement on the Protection of Rights for the Disabled of 2006. In the legal realm, therefore, the basic human rights instruments reiterate the protection of the family and the obligatory role of the State in providing that protection.

Political Instruments

Parallel to the strictly legal approach, it can also be argued that the United Nations has conducted work with a markedly political character that is set forth along two lines: the approval of a series of resolutions and the work of the Social Development Commission, under whose auspices the questions relating to families are included.

In the first case, The United Nations acts with the support of the mandate received by the General Assembly in article 13 of the Foundational Letter, which states: "The general Assembly will promote studies and make recommendations to the following ends: ... b) fomenting international cooperation in matters related to economic, social, cultural, educational and health issues while helping to make human rights and fundamental freedoms for all people effective regardless of race, sex, language or religion."

In 1989, the General Assembly approved resolution 44/82, which declared 1994 as the International Year of the Family under the slogan: *Family: Resources and Responsibilities in a Changing World*. The Resolution placed most of the responsibility for putting these activities into practice for the celebration onto local and regional entities and established that the Social Development Commission would be the entity within the United Nations system responsible for executing the approved decisions.

Since then, the reiteration of giving importance to the family has been given approval practically on an annual basis. The family was most assuredly in a difficult moment given that the meaning and the content of the term "family" was also being debated in world conferences at the same time, especially in the Conference on Population and Development (Cairo, 1994) and the IV Conference on Women (Peking, 1995).

The documents approved in the above Conferences establish that the family is the basis of society and that different types of societies have different types of families. This language is sufficiently loose to include any family profile, without excluding homosexual couples or polygamous relationships. The principle thrust of the wording was to achieve "the maximum with the minimum," turning to the national legislations to finalize the means of protecting the types of families that they deemed appropriate in each case.

As such, the debate that took place in the Conferences left its mark on the negotiating processes of all resolutions that have been approved since 1994. As stated above, the General Assembly had already approved Resolution 44/82, declaring 1994 the International Year of the Family, as well as Resolution 47/237, declaring May 15th International Family Day.

The report prepared by the Secretary in 1993 supported the establishment of three basic principles:

1) The family as the basis of all society.
2) Families assume different forms and functions depending on geographical zones, cultural traditions and existing religions.
3) All activities promoted for the 1994 Celebration must, as a rule, always seek shared responsibilities among men and women.

These principles have been reiterated in almost all resolutions approved in the seat of the Third Commission of the General Assembly up until the moment of the tenth anniversary of the International Year of the Family.

Precisely due to the polemic created in these world conferences, there were a group of countries interested in the United Nations explicitly recognizing the importance of family in the singular. This was is in order to avoid the situation of having families founded through the union between one man and one woman equated with polygamous unions or homosexual unions. Capitalizing on the event, a resolution was introduced in the Third Commission that reinforced the above recognition and gave the Secretary of the United Nations specific mandate to work along this line.

The proposal was followed by the presentation of a draft resolution in the Human Rights Commission, asking for the recognition of equality and non-discrimination for reasons of sexual orientation. Some of the Islamic countries threatened to boycott, introducing another resolution recognizing polygamy as a valid type of family structure. The result of the process was that no resolution in either direction was negotiated in the Human Rights Commission. And in the Third Commission, a long and bitter debate was opened.

Through this process, it could be said that an agreement was reached recognizing the family as the basis of society, but there were many points of dispute. First, there was a lack of a mandate for the Secretary, who did not receive instructions from the Member States to work on a singular definition of family. Second, there was a lack of adequate strategy in the most critical moments leading up to the debates from a political standpoint. Finally, there was an omission of cultural diversity references that condition family models in different geographical zones. It is also worth mentioning the errors in the negotiation process, although I will not delve into these as they lie outside the focus of this work. Having established the conceptual assumptions and the work conducted in the United Nations, we are now ready to analyze the situation in terms of the African Union case.

THE AFRICAN UNION

The choice of this organization is not accidental. The African continent probably has the greatest sociological variety in the world. The concepts of the family and the roles that women and men play in it vary widely from one end of the continent to the other. We should add ethnic and racial diversity to the cultural and religious traditions of all geographical areas, as these factors also condition the profile of a family.

As a result, I believe that focusing on the work conducted in the African Union can illuminate our objective of illustrating the idea and treatment of the family on the African continent. We must simply bear in mind a series of previous facts that facilitate the approach to a society as varied and plural as that in Africa.

The Role of Women

We should probably start by considering the possible function or functions that women carry out in an African society in order to establish the possible types of marital and family structures.

World Bank data confirm that Africa has integrated itself into the global system as a producer of goods it does not consume and a consumer of goods it does not produce. We should include in this description the fact that women earn less, possess less and control less than men even though they continue to bear the ultimate responsibility when it comes to food. For example, it can be cited that the women of Sub-Saharan Africa produce 80% of the basic food items, receiving 10% of the proceeds generated and controlling only 1% of the land. According to the latest data distributed by OIT, 48% of black African workers earn US$85 per month, while 65% of white men earn around US$500 per month.

Africa is made up of 48.8% men and 51.2% women. This represents 10.8% of the world female population and 14.7% of the female population in the Third World. The population growth rate is 3%, and the female population profile is basically young. However, we should bear in mind that this is not a homogeneous sector, given that there are important variations due to religion, social sectors, cultural sectors and generational overlap.

In many cases, marriage is considered more a union of clans or ethnicities than a union of two people. Normally (although there are differences from country to country) the dowry is one of the pivotal elements of marriage. Similarly, there are countries in which polygamy is the existing family model.

This structure denotes clear implications not only for women but for men as well. As such, the revision of the familial concept demands a revision not only of the role of women but also of the other half of society. We cannot omit the fact that Africa has the highest fertility rate, the highest mortality rate, and the lowest life expectancy rate in the world. It also is the continent with the highest number of armed conflicts in the world. On a brighter note, it also should be noted here that Africa has the highest rates of female parliamentary participation in the world.

Family Structure and Marriage

In Africa, family structure does not correspond to a single unitary scheme given the cultural and traditional differences in each country. However, geographically speaking, it could be stated that the concept of family corresponds more to an idea of parenting than a nuclear family.

The extended family that is so habitual on the African continent includes children, married children, brothers, wives, and occasionally widowed mothers or sisters whose husbands have left them. These family units tend to group themselves into a community, led by a head of the family who is recognized as having the rights of representation for the entire family.

From there, the principle that justifies the familial structure involves parenting ties. In many cases, the marriages are polygamous and arranged by a family representative when the woman is young. As such, there are times when marriage is perceived more as a commercial question than an emotional one. This is where the dowry plays a pivotal role. The more prestigious the woman is, the greater the dowry. Hence, the whole question is placed directly into the commercial realm.

In this sense, polygamy is justified in societies in which it seems necessary to ensure the survival of the family, clan or tribe, especially in zones of conflict. The more women a family head has, the greater his negotiating capacity given the fact that he can negotiate with a greater number of families. Furthermore, he has greater control over properties given the fact that he then governs the corresponding productive resources and labor force. Although there are differences between the Zulu and Mandinga tribes, for example, the approach to marriage is generally similar.

According to FAO data, nearly 50% of the marriages in Sub-Saharan Africa are polygamous with the exception of Lesotho, where this figure only reaches 9%. The number of women is different according to the region. For example, according to the same study, the majority of the polygamous households in the north of Sierra Leon have as many as 7 women, while in Zimbabwe that number is closer to 4.

There are also differences in terms of the age for entering into marriage, but the general criterion leans toward taking maximum advantage of the female reproductive cycle. According to FAO data, the marriage age for women spans from 17 to 21 years old, while that age spans between 23 and 25 among males. It should be noted here that polygamous marriages require an average age difference of 10 years between men and women in order to maintain the system, and women are much younger than their husbands as a general rule. According to the studies of Helen Warre that were conducted among the Konkomba in northern Ghana, the average difference between a woman and her first husband is 22 years. In northern Nigeria, the Kanuri women marry between the ages of 12 and 14 with men that can be two, three or even four times their age.

These differences grant men social positions that are different from women by endowing them with greater experience and power. This configures male/female relationships and, above all, affects the distribution of functions in the familial and marital structure that we have been discussing. It must be reiterated here that there are notable differences from country to country. Although I have referred to a few general profiles regarding familial structure, there are concrete cases like the Basa who live in the Cameroon zone and have small family structures that are very similar to the nuclear family. In these structures, the women have a greater margin of autonomy, and the men do not have the same power as those in the Mandinga communities. By citing this variety and the unified data referred to above, I now turn to an analysis of the terms in which the subject of family has been approached by the African Union.

Activities of the African Union on the Subject of Family

The African Letter on Human Rights and African Peoples, also known as the Banjul Letter, was promoted by the Organization for African Unity that has since been replaced by the African Union. The process began in 1979, when the Assembly of Heads of State and Government of the OUA decided to create an experts group to produce an instrument that guaranteed the protection of human rights on the African continent.

Once the group was constituted, it prepared a draft document that was unanimously approved in 1981 and entered into effect after the foreseen revisions on October 21st, 1986. The Letter is divided into three parts dedicated respectively to rights and obligations, guarantees and general dispositions.

The family is explicitly protected in article 18, which groups this protection with that of women, children and disabled people. The article is drafted in the following terms:

1) The family shall be a natural unit and the basis of society. It shall be protected by the State, which in turn shall look after its physical and moral health.

2) The State shall have the obligation of assisting the family, which is custodian of the moral and traditional values recognized by the community.

3) The state shall be responsible for eliminating any kind of discrimination of women and for protecting the rights of women and children exactly as stipulated in the international declarations and agreements.

4) The elderly and disabled shall also have the right to special measures for adequate protection of their physical or emotional needs.

In addition to recognizing article 18, the African Letter also assigns obligations to individual persons. Concretely, article 29 of the Letter affirms:

> The individual shall also have the obligation of:
> 1. Preserving the harmonious development of the family, promoting respect and cohesion to the latter, respecting one's parents at all times and caring for them should the need arise.
>
>   7. Preserving and reinforcing the positive African cultural values in relationships with other members of society in a spirit of tolerance, dialogue, consultation

and, in general, contributing to the promotion of moral
wellbeing in society.

This approach to the protection of families varies substantially with
respect to other international texts.

First, the recognition of rights is proposed as being linked to the
fulfillment of obligations. As such, the State is asked to protect the
family, and the individual is asked to preserve the harmony of the
family. Second, the existence of a general concrete framework is recognized. This framework is based on African cultural values that are
aimed at the moral wellbeing of society. This affirmation underscores
the contribution of the family towards improving society, reminding
us again that we are talking about the very basis of society.

From a conceptual point of view, this drafting provides a clear
difference regarding the conception of the family in western societies,
especially in Europe, not only for the firmness of its function in the
social group but also for the institutional and individual implications
regarding the support and defense of that social group. In this sense,
there are no precedents in other international texts.

We should add here some comment on the language emerging
from the African Letter concerning the rights and wellbeing of children. This Letter was approved July 11th, 1990, and its article 18 once
again proposes the protection of the family, this time under the following terms: "The family is the natural unit and basis of society. For
its establishment and development, it shall enjoy the protection and
support of the State. The States that are part of the current Letter shall
take the appropriate measures to guarantee the equality of rights and
responsibilities of wives in relation to their children during marriage
as well as in the case of the dissolution of that marriage. In the case of
dissolution, the necessary protection of the children shall be regulated.
No child shall be denied sustenance as a consequence of the civil status
of his or her parents."

This concept is completed with article 19, concerning the right of
children to enjoy the protection and care of their parents, and articles
24, 25 and 30 on the protection of children in the case of recluse
mothers, parents' separation or adoption processes. In all cases, the
State assumes the obligation of proposing alternative family formulas
to remedy possible absences of the biological family.

The last of the legal instruments to bear in mind is the Optional Protocol to the African Letter concerning the rights of women, which was approved in Maputo on July 11th, 2003. It is significant that on this date, when the United Nations had already approved the documents of the World Conferences as well as the resolutions relating to the family, an article on protecting marriage was included in which marriage is based on a nuclear structure involving a husband and wife to whom the option is given to choose the marital regime and place of residence. Sub-paragraph 5 of Article 6 states that, "the husband and wife shall, by mutual agreement, choose their matrimonial regime and place of residence."

Furthermore, the same article recognizes equal rights for men and women in sub-paragraph 7: "A woman and a man shall have equal rights with respect to the nationality of their children except where this is contrary to a provision in national legislation or is contrary to national security interests."

In case there were any doubts concerning the role of men and women, the second-to-last sub-paragraph of article 6 attributes the responsibility of protecting the family to them in the following terms: "A woman and a man shall jointly contribute to safeguarding the interests of the family, protecting and educating their children."

The wording in this article sheds light not only on the idea of the family based on marriage between a man and a woman but also underscores the responsibility of both in the project of protecting the interests of the family. To this we should add the fact that these references are made in the Optional Protocol dedicated to women's rights, centering attention on their function within the family environment without the prejudice found in some of the negotiations lead by westerners in which this would be completely impossible to propose.

As for legal instruments, The African Commission on Rights has not produced specific documents on the family, its situation or its rights. In United Nations negotiations, each African country has acted autonomously, advocating respect for national legislations. However, there have been clear positions on concrete topics such as the protection of children, recruitment of minors or the incidence of AIDS.

Given these arguments, and after having conducted a rapid assessment concerning the African situation on questions of family and the international texts approved in the African region, perhaps it could be concluded that a heterosexual version of the nuclear family exists in Africa. In this version, rights are recognized (protection and support of the State) as well as obligations (upholding African traditional values). Admittedly, the idea of the nuclear family is broadened in many places in Africa, where it is understood more as a web of individuals linked by kinship that goes beyond the nuclear family, which in the West is identified as based on marital relations and children.

In this sense, it would be interesting and useful to conduct more detailed research on the approach to defining family and, above all, the role assigned to the family in society's overall design for wellbeing.

References

Browning, D. 2004. Meaning of family in the Universal Declaration of Human Rights. Presented at the Asia/Pacific Family Dialogue for the Doha International Conference for the Family, in Kuala Lumpur, Malaysia.

Durán y Lalaguna, P. 2007. *La perspectiva de las Naciones Unidas en la protección de los derechos sociales*. Madrid: Aranzadi & Thomson.

_____. 2006. The United Nations and equal opportunities for men and women. UN-INSTRAW (UN International Research and Training Institute for the Advancement of Women).

ILGA-EUROPE. 2005. Directive of the European Union on free circulation and families formed by same-sex couples: Guide on the process of application. Brussels: International Lesbian, Gay, Bisexual, Trans and Intersexual Association.

Karim, A. A. 2005. Terminology's cultural differences: terminology of UN Documents related to Women and the Social Sphere. Organization of Islamic Conference.

_____. 1999. *Globalization issues: the problems of the next century*. Cairo: Samaa Publishing House.

Sauerbrey, E. 2004. The UN and Family Policy. Presented at the World Congress of Families III, Mexico.

Thuku, K. 2004. Silent relevance of African Trans-Family Ethnographies: realities and reflections on the African Family. Presented at the Asia/Pacific Family Dialogue for the Doha International Conference for the Family, in Kuala Lumpur, Malaysia.

Williams, C. 2004. Theory, tradition and contemporary marriage. Presented at the Asia/Pacific Family Dialogue for the Doha International Conference for the Family, in Kuala Lumpur, Malaysia.

Reports (2004), The Doha International Conference for the Family, Doha, Qatar.

—European Union: www.europa.eu.int.

—Food and Agriculture Organization of the United Nations: www.fao.org

—Organization of the African Unity: www.africa-union.org

—Organization of the Islamic Conference: www.oic-oci.org

—International Labor Organization: www.ilo.org

—United Nations: www.un.org

—World Bank: www.bancomundial.org; www.worldbank.org

Chapter 5

LEGISLATING MARRIAGE: GLOBALIZATION AND FAMILY LAW REFORM IN WEST AFRICA

Susanna D. Wing

Everywhere in the world, efforts to legally alter marriage practices inevitably give rise to heated debates concerning cultural norms and values. Nowhere is this more evident than in the recent debates surrounding the reform of Family Laws or Personal Laws in African states. These laws encompass marriage, divorce, child custody, and inheritance and the conflict over reform is often framed as "modernization" pitted against "tradition." Because gender roles are embedded in Personal Law any legal reform is threatening the status quo of a gender hierarchy that routinely positions a man as *chef de famille* (head of household) while a woman is viewed as "*la base de la societé,* the source of life, and the one responsible for transmitting to her children the fundamental values of community life" (Diallo 2008). The profound cultural significance of these responsibilities of women have important ramifications which often result in reinforcing the challenges to reforming family law despite the fact that women's constitutional rights, as well as those protected by international agreements signed by their governments, are in direct conflict with existing laws and daily practice.

This paper explores legal reform, globalization,[1] and shifting gender roles in Benin, Mali, and Senegal. In most instances laws change before social practices do, such as Benin's recent outlawing of polygamy and *levirate* (widow-inheritance), and the unintended consequences of these reforms may include a loss of rights for women. Ideally, it is believed, such reforms will lead the way to social change although the notion that law can work to reform society is widely contested and evidence from Senegal illustrates how slowly societal change might come, if it comes at all. In countries in which reform of Family Law is stalled, as in Mali, the culprit is frequently the resistance of conservative elements in society seeking to protect their own positions of power. In Mali this is represented by the *Collectif des Associations Musulmanes* whose membership includes religious authorities who play an important role in marriages and inheritance. In Senegal, reforms designed to rollback existing Family Law and impose Shari'a onto all Muslims in cases of Personal Law were proposed by the Islamic Committee for the Reform of Family Code in Senegal (CIRCOFS), a group led by the former presidential candidate Babacar Niang. In this unique case, progressive reforms were proposed by women's organizations but members of CIRCOFS took it upon themselves to propose the "*Projet du code du statut personnel*" in response to what they viewed as Western law that was inappropriately adopted by political leaders in 1972.

These three cases reveal the importance of leadership in the pursuit of progressive reforms and downplay the significance of religion by highlighting the political nature of debates concerning legal reform. As we will see, this political debate has most often been framed as a conflict between "Western" values and local traditions. Martin Chanock argues, "the invocation of the legitimacy and cultural importance of customary law has most often, in spite of its latter day harnessing to anti-colonial rhetoric, been in defense of conservative positions" (Chanock 1995: 184). Because the conservative arguments are framed in terms of cultural survival in the face of Western imposed values, this dichotomy creates challenges for those who see Family Law reform as integral to ongoing democratic transformations. The conservative stance is not surprising given the sweeping changes in some communities, particularly in urban areas, that are in part the result of globalization and liberalization. As Benjamin Soares has argued, following the collapse of Moussa Traoré's authoritarian regime in Mali, Islamic leaders in Bamako were angered by liberalization that they viewed as responsible for gambling on street corners (PMU kiosks popped up around the city and a casino opened), hotels by the hour located near mosques and madrasas, pornographic films in the city, and bars and nightclubs open during Ramadan (Soares 2005). In both Senegal and Mali, the effort to push these secular states to legally recognize Shari'a is in direct response to aforementioned societal changes.

Currently many African countries are revisiting Family Laws. In most cases (Senegal is a notable exception), reforms are designed to bring Personal law into accordance with international agreements ratified by states (such as the Convention on the Elimination of all forms of Discrimination Against Women, CEDAW and the Protocol to the African Charter on Human and Peoples' Rights on the Rights of Women in Africa) as well as their own constitutions. Globalization plays an integral part in the pursuit of increased women's rights. For example, the Millennium Development Goals are designed as a global blueprint for development and Goal 3, to "promote gender equality and empower women," incorporates multiple benchmarks for improving the status of women around the world. Central among these is the guarantee of land and property rights through legal reform. Legal reform of family law is frequently designed to give women access to property in marriage and inheritance. Not surprisingly, the wave of support for women's rights, which is particularly evident following the 1995 Beijing United Nations World Conference on Women and embedded in the Millennium Development Goals, has spawned widespread resistance to altering the status quo.

Globalization has destabilized family dynamics through the migration of workers to cities or foreign countries in search of employment. Economic opportunities for men and women have changed along with urbanization and increased access to formal education. These changes are perceived by some as placing customary and religious norms at risk. In many instances, women stay at home to raise families and depend on remittances from their husbands who have traveled in search of employment. The growing number of women-headed households includes those women who receive significant remittances that allow them to raise their families comfortably, or those who rarely see any support from their absent husbands. In other cases, these women are widows with few means of survival or they may be divorced women raising children, with or without the support of their former husbands. In many instances recently widowed or divorced women will seek to enter quickly into new marriages for emotional and/or financial support. In the countries analyzed here, it has often been the case that these women will enter into polygamous unions. Any one of these women is likely to face precarious and confusing legal environments that may or may not protect her as she seeks spousal support during marriage, the custody of children or alimony following a divorce, or inheritance of property following a death. The struggle between the effects of globalization and the persistence of traditional ways of life should be recognized as a struggle over power that has an important impact on gender relations and families.

Women who pursue professional lives, in response to increased opportunities available as a result of liberalization, are often faced with resistance at home to their greater independence. As Gerti Hessling and Marijke Van den Angel found, when women in Mali sought legal advice from the *Association des Juristes Maliennes* (AJM) for marital concerns, frequently these disputes were the result of husbands refusing to allow their wives to pursue their professional aspirations. Men threatened divorce or they claimed they would take second wives if their spouses did not change their ways. These social dilemmas were never acknowledged directly by the AJM councilors as they handled the legal aspects of women's concerns. As a result women often backed away from their professional activities in order to maintain peace in the household (Hesseling and Angel 2001). It is possible that because of the deep-rooted nature of cultural norms councilors did not question the resistance women faced, or because they concerned themselves only with legal nature of their clients' concerns, which were primarily marital disputes, they left the deeper issue of restricting women's professional opportunities alone. It is clear that while increased opportunities exist for women in public life, the divergent expectations of families and spouses often cause strife. This is not surprising, and is certainly a universal phenomenon. It does, however, underscore the urgency required to not only protect women's rights so that they are free to pursue as array of opportunities, but to conduct widespread educational campaigns concerning the rights of women and, more instrumentally, the benefits women's employment can bring to the household. To be sure, there are direct economic consequences to restricting women's professional activities because the extent to which women are prevented from participating in available opportunities inevitably reduces independence and economic activities available to a large segment of the population. This perspective does not deny the numerous sectors where women have been economically successful (such as markets) but rather emphasizes the restricted opportunities in formal businesses, the non-profit sector, and education, to name a few, which relate to existing gender roles and hierarchy.

Democratization and human rights, an integral part of the Millennium Development Goals and a central aspect of both CEDAW and the African Protocol on Women's Rights, destabilize gender roles within societies and this is played out in the debate over family law. It is not surprising that legal reforms are framed differently by opponents and supporters and that the wave of international support for Family Law reform has both positive and negative consequences. While donor funds are used to help promote public awareness of women's rights and provide a network of support for African women, there is frequently a backlash by those who perceive their actions as nothing other than cultural imperialism.

Prior to discussing recent attempts at legal reform in West Africa, I contextualize the debate by explaining the history embedded in colonial law as it relates to customary law in Francophone Africa and the legacy that this legal history imposes on current debates concerning Family Law reform.

LEGISLATING MARRIAGE IN AFRICA

Marlene Dobkin wrote in 1968 that women's emancipation through the Mandel Decree (1939) and Jacquinot Decree (1951) had wrecked havoc on marriage in Francophone Africa. She argued that these decrees, which required consent of both parties to marriage, regulated bridewealth, and set age minimums for marriage, led women to change husbands every 3 or 4 years leaving their children behind. She claimed that:

> Sudden emancipation of women without any adequate preparation resulted in new social mobility for women

who could travel about easily leaving their small compounds for the excitement of Yaoundé, Doula, or other
urban centers where they lived with little restraint or
surveillance. They often returned home with some savings
amassed from prostitution in the towns (Dobkin 1968).

The idea that women's emancipation would lead them to abandon
their husbands and children for urban excitement and prostitution
is an exaggeration. Fifteen years later in Cote d'Ivoire when deputies
discussed reforming the Family Code, several legislators defended
polygamy and levirate and "generally insisted that any deviation from
tradition could cause various social ills such as increased delinquency,
illegitimacy, and teen pregnancy" (Toungara 1997: 65). The responses
to reforms that promoted women's rights and independence were
similar in the United States where opposition to the Equal Rights
Amendment (ERA) prevailed by successfully portraying the ERA as
legislation that would wreak havoc on the household and marriage
(Mansbridge 1986). It is not surprising that revising Personal Laws
was perceived as profoundly destabilizing for Francophone Africa
as a whole. Arguments against reform often rely on the discourse of
protecting tradition; however, we must remind ourselves that these
very traditions are syncretic and have been constructed over time and
therefore they should not be held as sacrosanct norms. Customs are
embedded in power relations:

(I)t is important to remember that custom is not simply
what people do; that it is a set of values expressive not
simply of communal life, but of a way of maintaining order
and relations of power. This tends to be forgotten in situations in which custom derives its identity from a contrast
with, and an opposition to, and a rallying point against,
the law of the state (Chanock 1995: 173).

Those who hold power in customary regimes seek to maintain the
dichotomy between the law of the state and custom, thereby protecting
tradition in order to maintain their power.

The imposition of the French civil code during colonialism cleared
the path for capitalist growth by establishing patriarchal property laws
and male heads of household which facilitated tax collection among

other administrative necessities. During the colonial era Family Law was a compromise between colonial rule and African authorities or religious elders (Chanock 1995). The French were willing to leave Personal Law to the jurisdiction of these authorities so long as the practices in place did not threaten French notions of civilization. It should be noted that both levirate and polygamy had important social and economic functions within societies. Levirate ensured that a widow and her children were provided for by her husband's family and polygamy facilitated larger families, an asset in rural-based communities.

President Leopold Senghor of Senegal was one of the first heads of state in Francophone Africa to achieve family law reform. He hoped to create a "modern" and more uniform law, but was willing to do so only so long as religious leaders supported the changes. In this case, Senghor was balancing the pressures of uniformity placed on him by the process of modernization with the important position of religious leaders in supporting him as President. Fatou K. Camara criticizes Senghor arguing that "Lip service was paid to 'modernity' while greater concern for Muslim leaders' support is unashamedly clear" (Camara 2007: 788). Babacar Niang, the president of the Islamic Committee for the Reform of Family Code in Senegal (CIRCOFS) argued that religious leadership at the time remained opposed to the law. "Contrary to what certain people would have you believe, the Family Law was never accepted by our eminent Muslim leaders who condemned it without beating around the bush and rejected its application before as well as after its passage" (Niang 2008). A leader of the Muslim brotherhood of the Mourides claimed "The Code will not affect Touba. Because the law of God is translated into commandments and it will not be legislated by men, no matter who they are." The leader of the Tidjianes Muslim brotherhood argued that "The Code has no place in Senegal because a legislator should not impose onto citizens concepts and rules that are not their own, rules that frustrate their Muslim reflexes (Niang 2008)." Despite a relatively progressive law that passed in 1972, and was revised over time, Senegal illustrates challenges to reforming family law, but more importantly the inability of state law to have broad influence over daily practices of the country's citizens. Niang argues that the failure of the Family Code is evident in the fact that it is widely ignored by the practices of the majority of Senegalese people.

Colonialism left a legacy in Africa in which Family Law derived from European law applied to non-Africans, while the majority African population was subject to customary law (Chanock 1995: 172). Legal pluralism is not unique to Africa; however, "colonialism has overlaid the problem in Africa so that the law of the state appears to be 'white' law and the law of the people 'African'" (Chanock 1995: 172). This has led to a volatile debate at the root of legal reform that centers on the imposition of European or Western norms onto what has been labeled as African ways of life. To the extent that reform continues to be viewed as Western-imposed, change is unlikely and compliance with new laws is even less likely. Gwendoyn Mikell explains in *African Feminism* that any change in gender relations must emerge from within and not be imposed from the outside (Mikell 1997: 6). The problem lies in recognizing what has become a local movement for change and what might be viewed as imposed. Unfortunately, many of the organizations advocating for reform (discussed in more detail in the following section) are dependent on financial support from international donors making it difficult for African women to take ownership of the process of pursuing Family Law reform. Nevertheless, their ability to spearhead public awareness campaigns and frame this struggle for rights as their own struggle and not one that has been imposed from the outside will increase the likelihood of their success. If African women and men who support the protections of women's rights are able to establish these as their own convictions associated with increased democracy, then legal reform is more likely in countries in which many citizens are, for the most part, supportive of recent democratic changes.

REFORMING FAMILY LAW

Several African countries including Botswana, Cote d'Ivoire, Morocco, Mozambique, South Africa, Uganda, and Tanzania, among others, have pursued family law reforms. This section briefly explores the context of reform in Benin, Senegal and Mali. As we will see, in each case the debate over legal change is framed as "modern" versus "traditional" and political leadership plays an important role in the current status of reform. Both Senegal and Benin have adopted generally progressive personal laws, while Mali has not succeeded in efforts to replace its 1963 marriage law.

BENIN

In 2004, the National Assembly of Benin voted 57-0 (with 8 abstentions) in favor of a new Family Law. The new law consecrates monogamy as the sole form of legal civil marriage while permitting polygamy only in traditional marriages. While a man may take multiple wives, only the union that takes place in a civil ceremony will be legally recognized. The law outlaws *levirate,* does away with forced marriage and allows for a woman to keep her maiden name after marriage, a practice not previously permitted by the law (Boko Nadjo 2004). Supporters of the new law were backed by international donors such as the US Agency for International Development (USAID) as well as transnational movements such as WILDAF (Women, Law and Development in Africa). WILDAF-Benin and the *Association des Femmes Juristes du Benin* (AFJB) were two women's associations from Benin that actively lobbied for reform. Opponents to reform argued that their traditional ways of life were being undermined by this "woman's code" and that the intelligentsia were leading a coup against men (Kouton 2002). Traditional practices were defended by Houssoue Houenivo, a village chief, who stated that "Taking the wife of a dead brother is not a crime...It is tradition that demands it. Our parents practiced it...I say no to this law which wants to abolish this cherished practice" (Kouton 2002). Challenges to the new law were no match for the lobbying by proponents of reform.

Reform of the Family Code in Benin took place in the halls of the National Assembly with a great deal of lobbying on the part of women's associations. Indeed members of WILDAF-Benin were present in the Assembly when representatives voted on the law. Those threatened by reform did not organize in opposition to the cause. Whereas women have gained international support and have organized as a group politically, men have not. In 2002, the President of the National Assembly, Adrien Houngbédji promised to bring the reform to a vote and his influence on other deputies is certain to have influenced the outcome of the vote (Touré 2002). Houngbédji is a vocal supporter of women's rights arguing that:

> One cannot take a stand on respecting human beings if there is no respect for women and gender equality. It is through an openness to their ideas and demands that

this respect occurs. Women deserve more of a presence in public, representative proceedings and in groups of public and private decision-makers. The principle of the participation of half of the population is non-negotiable and cannot be subject to either substitution or shortcuts (Houngbedji 2002).

Houngbedji explicitly challenges the notion that democracy can move forward in Africa while leaving women behind.

WILDAF and Houngbedji were not the only strong advocates for reform in Benin. USAID played an influential role through its Women's Legal Rights Initiative (WLRI). WLRI is an important source of funding for organizations such as the AFJB that are at the forefront of public awareness campaigns regarding the new Family Law. USAID is straightforward about the purpose of the project. "Women's Legal Rights activities are aimed at overcoming resistance due to influence of traditions and customary practices...This new law marks a watershed in the history of Benin legal environment that is constituted of retrograde customs and traditions" (US Agency for International Development 2008). Unfortunately the customs and traditions practiced in Benin are practiced by the majority of the population and language such as "retrograde" only serves to underscore the view that this is a conflict between acceptable modern laws and backward traditions. Such an approach deepens the divide between those in favor of reform and those who are suspect of its relation to outside influence.

A revised code, passed in 2002, was declared unconstitutional by the Constitutional Court because it permitted polygamy (and not polyandry). The court then reworked the law which was presented to the National Assembly and passed in 2004. There are deputies who claim that the Court hijacked the law from the Assembly. The fact that a primary supporter of the reform, founder and former President of AFJB, Judge Clotilde Médégan Nougbodé was also the President of the High Court of Justice and a member of the Constitutional Court fueled the deputy's concerns. Judge Médégan Nougbodé's association with USAID and AFJB made her the face of the new Family Law.

Of the three countries examined here, Benin is the only one that does not have a majority Muslim population. This is significant only to the extent that Muslim associations and religious leaders are able to mobilize their followers in opposition to reforms by labeling them anti-Islamic, as in Mali and Senegal. The fact that the President of the National Assembly was a principle advocate of the new law and that no legislator would vote against it reveals a great deal of political pressure associated with the passage of the law and a good deal of political leadership on the part of the President of the Assembly. There were no interest groups lobbying in opposition to the Family Law.

The passage of the law was pivotal to Benin's attempt to change social practices through legal reform despite widespread resistance. Polygamy is still widely practiced but only a wife married in a civil ceremony will have any legal rights in case of divorce or the death of her spouse. Deputy Rosine Vieyra-Soglo argued, "You can have forty wives if you like, but know that if you die it is only the wife married in a civil ceremony who will have the right to inheritance, all the others will have nothing" (Touré 2004). Many women are unaware of the Family Law and may choose to enter into polygamous customary marriages and could easily find themselves with few legal rights if their marriages come to an end. Because customary law required maintenance of each wife the fact that a husband can legally deny support to any wife not married under civil law has serious consequences for women who continue to expect traditional practices to protect them. While compassion and social pressures may lead most husbands to support their spouses, he has no legal obligation to do so and in effect those women not married by civil ceremony have no status as wives and become concubines in the eyes of the law. The response to this dilemma has been to raise public awareness of the importance of civil marriages.

Since the passage of the law its implementation has been a primary concern. Legal compliance remains the Achilles heel of new legislation that challenges social norms so profoundly. A 2006 survey conducted by the National Institute of Statistics and Economic Analysis reported that polygamy was no longer the norm in Benin. The percentage of married women in polygamous unions dropped from 50% in 1996 to 42% in 2006).[2] This drop may have more to do with economic means than with a social transformation regarding multiple marriages or compliance with the new family law. In addition, now that polygamy is not legally recognized, it is possible that respondents are not forthcoming in acknowledging that they are in a polygamous union. Benin has pursued change through democratic means. Leaders in Benin are relying on legal reforms to have an impact on daily practices of the general population of the country. This is likely to be a lengthy process, the outcome of which remains undetermined.

SENEGAL

The 1972 Senegalese Family Code has been revised in 1974, 1979, and 1989. The 1972 Law renounced repudiation, forced marriage and early marriage (girls must be at least 16 years of age and males 20). The groom is required to choose the marital regime prior to his first marriage and the choice is for life. He can select monogamy, limited polygamy, or polygamy (up to four wives). Because he alone commits to this decision and the choice is for life, most men select polygamy. The law allows women to work outside the home without the consent of their husbands. Men remain the *chef de famille* (head of household) and *puissance paternelle* (paternal power) is invoked in Article 152 as the authority in the household rather than the gender neutral *autorité parentelle* (parental authority) which has been advocated by WILDAF (2004). It is not surprising that critics of the law argue that it is imported from the West, violates the rights of Muslims, and is labeled a "feminist code" (Sowsidibe 1993-94: 427). In both Mali and Benin the proposed laws were referred to as the "women's code."

In 2003 the Islamic Committee for the Reform of the Family Code in Senegal (CIRCOFS) submitted a revised version of the Family Law to the government. After President Abdoulaye Wade announced that he would not permit Personal Law to be based on the shari'a and the National Assembly would not adopt such a code (his party held the legislative majority), CIRCOFS continued to push for its adoption. While pleased with the prevention of Shari'a as Senegal's Family Law for Muslims, the transnational organization "Women Living under Muslim Laws" argued that by opposing the reform President Wade was able to present himself as a defender of women's rights while at the same time avoiding changes to the law that advocates of women's rights have supported for a long time. NGOs in Senegal fear that the President will use the pressure from CIRCOFS as a pretext to prevent further changes to the law. Women in Senegal are expected to be grateful for avoiding the adoption of the shari'a with respect to Family Law and therefore the government does not expect them to continue to seek reforms to the existing law (Women living under Muslim laws, 2003).

There is a great deal of evidence that shows the extent to which personal laws in Senegal have failed to alter societal practices. From 1974 to 1985, 4607 judgments were made on inheritance and only 452 of these were based on statutory law, the others were decided according to Islamic law (Sowsidibe 1993-94: 427). With respect to marriage, the Law of February 24, 1967 fixed dowries at small amounts not to exceed 3000CFA and wedding ceremonies were not to exceed 15000 CFA. This was quickly put aside as powerful families (including the very deputies who passed the law) sought to celebrate marriages with ceremonies they deemed as appropriate to the occasion (Sowsidibe 1993-94: 428). In cases in which legal protections existed they were not always observed by the judicial system.

The laws that were established by President Senghor and revised over time do hold the possibility of protecting women, although more needs to be done in this regard. If courts do not uphold the law and women no longer have the ability to seek protection from customary law then indeed women are left with very little protection. It is likely that the family code was passed in 1972 because it was widely understood that it would have very little impact on daily practices across the country. The notion that what currently exists is a "hollow law" was central to CIRCOFS push for a rollback of the current legislation.

President Wade was an important voice promoting the Protocol to the African Charter on Human and Peoples' Rights on the Rights of Women in Africa. He played a significant leadership role in seeing the Protocol ratified by several of his peers across the continent. Without intending to overemphasize his feminist credentials, it is clear that his forceful refusal to consider Shari'a as the basis for family law in Senegal prevented the CIRCOFS initiative from gaining ground. In all likelihood, Wade's position on this subject had more to do with broader political calculations in which he recognized the importance of supporting the human rights and donor communities as opposed to religious conservatives represented by CIRCOFS. Nevertheless, both Senghor's and Wade's political leadership were critical to support for family law in Senegal. Unfortunately, there continues to be a vast gap between the law and daily practice. Urban compliance with family law is significantly higher than compliance in rural areas where the law is largely ignored and likely unknown (Gellar 2005: 118).

MALI

In Mali the 1963 *Code du mariage et de la tutelle* governs marriage and there is no civil code to govern inheritance which is decided by the traditional or religious law that best applies to the deceased. The *Code du Mariage* restricts women's activities and states: "The husband owes protection to his wife, and the wife owes obedience to her husband". As Hessling and Angel argue:

> In practice, this gives the husband unlimited and uncontrolled power to restrict the freedom of movement of his wife. A married woman who is legally separated from her husband, is also restricted in her activities by her husband. In 2000, this led to a famous case in Mali. A woman wanted to start an international trade business. Her husband, from whom she was legally separated, went to court in order to prevent this, and asked the judge to withdraw his wife's passport. The claim was sustained. When the woman refused to give the passport, she was convicted to two years imprisonment (Hessling and Angel 2001).

This discrimination against women has clear ramifications for not only women's freedom of movement, but for economic development more broadly considered.

There has been an ongoing struggle between women's associations seeking reform of marriage and inheritance laws and the *Collectif des Associations Islamiques du Mali* who are strongly opposed to reforms that would not legally recognize customary or religious marriages, and could outlaw polygamy. Women's associations such as AJM, *Groupe-Pivot Droits des Femmes, Coordination des Associations et ONGs Feminines du Mali* (CAFO), and the *Association pour le Progrès et la Defense des Droits de Femme Maliennes* (APDF) all lobbied for change and the Ministry for the Promotion of Women, Children, and Family spearheaded the *Projet de la Reforme du Code de la Famille*. While a new law was proposed to the *Conseil des ministres,* it was not brought to the floor of the National Assembly. In 2002 during his last days in office, president Alpha Oumar Konaré attempted to reform the code by decree. This followed a series of *concertations* or local and regional meetings that incorporated civil society and members of the *Collectif.*

The decree was viewed by the *Collectif* as a denial of their concerns expressed in the dialogue that had taken place in the *concertations*. The *Collectif* threatened violence in Bamako, Mali's capital, if President Konaré signed the decree. Several imams used their positions to mobilize opposition to women leaders who pushed for reforms (as well as other culturally sensitive topics such as outlawing excision).

The opposition to reform can be linked, in part, to the loss of power on the part of religious authorities who currently play an important role in marriages and inheritance. With the 2002 election of President Amadou Toumani Touré, women's associations have become less vocal and no longer actively lobby for the government to reform the law. This, I argue, is the result of the cooptation of many NGOs and the lack of continued pressure from the Ministry for the Promotion of Women, Children and Family (to be referred to as Ministry for the Promotion of Women). The political climate changed such that women leaders clearly did not believe it was in their best interest to continue to pressure the government for change and there was a long silence that followed with respect to reforming family law.

It is relevant that there has also been an ongoing struggle between the Ministry of Justice and the Ministry for the Promotion of Women. The Ministry of Justice did not support the fact that the Ministry for the Promotion of Women spearheaded the *projet du loi* during Konaré's time in office. Some people argued that the law was about individual rights and justice and should rightly be handled by the Ministry of Justice. Interestingly the project has been taken out of the hands of the Ministry of for the Promotion of Women and given to the Ministry of Justice which established, on January 10, 2008, a 19 member commission to reevaluate the Family Law. As one journalist noted, this commission must reconcile modernism and tradition. In addition, their actions affect not only women, but family, society, and are a question of good governance and democracy (Camara 2007: 2). The revised code, created through dialogue that incorporated both members of the *Collectif* and women's associations, was passed by the National Assembly in August 2009. In response, thousands of protestors marched in Bamako and across the country. Imams encouraged religious marriages to continue although the proposed law did not recognize them as legal unions (Soares 2009). In response to the outpouring of discontent over the new Family Code, President Touré refused to sign it into law.

Although the most recent revision of the *Code* pursued a Moroccan style approach—that is, one that relies heavily on the Koran to support proposed reforms—it was still perceived as a direct threat to many in the Muslim community.

Each of these cases underscores the debates surrounding reform of Family Law and shows the extent to which the relative power of men and women comes into play as men seek to maintain power that rests in the status quo and women leaders pursue protection of their rights. It also reveals the language of "traditional" and "modern", "African" and "Western" that arises in these debates. Changes to families are taking place in Africa as a result of changing economies and democracy has created an environment for increased protections of citizen rights. Despite the spread of democracy, women's rights are routinely presented as being imposed by the West. This places women of all classes in a precarious situation in which customary laws that may have protected them in the past are eroded while new laws are either not put into place or are simply ignored.

GLOBALIZATION AND OWNERSHIP OF LEGAL REFORM

Globalization has an important effect on the laws that protect families in Africa, and women in particular. Economic liberalization and political liberalization are intertwined and integral aspects of globalization in Africa. Economic liberalization has provided opportunities for men and women at the same time that it has made life more difficult for many and therefore required a change in gender roles as men and women seek alternative forms of income. Political liberalization has brought democracy and increased demands for equality and women's rights. The influences of globalization have affected family structures at different rates across the continent but everywhere those representing customary and religious norms have resisted change. In Benin and Mali, opponents to legal reform framed the proposed Family Law as threatening to communities and cultural ways of life. In Senegal legal reform proposed by CIRCOFS was in essence an effort to prevent further changes to the legal environment that would promote women's rights, but also an example of an attempt on the part of an Islamic group to bring the legal structures in line with everyday marital practices in the country. Indeed Shari'a is widely respected across the country and Family Law does not reach the lives of many living in rural areas who are unaware of the state laws. In defending their *projet du loi* CIRCOFS argued that the secular state in Senegal was a fallacy and that the political leadership of Senegal had merely mimicked France, thus framing the entire constitution as being alien to Senegalese customary ways of life. CIRCOFS placed tradition in direct opposition to the state and attempted to undermine the legitimacy not only of Senegal's Family Law but of the constitution itself:

> One has become familiar, in the current contentions between feminism and patriarchy, with appeals to what is 'natural,' supported by reference to 'science,' by those who resist the movement towards greater gender equality. Africans, too often in the recent past on the receiving end of pseudo-scientific invocations of a natural order of things to justify oppression, tend to take refuge in 'custom' as the over-arching endorsement of inequities. The similarity of these arguments must be recognized. Both are attempts to avoid discussion of the essential political issues by invoking a greater and determining reality (Chanock 1995: 175).

Chanock's observation raises important similarities in societies undergoing change.

The extent to which the status quo can be out of the hands of people—whether because the laws are natural or traditional—the easier it is to argue that they ought to be left untouched. All societies change overtime and just as the concept of a natural order of things was used as a rationale for oppression so too is the notion of stagnant tradition.

If proponents of reform can effectively argue that Family Law reforms are integral to democracy they are more likely to achieve reforms. In young democracies such as Benin and Mali there is still a great deal of pride in the transition away from coups d'états and arbitrary rule towards democracy.[3] These countries are models for democracy in Africa following their national conferences and transitions that began in the early 1990s. Senegal has long been held as a quasi-democracy since the time of President Leopold Senghor who was recognized as an "enlightened" leader among Africa's dictators (of course this "enlightenment" had everything to do with his willingness to assimilate to French notions of civilization). In 2000, Senegal, for the first time in its history, saw a change of political party in power with the election of President Abdoulaye Wade and the 2001 constitution restricted the president's term in office to two five year terms. The government of Senegal faces the challenge of balancing the demands of those who wish to integrate Shari'a more formally into the legal structure of the country and those who seek to further protect women's rights. Ultimately, the state must address the conflicts that exist between the law and daily practice.

Just as colonialism strained gender relations and institutionalized patriarchy, globalization has continued to further divide societies. Since the 1995 UN World Conference of Women in Beijing and the growing effort to place women at the center of development (Women in Development agenda) and to recognize women's rights as human rights, conservative groups in Mali and Senegal have been threatened and mobilized to action. In Benin those opposed to reform were not well organized whereas in Mali and Senegal the existing religious organizations and could rely on sermons to raise the issue of threatened ways of life with their constituents and bring "cultural survival" to the public eye.

Women's transnational organizations such as WILDAF and the Fédération Internationale des Droits de l'Homme (FIDH) as well as local organizations such as AJM, CAFO, AFJB are the critical players in achieving reform as well as in the critical phase of public awareness following reform. However, given the fact that these organizations are generally funded by outside donors they invite the criticism of being labeled Western. Women will have to make every effort to form networks within their own countries that mobilize across class divides to bring support to their cause. Public awareness campaigns will need to include both men and women. Unfortunately, in the case of Mali, some women leaders have been co-opted and have not illustrated the necessary conviction required to maintain pressure groups in turbulent times. Others have gained positions of power and have launched new international careers that take them from the struggles at home. These women are to be congratulated for achieving international prestige and it is hoped that their example will have both an effect on the international community but also inspire women in their own communities to become leaders at home.

The recent democratic openings provide the essential platform for ongoing community discussions concerning issues of Family Law reform, culture and citizenship. It is also important to increase women's public presence in elected office at all levels. Women in decision-making positions are well placed to argue for democracy and human rights. The deep-seated resistance to women in elected office is evident in the numbers of women in leadership positions which are slow to change. Postcolonial states are placed in a difficult context from which they must continue to negotiate which values and laws will be respected within their societies. Only through ongoing dialogue and debate from within will this take place. Culture and religion ought not be placed on a pedestal as sacred values free from hierarchies of power, nor should democracy be viewed as a panacea. Donors must gauge their contributions carefully in an effort to permit women to be at the forefront of their own struggle for legal protections that democracy affords them. There is no doubt that financial support for women's associations is necessary and yet the danger lays in associations that simply compete for funds in order to merely exist without achieving their mission goals.

In each of these cases we can see how destabilizing legal reform relating to families can be. Despite this, most families in Mali, Benin, and Senegal are unaware of the legal codes that govern their relations. Indeed, many individuals seeking resolution to family conflicts will find the answer within their own compounds and will rarely seek outside input. The problem rests for those who do seek the protection of the legal system and find a precarious mix of laws that can be used to restrict their own rights. It is not surprising that the French left personal law to the jurisdiction of religious and customary norms. Nevertheless, the social upheaval of colonialism did impact family relations and has had a lasting effect on how legal reforms are perceived within postcolonial states. Women and men in Benin, Senegal, and Mali who support women's rights will need to lead the way in convincing their fellow citizens that their struggles are their own, that they are grounded in democratic aspirations and are not a threat to families in Africa.

Notes

1. In this chapter globalization refers to the increasing social and economica integration of peoples and cultures. Economic and political liberalization policies are key aspects of globalization. In Africa, "Westernization" and "modernization" are frequently viewed as synonymous with globalization.

2. *Jeune Afrique,* "Les Béninois de moins en moins portés vers le ménage polygamique," May 15, 2008.

3. This position is evident in interviews conducted by the author in Mali and Benin as well as in the Afrobarometer public opinion surveys.

References

Afrobarometer Network. 2004. Afrobarometer Round 2: Compendium of Comparative Results from a 15-country Survey, Working Paper no. 34. Comp. Michael Bratton, Carolyn Logan, Wonbin Cho, and Paloma Bauer. www.afrobarometer.org.

_____. 2005. Afrobarometer Round 3: Survey in Benin, 2005, Summary of Results. www.afrobarometer.org.

_____. 2007. Citizens and the State in Africa: New Results from Afrobarometer Round 3, Working Paper no. 61. Comp. Carolyn Logan, Tetsuya Fujiwara and Virginia Parish. www.afrobarometer.org.

AFJB (Association des Femmes Juristes du Benin). 1995. *Guide juridique de la femme Beninoise.* Porto Novo: Presses du J.O.R.B.

An-Na'im, Abdullahi Ahmed. 2002. Shari'a and Islamic Family Law: Transition and Transformation. In *Islamic Family Law in a Changing World: A Global Resource Book*, ed. Abdullahi Ahmed An-Na'im, 1-22. London: Zed Books.

Appleton, Simon. 1996. Women-Headed Households and Household Welfare: An Empirical Deconstruction for Uganda. *World Development* 24.12: 1811-1827.

Benin Constitutional Court Decision DCC-0063, September 26, 1996.

Benton, Lauren. 2002. *Law and Colonial Cultures.* Cambridge: Cambridge University Press.

Boko Nadjo, Geneviève. 2004. *Persons and Family Code of Benin.* Ethiopia: NGO Forum Addis Ababa.

Botimela, Loteteka. 2006. L'experience d'intermediation au tribunal pour enfants de Paris, l'histoire de Mamadou. *Juridicités, Cahiers d'Anthropologie du droit, hors série*, 45-50.

Camara, Dado. Révision du code de la famille: Quel sera le nouveau statut de la femme, Mali. http://www.wluml.org/french/newsfulltxt. shtml?cmd[157]=x-157-559874 (accessed January 21, 2008).

Camara, Fatou K. 2007. Women and the Law: A Critique of Senegalese Family Law. *Social Identities: Journal for the Study of Race, Nation and Culture* 13(6): 787-800.

Chanock, Martin. 1995. Neither Customary nor Legal: African Customary Law in an Era of Family Law Reform. In *African Law and Legal Theory*, ed. Gordon R. Woodman and A. O. Obilade, 171-190. New York: New York University Press.

_____. 1991. Paradigms, Policies and Property: A Review of the Customary Law of Land Tenure. In *Law in Colonial Africa*, ed. Kristin Mann and Richard Roberts, 61-84. Portsmouth: Heinemann.

_____. 1989. Neither Customary nor Legal: African Customary Law in an Era of Family Law Reform. *International Journal of Law and the Family* 3: 72-88.

Chant, Sylvia. 2003. Female Household Headship and the Feminization of Poverty: Facts, Fictions, and Forward Strategies. Gender Institute.

De Langen, Maaike. 2001. Les Assesseurs et la Justice: configurations du droit et de la coutume dans les conflits fonciers à Douentza. Mali: Cooperation Juridique Malienne Néerlandaise.

Diallo, Ibrahima. 2008. Rentree solonnelle des cours et tribunaux: Le statut de la femme au tableau. http://www.sudonline.sn/spip.php?article8468 (accessed online January 24, 2008).

Dobkin, Marlene. 1968. Colonialism and the Legal Status of Women in Francophonic Africa. *Cahiers d'études africaines* 8(31): 390-405.

Ekeh, Peter. 1975. Colonialism and the Two Publics in Africa: A Theoretical Statement. *Comparative Studies in Society and History* 17: 91-112.

Gellar, Sheldon. 2005. *Democracy in Senegal: Tocquevillian Analytics in Africa*. New York: Palgrave.

Hesseling, Gerti, and Marijke Van den Angel. 2001. Inegalités de Droits: Gender and Law in Mali. Paper presented at the International Colloquium: Gender, Population and Development, July 16-21, in Africa. http://www.ined.fr/coll_abidjan/publis/pdf/session3/hesselin.pdf (accessed January 16, 2008).

Houngbedji, Adrien. 2002. Approfondir la Démocratie dans un monde fragmenté. Cotonou. http://www.undp.org/surf-wa/nepad/parliamentarians/docsfr/houngbedji.htm.

Howard, Rhoda. 1990. Group versus Individual Identity in the African Debate on Human Rights. In *Human Rights in Africa*, ed. A. A. An-Naim and F. Deng, 159-183. Washington: Brookings Institution.

Islamic Family Law Project. Emory University. http://www.law.emory.edu/ifl.

Jeune Afrique, "Les Béninois de moins en moins portés vers le ménage polygamique," May 15, 2008.

Kouton, Emile. 2002. "Moves to outlaw archaic marriage customs stirs storm in Benin," Agence France Press, July 26, 2002. Lexis-nexis, load date October 21, 2002.

Kouton, Emile. June 23, 2004. "Trouble and strife among Benin's menfolk as new law bans polygamy." Lexis-nexis, load date June 24, 2004.

Le Vine, Victor. 1997. The Rise and Fall of Constitutionalism in West Africa. *Journal of Modern African Studies* 35(2): 181-206.

Lloyd, Cynthia B., and Anastasia J. Gage-Brandon. 1993. Women's Role in Maintaining Households: Family Welfare and Sexual Inequality in Ghana. *Population Studies* 47(1): 115-131.

Mansbridge, Jane. 1986. *Why We Lost the ERA*. Chicago: University of Chicago Press.

Mikell, Gwendolyn. 1997. *African Feminism: The Politics of Survival in Sub-Saharan Africa*. Philadelphia: University of Pennsylvania Press.

Niang, Babacar. January 23, 2008. "L'echec du Code de la famille." *Le Quotidien* (Senegal), http://lequotidien.sn/dossiers/article.CFM2article_id=67&var_doss=13 (accessed January 24, 2008).

Royce, Ed. 2002. Recognizing the Importance of Inheritance Rights of Women in Africa. Presented by the US House of Representatives Subcommittee on Africa, July 23, Washington, D. C. http://allafrica.com/stories/prinatble/200207230672.html.

Schulz, Dorothea E. 2003. Political Factions, Ideological Fictions: The Controversy over Family Law Reform in Democratic Mali. *Islamic Law and Society* 10(1): 132-164.

Soares, Benjamin. 2005. Islam in Mali in the Neoliberal Era. *African Affairs* 105(418): 77-95.

---. 2009. "The Attempt to Reform Family Law in Mali." *Der Welt des Islams* 49: 398-428.

Sowsidibe, Amsatou. 1993-94. Senegal's Evolving Family Law. *University of Louisville Journal of Family Law* 32(2): 421-430.

Sow, Fatou. 1995. *Femmes rurales chefs de famille en Afrique Subsaharienne.* Rome: Food and Agriculture Organization.

Toungara, Jeanne Maddox. 1994. Inventing the African Family: Gender and Family Law Reform in Cote d'Ivoire. *Journal of Social History* 28: 37-61.

_____. 1997. Changing the Meaning of Marriage: Women and Family Law in Cote d'Ivoire. In *African Feminism: The Politics of Survival in Sub-Saharan Africa,* ed. Gwendolyn Mikell, 53-76. Philadelphia: University of Pennsylvania Press.

Touré, Ali Idrissou. 2004. Droits-Benin: Le code de la famille consacre la monogamie, mais n'interdit pas la polygamie. Inter Press Service. http://www.ipsnews.net.fr/internat.asp?idnews=2238 (accessed June 17, 2004).

_____. 2002. Benin: Les ONG de femmes present parlement de voter le nouveau Code de la famille. http://www.famafrique.org/nouv2002/nouv26-04-12b.html (accessed April 23, 2002).

Tripp, Aili Mari. 2004. Women's Movements, Customary Law, and Land Rights in Africa: The Case of Uganda. *African Studies Quarterly* 7(4). http://www.africa.ufl.edu/asq/v7/v7i4a1.htm.

United Nations Human Development Report, 2001 and 2003.

UNICEF. 2005. At a Glance: Senegal. New York: United Nations Children's Fund. http://www.unicef.org/infobycountry/senegal_statistics.html (accessed May 11, 2005).

US Agency for International Development. 2008. Gender: Promoting Women's Legal Rights in Benin. http://www.usaid.gov/bj/gender.html (accessed January 14, 2008).

US Department of State Human Rights Report 2001.

Varley, Ann. 1996. Women Heading Households: Some More Equal than Others. *World Development* 24(3): 505-520.

Wing, Susanna D. 2002a. Women Activists in Mali: The Global Discourse on Human Rights. In *Women's Activism and Globalization*, ed. N. Naples and M. Desai, 172-185. New York: Routledge.

_____. 2002b. Questioning the State: Constitutionalism and the Malian *éspace d'interpellation démocratique. Democratization* 9(2): 121-147.

Women in Law and Development in Africa (WILDAF/FeDDAF). 2004. Situation des femmes Sénégal. http://www.wildaf-ao.org/fr/print. php3?id_article=47 (accessed January 14, 2008).

Women living under Muslim laws. 2003. Senegal: Victoire pour les forces progressistes mais pas forcement pour les femmes sénégalaises. http://www. wluml.org/french/newsfulltxt.shtml?cmd%5B157%5D=x-157-15172 (accessed January 2008).

Wooten, Stephen. 2003. Women, Men, and Market Gardens: Gender Relations and Income Generation in Rural Mali. *Human Organization* 62(2): 166-177.

Chapter 6

MATRIFOCALITY, PATRIARCHY, AND GLOBALIZATION: CHANGING FAMILY FORMS IN A SOUTH AFRICAN CITY

Leslie Bank

Strangely the everyday rhythms of domestic life have rarely counted as part of the 'urban,' as though the city stopped at the doorstep of the home. But domestic life is now woven routinely into the urban public realm... The rhythms of the home are as much part of city life as, say, the movements of traffic, office life, or interaction in the open spaces of the city. Its rhythms, too, need incorporating into the everyday sociology of the city.

(Amin and Thift 2002: 18)

INTRODUCTION

This chapter focuses on globalization and changing family structures in the coastal South African city of East London. In this chapter, I am especially interested in the fate of the multigenerational, matrifocal family, which was ubiquitous in the townships across South Africa in the 1940s and 1950s, but disappeared in the era of Apartheid urban planning and restructuring. This paper seeks to explain why this family form came to predominate during this period, why it collapsed under apartheid, and what evidence we have of its re-emergence in the current period of post-apartheid planning and globalization. To develop my argument, I focus on changing family structures and especially the matrifocal family in the townships of a single South African city, the coastal city of East London in the Eastern Cape province since the 1950s. There are two reasons why I start my discussion after the Second World War, the first is that this was a critical first period of transition towards globalization in the South African economy, the second is that we have an excellent account of family life in East London's locations in the ethnographies of a number of social anthropologists, who worked in the city's locations in the 1950s (Reader 1960; Mayer 1961; Pauw 1963). This work provides us with useful baseline from which to assess and measure social and cultural change.

One of the weaknesses of these classic anthropological studies was that they were more interested in the 'reinvention of tradition' in the city, the way rural Xhosa identities and social relations were reconstructed in town, than in the social impact of globalization on urban social life and gender relations (Bank 2005). The late 1940s and 1950s was a period of very rapid change in South African urban areas. It was a time of secondary industrialization, when manufacturing started to compete with primary production for the center of the economy and new goods and commodities flooded into South Africa from all over the world, especially America. Port cities, like Durban, Cape Town and East London, became centers through which these goods flowed into a hinterland, which included former colonies like Southern and Northern Rhodesia (now Zimbabwe and Zambia). New media and magazines, such as *Drum* and *Bona*, reshaped the way urban Africans viewed themselves and responded to urban social life and modernization. My paper begins in the 1950s with the impact of globalization and cultural change in East London and the emergence of new gender identities and family forms amongst the black urban working class.

In what follows, I contrast the 'new families' created in the post-war municipal housing estates and those of old urban locations. Building on the work of Pauw (1963), I reflect on the growth and consolidation of the matrifocal family after the Second World War. I try to explain why this family form became so socially and economically powerful, and also explore how it threatened urban patriarchal power, being vilified both by black mission-educated location elites and local officials, who blamed the 'fatherless family' for 'juvenile delinquency,' crime and political unrest. As a result of these criticisms and a shift to new forms of urban planning with the advent of apartheid, the extended, multi-generation matrifocal family was destroyed with the old locations. I argue that apartheid urban planning, as with other variants of modernist planning, was deeply patriarchal in its structure and orientation and offered no place for matrifocal families in the newly constructed urban townships. Large numbers of matrifocal families were thus broken up and relocated to the homelands. In the case of East London, many ended up in the commuter township of Mdantsane in the Ciskei.

The third section of this chapter focuses on the post-relocations adjustments in family structures in East London, both inside the city and in the more distant (but connected) commuter township of Mdantsane. In the 1960s and 1970s, new notions of masculinity and femininity were promoted in the city to accommodate men as breadwinners and women as homemakers, while in Mdantsane single women were forced to take up factory jobs in low-wage sweatshops to survive. I show how mothers and daughters stuck together through this difficult period, cobbling together a living from factory wages, domestic work, odd jobs and small-scale neighborhood *spaza* shops. In the 1980s, urban households in the city townships fragmented and 'decompressed' as youth men and women broke away from the parental homes to move into shacks areas. Younger women often stayed behind and built shacks in the backyards of their parents houses, which led to a re-aggregation of female headed household in the yards. In Mdantsane, two- and three-generational female-headed households generally held together, with daughters clinging onto their factory jobs and their mothers adding whatever they could through welfare grants, pensions and occasional earnings. From the mid-1990s, however, widespread de-industrialization due to global competition led to the loss of thousands of jobs in the feminized textile sector, leading more and more female-headed households into unemployment and poverty. In this chapter, I also explore the impact of these processes on individual and families.

In conclusion, I argue that, although the patriarchal controls that defined the apartheid years have been lifted and women can now again operate as independent agents whose rights are protected under the country's constitution, the impact of globalization and the associated large-scale jobs loses in feminized sectors of the local industrial economy, combined with the trend towards domestic fragmentation inside the city, has made it very difficult for women to rebuild socially and economically powerful matrifocal households. This is not to suggest that women have been unresponsive to new local economic opportunities in the post-apartheid period, nor that they been unable to construct new social networks, it is rather to note that they have never been able to re-acquire the kind of power, authority and upwardly mobile class position many matrifocal households enjoyed across South Africa in those boom years of the 1950s.

GLOBALIZATION AND DOMESTIC DESIRE IN THE 1950S

After the Second World War, a story about the emergence of new nations via processes of modernization or development provided a new grid for interpreting and explaining world inequalities. In this optic, a modern form of life encompassing a whole package of elements— including such things as industrial economy, scientific technology, liberal democratic politics, nuclear families, and secular world views— would become universalized across the globe as democracy spread and former colonial countries achieved independence. A basic element of the modernization trope was that of global *convergence,* a situation where societies would eventually move closer together. In the 1940s, urban black South Africans believed in this convergence and were filled with a new sense of optimism and self-confidence, which was inspired by the outcome of the war, the destruction of fascism in Europe, and the promise of global modernization and equality (Dubow 2005).

The post-war years ushered in an economic boom in South Africa as the economy made the shift from primary to secondary industrialization with the rapid growth of processing and manufacturing. The new economic regime that drove manufacturing has been described by some scholars as a system of 'racial' Fordism (Gelb 1991; Beall, Crankshaw and Parnell 2002). In the West, Fordism is classically associated with industrial development from the 1930s onwards and with trade unions, collective bargaining and generally high wages for the working class. In South Africa, the term *racial* Fordism is used to refer to the period from roughly the end of the Second World War to the world oil crisis of the mid-1970s, when factory-based manufacturing along Fordist lines began to compete seriously with mining for dominance of the South African industrial economy. The high water mark of this period was the boom years of the 1960s, when the South African industrial economy grew rapidly and diversified. Under racial Fordism, the division of labor followed clear racial lines: whites dominating skilled, semi-skilled and managerial positions in the economy, while blacks were generally limited to unskilled positions.

At a political level, African National Congress (ANC), as the main black political party in South Africa, asserted a universal rights-based discourse and extended demands for popular democracy. The new political agenda was expressed through the ANC Youth League and was invigorated by the 'Programme of Action' initiated by the ANC in the late 1940s that led to the Defiance Campaign of the early 1950s. On the shop floor, the 1946 Mine Workers strike proved to be a watershed in the struggle for greater equality and recognition for African workers. Africans across the country expressed solidarity with the miners and demanded that aspects of the old Color Bar be repealed. Dubow (2005) contemplates this new political confidence and concludes that it was fuelled by a *new cultural politics*, in which 'a youthful and volatile city-based population expressed its hopes and aspirations in new literary and musical forms, as well as through participation in independent churches and self-help groups.' He goes on to state that: 'The deferential attitudes of politically cautious mission-educated Africans, as well as the paternalism of well-meaning white liberals were [increasingly] dismissed with amused disdain' by the township youth and new working class' (Dubow 2005: 14).

Although Johannesburg and the Reef townships are presented as the epicenter of this new cultural politics or urban cultural renaissance, the Eastern Cape, home of the country's best mission schools, was also a critical site where local communities were being reshaped by broader changes in the political economy. The economy of East London was fundamentally transformed after the war with secondary industrialization. In 1946, there were only 135 manufacturing plants employing

3800 people in the city of East London. By 1958, this number has grown to 323 and the size of the workforce had increased to 12,913. In the mid-1950s, it was reported that the total industrial work force in the local region was 17,500 employees, of whom 85% were male and more than 75% of whom lived in the East London and King Williams Towns areas. The industrial base of the city was structured around the food, textile, motor vehicle, furniture and chemical producers. The promise of jobs brought thousands of new work seekers into the city, which saw the size of the cities' black locations swell to around 40,000 people in the mid-1930s to over 60,000 people in the 1950s. This growth is significant given that the national African urban population in the 1950s was only approximately 500,000 (Butler 2007: 3).

In the East London locations, there was well-established elite of mission-educated African families, the cream of the crop of the rural mission school, who had moved to the city to work in local hospitals, schools and service sector jobs. The East Bank location in the city had one of the most outstanding black high schools in the country, the Welsh High School, which competed favorably with Lovedale and Healdtown. The city also attracted many visitors from other towns, including large numbers of students from Fort Hare University in Alice, who came to the city at weekends to listen to jazz, watch sports and participate in the social clubs and events. The latter were also active in spreading the doctrine of popular democracy and were champions of the 'new cultural politics' of the time. On the other hand, and at the opposite end of the cultural spectrum, East London locations also housed a large number of conservative rural migrants who came from areas which had not be affected by missionary activity and many viewed themselves as Xhosa traditionalists. They would say that they had come to the city for one reason only, to earn wages to reinvest in the rural homesteads (*umzi*) in the countryside. These migrants were known as *amaqaba,* and mostly lived in rented backyard rooms in the locations. They tended to avoid urban influences and modern values, associating mainly with their own *amakhaya* (home mates) in the location. The adaptation patterns and urban lifestyles of this category of migrants are analyzed in detail in the work of Philip and Iona Mayer's (1963) book *Townsmen or Tribesmen.*

The views and attitudes of the Red migrants, while sociologically interesting, were marginal to the cultural dynamics of the locations, which were dominated by the youth and their infatuation with popular American culture and its South African derivatives. This new popular culture cohered around music, sports and politics. Indeed, far from being a rural backwater, East London developed a reputation for itself in the 1950s as a 'happening place' with a dynamic modern cultural scene. There were numerous public halls and sports complexes that served as venues for music and social events every weekend. In addition, the locations were awash with new commodities and aspirations. Burke (1996) has shown that the post-war period saw a flood of new cosmetics and domestic products enter the market throughout southern Africa. As a growing port, East London was an immediate beneficiary of these developments, and the high street was full of new department stores and fashion shops in the 1950s. Sybil Hans, a local East London resident, recalled that there was suddenly a whole range of new household products directly available to East Bank residents:

> In the 1950s the shops were crammed with new products which were not difficult to get if you had the money. I remember that most of the latest creams and detergents were displayed in the windows of local shops, like Masuali's store, on our corner. You did not even have to go to Oxford Street [the high street] to get the latest stuff.

The marketing of these products was associated with a new set of images for the modern African housewife that highlighted hygiene, cleanliness and domestic efficiency. The message was that housewives, who used the new products, would stand a better chance of keeping their men and caring for their families. For example, a popular Sunlight soap advertisement directed at African urban women said, 'I was losing Tom's love ... until I talked to a friend,' with the story of how a housewife's use of Sunlight stopped ruining her husband's clothes and how this made her husband exclaim that she was a 'wonderful wife' (Kallman 1998: 106). Surf and Omo offered women 'the cleanest whiteness wash in the world,' while various body creams and skin lighteners promised to keep them beautiful for longer. The dominant image of mature women in the media was that of active home-makers, directly responsible for cleanliness, beauty, and keeping a home. Younger women, by contrast, were usually presented as hard-working, not yet home-makers, who were seeking good husbands (Burke 1996; Kallman 1998).

In the 1950s these new images of modern African housewives circulated in East Bank through magazines such as *Drum,* which was selling a 100,000 copies an issue in 1954, and on daily radio programs including Sis Barbara's *Ezamakhosikhazi* ('For women'). Joyce Tjali recalled that listening to the radio had become very popular in the locations and Sis Barbara was a 'hot favorite among East Bank housewives.' Her programs, she said, 'gave women all sorts of new ideas and hints on cooking, washing, childcare and household hygiene.' She explained that, in terms of the media images of the day, womanhood for urban Africans was associated with home-making and child-care, but not in the ways that women had been used to those roles. They were now 'glamorized,' she said, 'with women using the latest lotions, detergents and time-saving domestic commodities.'

In the early 1950s, Clovers (2005) argues that men were portrayed in magazines like *Drum* as still having strong emotional and social ties with the home, and were presented in both adverts and stories as being intimately involved in domestic matters, household chores and even child rearing. Adverts for baby foods, such as *Incumbe* or *Nutrine,* had men holding babies, asking whether the formulae would make their children 'healthy and strong' (Clovers 2005: 97-98). Family and studio photographs in East London reproduced these images (see Plate 1 and 2). There was also a tendency during this period for the camera to catch informal, intimate moments between young couples. Images of young couples posing together in a modern domestic setting with props, like radios and appliances, were indicative of how deeply entrenched new notions of gender identity had become by the 1950s. Clovers (2005: 98) states that 'in the early *Drum*, it seemed that males became men through social recognition of their richly complex roles as sons, grandsons, fathers and husbands, brothers and uncles, a recognition rooted in a wide variety of domestic obligations inherent in these roles.' However, she goes on to note that, it was not just social recognition within any social group that mattered, it was the ability of young men and women to position themselves within the modern nuclear family that emerged as the dominant progressive image of the 1950s.

In post-war period then, young working class households in East London's locations aspired to set up modern nuclear households along the lines of those seen in magazines and on films, where men and women played their different but complementary roles surrounded by the trapping of modernity. The new urban housewife was a young mother who wanted to improve her homes and adopt new, more modern domestic routines and appliances. She wanted a clean and hygienic environment to support her role as a modern and efficient housewife. The problem was that the old locations, where the majority of urban black families lived in the city, was that they were overcrowded and congested. The streets were dirty and the available services were extremely basic. Sewerage flowed onto the streets and only a handful of houses in the older parts of the location had access to electricity or on-site water and flush sanitation.

As a result of these conditions, many of those who desired new forms of domestic modernity turned their attention to the new Duncan Village housing scheme, which produced several hundred new brick and mortar houses for new working class families in the 1940s. In the new house schemes, there were opportunities for young working class families to embrace a new style of urban living (if their wages allowed them to purchase the host of new goods, appliances, and furnishing on the market). Reader (1960) conducted a social survey in the municipal houses in August 1955. He found that most of those living there were young nuclear families. In fact, a third of the household heads were under 30 years of age and the remainder between 30-59 years. No-one was over 60 years and almost all of those who lived there stated that they were born in the city. Most of the households were male headed, and over 80% were nuclear families. The visual and oral evidence collected for the 1950s suggests that it was in these new houses that the domestic desires and aspirations of the new working class families could be expressed. However, one of the factors that inhibited the new working class from improving their homes and furnishing was the very high monthly rents of £1.20 charged for the houses by the municipality, which was almost half the average monthly wage.

Matrifocality, Property and Accumulation

The conditions in the neat new municipal housing estates contrasted starkly to those in the sprawling wood-and-iron sections of the old East Bank location, where the vast majority urban families lived.

When the anthropologist Pauw (1963) visited the East Bank location in the mid-1950s to investigate the social lives of the 'second generation,' those who had been born and brought up in the city, he found that there was a strong tendency towards the construction, not of nuclear families, but what he viewed as 'matrifocal families,' especially in the wood and iron sections of the location. Matrifocality, as we know, occurs when households cohere around a mother figure, who is the household head and key decision-maker in the family. In matrifocal families, the household development cycle does not hinge on the maturation of the married couple and eventual dispersal of their children into separate units. It is inextricably connected to the fate of mothers and other senior women, who do not necessarily allow or encourage their children, disperse as their mature. As a result these households tend to develop as multi-generational units with at least three generations of women living together (Smith 1988, 1996). Typically, Pauw (1963) found that there are mothers, daughters and granddaughters all living together in the same household, often without any male presence. In the mid 1950s, there were *twice* as many female-headed, multi-generational households as male-headed ones and a strong tendency for women to want to set up households without a male presence.

In this context, Pauw (1963: 52) declared that there was an 'unmistakable trend towards the matrifocal family among Xhosa households in the city of East London.' He found that increasing numbers of women in the city's locations setting up their own households 'without effective male participation' and argued that this trend was undermining the urban growth and expansion of the 'normal nuclear family.' For Pauw, the key to matrifocality was the growing economic opportunities available to women in the city. He argued that the improved access that women enjoyed to the labor market (which I would say was still very limited) and other income-earning activities, especially those related to the control of residential property meant that the Xhosa husband-father figure had become *dispensable*. He explained:

> For their income, households depend mainly on labor, trading and rentals; none of these are controlled exclusively by the husband-father. Mothers freely take up employment, venture into large- or small-scale trading and can own properties through inheritance or purchase. Even an unmarried mother can manage to rear her own

family without a husband-father and even without her
own mother (Pauw 1963: 162).

At a socio-cultural level, Pauw (1963: 145) suggested that the *disarticu-
lation* of domestic and public power in the city encouraged the growth
of the matrifocal family. He suggested that in rural Xhosa society, the
father figure constituted the critical link between the matricentral cell
of mother and child and the wider society. In this system, it was the
father who gave the mother and children their jura-politico status and
linked the household to productive land and other resources in the
village. The male household head thus defined the social, economic
and political status of the family in rural society. In the city, though, the
father role was essential neither in upholding the jura-political status
of the household, nor in determining access to economic resources. In
theory, this meant that women with access to their own houses and
properties could bypass male-dominated circuits of power and authority in the location and quietly get on with the business of making a
living and running their fatherless families.

It is this latter point that is critical for understanding the different forms of *matrifocality* that emerged in the East Bank in the 1950s.
There were clearly a growing number of female-headed households in
East Bank at this time, but not all of them were powerful matrifocal
families. In fact, many female-headed households in the location poor,
weak and vulnerable, especially those located in backyard rooms. The
real engine behind the economic success for matrifocal families was
the ownership or control of residential property, which offered women
a significant measure of independence from male authority as well as
a vital means to make money, not only from backyard rentals, but also
from other entrepreneurial activities. Nomathemba Sontji recalls that
matriarchs would do everything in their power to get hold of the 'site
permits' on which property ownership was based. She remembers that
senior women would even send their young daughters to the *Kwa-
Lloyd* (the municipal offices) dressed to the nines, hoping to attract the
attention of influential white officials. She explained:

> In those days the most cherished possession for a woman
> was a site permit for your own house. Rents were high and
> it was an easy way to earn income. You could run a small
> business selling liquor, which we used to hide under the

floorboards, or other soft goods, like food, *vetkoek* (dough buns) and cooldrink for the kids. I remember that women would do virtually anything to get this site permit. If you had money you could try to buy one for somebody who could not pay their rent, but women also knew that some officials at the Kwa-Lloyd offices liked our nice thighs. Women would go there in their most alluring dresses and skirts to satisfy these officials in the hope of getting a site permit.[1]

The offering of sexual services for municipal privileges apparently extended to others areas, such as exemption from pass arrest or permission to stay in the location without a lodgers permit. But matriarchs also used their own houses to offer sexual services to migrants and other men in the location. Luise White (1990) in her work on sex work in Nairobi has suggested that transactional sex work took many forms, which included *watembezi,* or street walking, *malaya,* where women waited in their rooms for men to come to them, or *wazi wazi* where women call for clients off the street from the house. In her work, White shows how the control of *property* benefitted those engaged in using sex work for profit. This same was true in East London, where most men in the city were migrants. They were generally not looking for permanent urban unions and the associated financial and social responsibilities. Instead they sought lovers—*khwapheni* ('a thing that is hidden away'). This created a demand for sexual services and companionship that encouraged sex work that took similar forms to those documented by White. In the case of East Bank, houses that sold liquor were often also places were sexual services were also offered. If matriarch could control younger women they could also control the profits from this trade.

Property owning matriarchs were also known to extend dwellings to suit their business interests, building on as many extra rooms as possible and often restructuring the internal lay-out of their houses to maximize business opportunities. Shebeen owners were known to store liquor under their floorboards in order to keep it out of view from prying officials and to save space. The residential conversions that these women made to their dwellings were not always popular with their neighbors. In the wood-and-iron sections of the location, all sorts of families lived cheek by jowl, and it was quite common for the rambling tenements of a self-employed matriarchs and their family to be situated next door to a families with a different social and cultural backgrounds. In fact, there was considerable tension throughout this period between location matriarch and established male working and middle class male-headed households, who objected to the constant noise and activity on their streets. Devout Christian families did not approve of what they viewed as the 'moral degradation' of their neighborhoods and made their objections known to the Location Advisory Committee, which was made up of local elites and senior white officials.

In East London, the rise of the matrifocal family from the 1930s onwards generated a great deal of public concern and debate. In the minds of white politicians and planners, the single mothers and matriarchs of old "tin town," the *amakazana* (unmarried mothers) as they were called, were anathema to order, discipline and progress in the city. In fact, they seemed to provoke fear and anxiety in minds of city officials who saw these women and their bodies as tempting, but also threatening to male order, male self-discipline and to their ability to discipline the city. The ability of single town women in town to use their sexuality for personal gain and to spawn "fatherless families," horrified many senior bureaucrats and fuelled demands in the city for these menacing sexualities to be brought under control. There was also a long history of blaming the matrifocal family and single mothers, in particular, for the social and political instability of the township. The argument made by the Thornton Commission in 1937 and repeated strong by the Welsh Enquiry of 1949 was that 'juvenile delinquency' and *tsotsism* was a direct result of the growth of the 'fatherless family' and the fact that young men were growing up without the disciplinary presence of a father figure. Officials went on to suggest that many single mothers (many of whom made a living through 'illegal activities' such as beer brewing and petty trade) actually encouraged and protected their sons in their criminal lifestyles. Christianized African elites, who felt threatened by the social styles and material wealth of many matriarchs, echoed the concerns of city officials, calling for action to be taken to bring this 'unruly' segment of the township population under control.

But despite these objections and complaints, East Bank matriarchs proved to be extremely successful business operators and accumulating resources and property, either as substitute owners or as site holders. There was an active market in site permits and they were exchanged between individuals with the permission of the municipality. Reader

(1960) reports that there was a lot of movement of residential market in the mid-1950s, with most of the site permits being acquired by location matriarchs. One factor which forced site permit holders to relinquish their permits was indebtedness and successful matriarchs took advantage of this situation by offering to pay off household and business debts in exchange for the transfer of the site permit. Whatever mechanisms were used, the reality was that *independent women owned approximately half of all the site permits in the location in the mid-1950s*.

The power and presence of women in the property market is reflected in Minkley's bold assertion that:

> Independent and single/unmarried women 'owned' the East Bank Location and the men in it. These women were able, over the period, to shape the location in material, social and cultural ways with a great deal more effect and endurance than men from the location elite, factories and rail-yards, male migrants from the rural areas, or the masters of the local state. The community of the location cohered around these 'matrifocal family structures,' although it was seldom consciously or publicly asserted (Minkley 1996: 156).

The trend towards a certain form of matrifocality was therefore less an issue of kinship preference than one of *incipient class formation*. Women with property were able to pull in female kin and clients to assist them with their urban enterprises and in the process strengthened their own economic and social standing. One of the keys to economic success, as Pauw (1963) shows, was the ability of senior women to hold their families together as close-knit social units where power and authority was ordered along generational lines. In multi-generational matrifocal households, power cohered in the 'mother figure' and other senior women who expected respect and obedience from junior women. The strongly centripetal tendencies in these units appear to have allowed them to operate like closed business corporations which lay beyond the reach of male-dominated authority structures in the location.

If the cultural scripts that informed the construction of new young male headed, working class families were being read off the pages of magazines like *Drum*, this certainly could not be case for matrifocal families. The matriarchs who ran these units deployed a *house model* of accumulation very similar to that used by rural patriarchs in the communal areas. It was one that was built on thrift, saving and constant and strategic reinvestment in property. Middle-aged East Bank matriarchs had little time for the consumerist impulses that had gripped the youth or for the labor-saving appliances so desired by young housewives. They regarded these items as unnecessary frills. They showed no appetite for the worldly cosmopolitanism, except as a business opportunity. They were urban *localists*, to use Ferguson's term (1999), who worked their turfs for small and sometimes large profits. Their main quest was for urban permanence and security, not worldliness, fashion or education. These women also had no interest in returning to the countryside. In fact, many had arrived in the city as runaway girls, fleeing rural patriarchy and domestic violence (Mager 1999). They understood clearly that their future lay in the city, and they would do whatever was needed to secure it.

Ironically, then the survival and accumulation strategies of urban matriarchs to build on a feminized version of the rural, male migrant model of 'building the *umzi*' (homestead) (McAllister 2001, 2005). For urban matriarchs, urban property and small businesses replaced cattle and fields as their desired source of wealth. The social logic of the matrifocal family house economy was based built on generational power and respect, on the desire and need of senior women to manage and control female labor and to ensure that it remained loyal to the house (Gudman 1990). Powerful matriarchs were women who controlled the labor of young and even other older women, and were able to deploy their labor for their own interest, whether offering sexual favors to migrants, or selling beer, or acting as 'substitute owners' and rent collectors in their second and third properties.

In the section below, I discuss the demise of the property-owning, matrifocal family in the period of apartheid planning in the city. In this section I want to assert that historians and sociologists had generally placed too much emphasis on the racial underpinnings of apartheid urban planning and said too little about the patriarchal project that was so central to urban apartheid.

PATRIARCHY AND URBAN RESTRUCTURING

Overcrowding, worsening living conditions and political frustrations exploded into unrest in East London in 1952, when police opened fire on a crowd of several thousand people gathered at the central square in the East Bank location to campaign against unjust laws. Officially it was reported that the police had only killed 9 people on that day, but unofficial counts place the actual death toll at over 200, making the East Bank massacre one of the worst in the history of apartheid. In a context of rising political dissatisfaction, the city fathers announced their desire to removal all wood-and-iron dwelling from old location, leaving only the newly erected brick and mortar municipal houses. The city's first plan was to deliver 1500 new serviced sites next to East Bank to replace poor quality housing stock in the old location. Unfortunately, this scheme never materialized as the proposed development site was declared a 'white group area' under the Group Areas Act of 1951. In November 1955, the regional Divisional Council wrote to the East London City Council stating that 'there appears to be no real need for this Council to establish a [new] native location at this stage, or in the foreseeable future' (Reader 1960: 32). Desmond Reader summed up the situation as follows: 'the reply to the riotous demonstrations of 1952 was a statement of restriction, both in urban development and in wood-and-iron capital investment. The authorities, it seemed, had screwed the safety value hard down' (Reader 1960: 31).

But, after 1955, when Dr Hendrick Verwoerd personally visited the city, the official position on the fate of East Bank residents shifted decisively away from urban accommodation to forced removal. Verwoerd marveled at the possibility of creating a new township in the Ciskei homeland, but still within reach of East London. It was an ingenious apartheid scheme, which aimed to strip a large section of the East London African working class of their South African nationality, while retaining access to their labor. In the end, the state decided on a two-pronged strategy: on the one hand, it would continue to build new municipal bungalows for stable, male-headed working class households in Duncan Village, while at the same time relocating the majority of the city's black 'surplus population' into a new Ciskei township of Mdantsane. In terms of the new settlement policy, it was no longer possible (as it had been prior to the 1950s) for women to get access to municipal housing in Duncan Village as widows or single women. This was expressly prohibited, and it was clearly stated that divorcees, widows and other single women would no longer be permitted to stay on in the city. All households in Duncan Village would have to be male-headed.

For the matriarchs and landlords in the East Bank, the township restructuring programmed was a complete disaster. By the late-1950s it was clear that the state would proceed to demolish the old wood-and-iron sections in all the locations in East London (not only East Bank) and would offer *no compensation* for those who lost property or houses in the process. Matriarchs that owned property and ran businesses were particularly disadvantaged because they were excluded from acquiring new accommodation in the city, even though they had been born there. Those born in the city were generally sent to Mdantsane, while those without urban birth certificates were often simply relocated to their home homes in the Ciskei and Transkei homelands. In the accounts we have of apartheid dispossession, it is my view that the particular forms of discrimination and expropriation from women have not fully been recognized. In order to appreciate this point more fully it is useful to try to locate, the kind of restructuring attempted in East London within a border perspective.

Bozzoli (2004) has classified apartheid restructuring as a form of *racial* modernism. The emphasis in Bozzoli's work, as it has been in many other studies of urban apartheid planning is on the racial dimensions of the policies and programs rather than on their gender politics. To step back for a moment, we might recall that Rabinow (1989) suggested that a key departure point for modernism as a form of urban planning is that it no longer focuses on 'regulating and ameliorating a locale and its inhabitants, but rather on treating both as 'a matter to be *formed and normed at will*' (Rabinow 1989: 345). Modernism is not concerned with 'the isolation and rectification of islands of pathology' but with providing 'a blueprint for the scientific administration of modern life' (Rabinow 1989: 344). The intention is to create abstract sites where "all reference to older modes of life, to history, to the sedimented place of memory, and to sociability had been eliminated" and where the "the central point of the city had been reserved for public administration" (Rabinow 1989: 358). A key feature of all urban modernist planning regimes, Rabinow (1995: 60) continues, is the desire to 'create New Men freed, purified and liberated to pursue new forms of sociality which would inevitably arise from correctly designed spaces and forms.' But, one might ask, do such regimes say about women?

One of the explicit aims of the urban restructuring programmed in East London was to break down the social power and influence of matrifocal families, particularly multi-generational ones led by strong and independent women. The first part of this process, as we have seen, was to flatly deny female-headed households access to accommodation in the city. The second was to restructure these households through the process of relocation. The layout and plan for Mdantsane mirrored that of many of the new apartheid townships of the 1950s and 1960s. It was based on the construction of thousands of four-roomed bunga-lows to accommodate the tens of thousands of surplus African living in East London's old locations and other 'surplus Africans' from small towns and urban areas. But, unlike places like Soweto, the aim of those who planned Mdantsane was to create a semi-rural township, using the idea of the "garden city"—a concept developed by the turn-of-the-century British modernist planner Ebenezer Howard. As Howard (1906) argued: "There are not in reality only two alternatives—town and country life—but a third alternative in which all the advantages of the most energetic and active town life, with all the beauty and delight of the country may be secured in perfect combination" (Taylor 1998: 124). It was this image that state planners embraced when considering urban development in the new rural Ciskei homeland. They wanted to create semi-autonomous, inter-linked commuter township that were politically and socially detached from the city, but economically inte-grated into white urban areas.

In the same way as Ebenezer Howard felt that his idea of the 'garden city' would address some of the social pathologies of the over-crowded Victorian slums, apartheid planners saw the creation of townships like Mdantsane as a means of influencing and reforming African social life in more 'progressive directions.' Mager (1999: 46–71) suggest that urban planning in the Ciskei:

> ... opened up the discursive space for remodeling "the African family." NAD [Native Administration and Development] displayed enormous faith in the ability of tight administra-tion; decent homes and industrial work to fashion western-ized families. Their zeal reflected not so much the function-ality of the nuclear family to capital but the convergence of an idealized view of white, middle-class notions of morality, family and work in segregation-developmentist thinking. It was tied to a belief that social engineering could repair the ravages of social change (Mager 1999: 49).

These concerns were reflected in the planning of Mdantsane. The aim was to try to create as many new nuclear families as possible and to cleanse individuals and families of social pathologies and moral degeneracy of slum life. However, in the case of Mdantsane, it was also realized that, due to the nature of the East Bank population, the homeland township would have to absorb large numbers of female-headed households. Widows and single women were not welcome in Duncan Village, but the state was prepared to absorb them in Mdantsane as long as they were fragmented into smaller units. As a result many matrifocal families were broken up in the process of relocation. The initial dislocation came when East Bank residents destined for Mdantsane were housed temporarily in one-roomed structures in a temporary housing development outside Duncan Village (see Plate 4). When Pauw (1973) visited Mdantsane in 1972, 15 years after his original fieldwork in East Bank, he found that one third of the new households he interviewed were female-headed, but that most of them were two-generational units rather than the extended, multi-generational families in had found in East Bank. Pauw also confirmed that officials in Mdantsane (unlike those in Duncan Village) were prepared to classify unmarried mothers as "fit and proper" family heads that were legal entitled to homeland government housing. He concluded that his follow-up visit showed that, although female-headed households in Mdantsane were much smaller than in East Bank, the trend towards matrifocality had continued in Mdantsane, with unmarried women still constituting their own families without an effective male presence.

Mamdani (1996) in his masterful analysis of the dualism between subject and citizen in Africa and South Africa suggested that racial discrimination was the main barrier to blacks achieving civil and political rights and liberties in the city. In the countryside, he stressed the role of customary power and patriarchal proprietorship predominated, while in the city race was the primary barrier to back advancement. What Mamdani and many others who write about South African cities have missed is the extent to which the version of apartheid modernization was based on patriarchal proprietorship in *both* town and country. In the urban setting, African men were actively empowered through apartheid planning, not only in the village as headmen and chiefs, but in the township too as household heads. The urban administration had decided that it would only negotiate with male household heads in the city. Rather than dividing the customary and the civil, it might be argued that apartheid tried to *synchronize* patriarchal domination across towns and country, and to actively disempower and dispossess women in both spaces. In fact, feminist scholars like Wilson (1991), Hooper (1995) and Sandercock (1998) argue that modernist planning everywhere was underpinned by a patriarchal master-narrative. Hooper reads modernist urban plans as 'poems of male desire,' fantasies of control. I would like to suggest here that the racial modernist planning of the apartheid state should be viewed in the similar light, as an assault on the rights and power of women in the city.

The second and related cataract in our blurred vision of the apartheid city has been our failure to acknowledge the extent to which post-war planning de-commodified the township by shutting down the market in black urban areas. The closure of formal, licensed black business owned businesses in the old locations was only the tip of the proverbial iceberg. Many local enterprises and livelihoods were made from informal home-based businesses. The latter were usually owned and run by women, often single mothers, who supported themselves and their families off these enterprises. It is only when we consider the role of these enterprises to urban livelihoods and accumulation strategies that we begin to realize the full implications of apartheid planning for urban women. In some ways apartheid urban planning bore some resemblance to socialist restructuring in Eastern Europe, which aimed to eradicate bourgeois and petty bourgeois tendencies and shut down the free market. Verdery and Humpheries (1999) have shown, that, although 'hidden markets' continued to operate behind the 'iron curtain,' spatial and social restructuring made any form of private entrepreneurship very difficult in new socialist countries. The same occurred in the townships of East London, after the old locations were demolished. The hard earned wages of black workers that had circulated many times over in the convoluted circuits of informal economy now disappeared straight out of the townships either into the coffers of the local authority or onto the high street, where it was used to benefit white businesses.

MALE BREADWINNERS AND DESPERATE HOUSEWIVES

If racial modernist planning in South African cities was about creating 'New Men,' then what kind men (and women) did it seek to create? Lindsay Clovers (2005) argues that if one analyzes media images of black masculinity in the 1960s it is possible to note a distinct shift in the late 1950s away from the notions of the family man and father as an intimate and socialized being towards an image of man as breadwinner, as provider and as socially disconnected. In media images and stories in magazines, such as *Drum*, men are no longer presented as caring and socializing with their wives and children, but appear now as upright, responsible and alone. She sees men as more directly connected to public space at this time and women and children pushed into the background, if not removed entirely from the representation of masculinity. Clovers suggests that this more individualistic and modern notion of masculinity had much to do with the entrenchment of the migrant labor system and the separation of husbands and wives, and with changes in the advertising industry in the 1960s.

My own reading of this representation shift would be that it is consistent with urban policy and restructuring measures which insisted that men should stand up as the providers for their families, as real breadwinners, and not lean on their wives for financial support (as was often the case in the old locations). This image was consistent with representation of in the Western media of new gender roles in suburbia. This is not inconsistent with what the apartheid state wanted to achieve through its program of township restructuring. It aimed to airbrush women out of the picture, except as housewives, and promote men as responsible, hard-working industrial workers and breadwinners.

From the point of view of the new working class in Duncan Village, these images were all good and well, as long as industry was prepared to pay its male labor force sufficient for them to realize their roles as breadwinners and providers. This was not the case. Black wages were kept low during the 1960s. To compound matters, wages in East London consistently fell below the national average. This had profound implications for new working class families that wanted to realize their dreams of suburban style living in the new Duncan Village Extension. My interviews with those who had acquired modern new houses in Duncan Village Extension (especially younger couples who had been living in rented rooms in the old location) revealed that they had an enormous sense of expectation. Many young men and women actually said that they looked forward to the prospect of moving into modern, better quality brick and mortar housing. They said that they liked the idea of living in better-serviced houses with new rooms to furnish and decorate. They had, in any event, been nourished on images of the modern housewife in the media for more than a decade. Many women were simply bursting to get into their new houses and express themselves by creating modern interiors to match the glamorous images they encountered in magazines like *Drum* and *Bona*, and put into practice the advice that of the likes of Sis Barbara on the radio (see Plates 5&6).

For many the disappointment was palpable. The houses they received were often not as well made as they expected. There were leaks and cracks, and sometime doors and windows were not properly fitted because of the speed at which the state was trying to deliver new houses. But there greater disappointment came when they found it difficult to fill these spaces with the types of appliances and furnishings they desired. One woman explained: 'The thing I found most difficult about the new houses was that feeling of emptiness, not only on the streets, but in my house. Those brick walls and hollow rooms echoed, and I had nothing to fill them with. It made me long for our old crowded house in East Bank.' Audrey Jokazi emphasized the same point:

> Many of us could not wait to get into our new houses. We had really felt the overcrowding in the East Bank and couldn't wait to get some more space to ourselves. If you ask people now what they thought then, many will say that they never wanted to leave East Bank. This is not entirely true because many of us did not like the idea of having our community broken up, but at the same time we could see that the new houses were going to be better—new, clean and spacious.
>
> It was such a strange feeling when we eventually moved into these houses. They were empty and cold inside with cement floors. We were so far away from each other and everything was neatly arranged. It felt very strange to me not to have the hustle and bustle of a busy house ... I started to feel very isolated and alone in my new house, although I wanted a four-room house. My husband was away at work all day and the streets were quiet. There were hardly any visitors and the hours dragged. I used to listen to the radio—there was no TV in those days—while I washed clothes, cleaned the house and ironed, but this was not

> the same as talking to friends or watching people go by on the street. To my surprise, I started to get very lonely and started to wish that we had not been moved at all. More and more, I felt that I wanted to get a job myself just to get out of the house, but my husband did not like that idea.

These feelings were compounded by the vulnerability of women felt after the state had pulled the carpet of informal earning from under their feet. They were now entirely dependent on the husbands for 'house money.' Without access to their own income earning strategies, urban housewives turned their attention to the tactics of the house, to 'small maneuvers' and 'acts of wit' within that dominated space. They championed an ideology of fatherhood and masculinity acknowledged the role of men as breadwinners, but asserted that women were responsible for household management and required a decent size allowance from the husbands to get on with their jobs.

In Duncan Village Extension in 1960s and 1970s, women insisted that, if they were to be the homemakers and housewives of the new township, they needed a weekly 'allowance' to perform their tasks effectively. They endorsed the discourses presented in the media of black men as breadwinner and providers, and colluded in their own subordination in order to extract income from their spouses. By dividing household expenditure into recurrent bills, such as rent, and then insisting that most of the rest be given over to them to 'manage the house,' urban women tried to show their husbands that they had retreated from the consumerist tendencies that had so threatened them in the 1950s. They suggested that they were now approaching the tasks of housekeeping with the same frugal determination of the urban poor of the old location. They emphasized the importance of thrift and embraced the new bargain chain stores, like OK Bazaars, Pep Stores and Russells in Oxford Street, rather than the specialist, cash only shops that had captured their imagination in the 1950s. By showing restraint, women set out to demonstrate that they could manage money efficiently and were not the spendthrifts they had been labeled in the 1950s.

Many women in Duncan Village (Extension) resented the level of their dependence on male earnings in the post-1960 period and remembered the 1950s with nostalgia as a period when women controlled their own incomes and destinies. As Tombi Dlwani recalled:

> There was something very disconcerting about always
> waiting for money from our husbands, who were reluctant
> to tell us exactly what they earned. They would try to be
> secretive and vague about money and just give us what
> they thought we needed for the house. But we found out
> what they were paid at the different factories so that we
> knew exactly what they earned. We would use this infor-
> mation to get more for ourselves.

Tombi went on to explain that there was always the danger of demand-
ing too much, which (she said) could lead to men losing interest in the
wives and starting up relationships with other women on whom they
would lavish gifts.

Domestic struggles over the control of income along the lines suggested above thus emerged as a central feature of post-relocation domestic life in Duncan Village. It was a struggle that occurred in the context of
very unequal power relations within domestic groups. Unlike the 1950s,
when women exercised considerable social and economic power in the
old location, men now ruled the roost, they were the official tenants of
all municipal houses and they monopolized the formal-sector jobs in the
city. Female employment opportunities inside East London were still very
limited during this period, although as we will see below there were some
important changes in this regard occurring on the outskirts of the city.
In this we have seen how, when the state drew down an 'iron curtain' on
female entrepreneurship in the townships, it had significant implications
for the urban working class aspirations. Most working class households
(whether female-headed or not) had supplemented household income
in the old location through petty trade and commodity production. The
removal of the latter income sources slashed the disposal income of many
households and, all of the sudden, desirable consumer goods, the 'wanna
gets' became 'can't gets' for everyone trapped in low-wage formal sector
employment in East London.

DOMESTIC FRAGMENTATION
AND BACKYARD MATRIARCHS

By the 1980s, Duncan Village had been turned upside down political structures and intense generational conflict. Apartheid appointed
officials and councilors were no longer welcome in the township and,

within a few short years in the early 1980s, the state had lost complete control of the township. The new democratic structures were dominated by young men, comrades or the *amaqabane*, who felt a real sense of power, purpose and entitlement. The story of the rise of the comrades and their political impact on the South African township scene is well-documented (Seekings 1993; Mayikiso 1996), but what is less understood is the impact of these broad political changes and shifts in generational power on family structure and gender identities.

The first point to note about the 1980s in Duncan Village was that the domestic politics surrounding household income in Duncan Village began to change. Increasing numbers of men in the township found they were unemployed as retrenchments followed a wave of strikes and industrial action in East London in the early 1980s. Automotive workers at the Mercedes Benz plant and workers at the Wilson and Rowntrees (later Nestle) sweet factory were both engaged in protracted industrial disputes throughout the 1980s. Urban housewives could no longer rely take their husbands' wages and started to take greater responsibility for earning household income themselves. By the mid-1980s women were more active in the formal sector job market (than they had been in the 1970s) and now also sought to extract backyard rent from new arrivals in the township, who came flooding into the township again after 1980. Unlike the 1950s, however, the street committees controlled the rents, keeping them down to make urban residence affordable for new arrivals. This angered some older residents who felt they had every right to set their own rents. But they did not have the power to change the situation. Indeed, as the backyards filled up with shacks and new makeshift dwellings were erected on every piece of vacant land in the township, there was suddenly enormous pressure on the available urban services, which were designed to cope with a settled population of around 30,000. By the mid-1980s there were well over 70,000 people in Duncan Village.

Women's domestic routines and consumption patterns were also affected by the introduction of a consumer boycott of white-owned stores in the 1980s, which prevented them from buying goods in town. The entire township now relied on a few local general dealers, who stocked only basic goods and were often unable to get supplies. Gangs of male youth roamed the streets in packs and could enter township houses at will to demand food or shelter. As the comrades asserted their power and the rule of the street became the rule of the house, mothers found they could no longer control their sons and their daughters. They also witnessed their desires of suburban domesticity whittled away with new arrivals, increasing poverty and residential overcrowding. Woman's talk of plushly furnished and well-maintained urban homes with labor-saving appliances vanished as the smell of paraffin and uncollected garbage once again engulfed the township. Crowds now swelled at communal toilets and water points, and the shelves of overused township shops emptied almost as quickly as they were filled. The dream of black suburbia, once cherished by so many township mothers, had evaporated into thin air as the political mood swung way from middle-aged desires for consumerism to the youthful call for sacrifice, socialism and liberation.

The new pressures on urban mothers created tensions within the house. Disputes between men and women over allocation of funds to domestic expenses, and the desire amongst women to expand their own earnings either through engagement in wage labor or by selling commodities in the township created conflict. As economic conditions worsened, women increasingly took matters into their own hands, trying by all means to supplement household income. Men often objected, saying that their lovers and wives should concentrate on their responsibilities as mothers and stay at home (as they promised to do in the past). The establishment of home-based businesses, such as *spaza* shops, was considered by many to be a fair compromise since it kept women focused on their primary activities of home-making and relieved men of some of the responsibility for supporting the family.

One of the critical differences between the 1980s and 1990s and the earlier period of township planning was that men and women could now resolve domestic disputes *spatially* by moving away from each other. This was not the preferred option for older women because it meant relinquishing rights to a house, but a dominant tendency was for young men to move away from the parent's home into the shack areas to create 'living together' or *ukuhlalisana* relationships. This was not recognized as marriage, but a form of living together which involved young men and women co-habiting without bride-wealth or compensation between transacted between the young man's and the woman's family. No permission was sort from the parents to set up these relationships and access to land/sites on which to erect new shacks was negotiated through the youth dominated civic structures. In the 1980s there was an explosion of *ukuhlalisana* relationships in Duncan Village as the youth asserted their independence and larger families, which had started as young nuclear families in the 1960s, but grown into three-generational units, suddenly 'decompressed.' This tendency towards 'domestic fragmentation,' or what some sociologists have called 'household decompression,' has been widely noted in the urban literature on the post-apartheid city (Hindson and McCarthy 1994; Morris 1992).

Anthropological studies in the 1990s picked up on the theme of domestic fluidity within urban households, especially in informal settlements. These studies argued that household-level social relations appeared to have become increasingly individualized, blasé and amoral and that households themselves started to collapse as cohesive units of social interaction (Ross 1993, 1996; Spiegel 1996). In Duncan Village, mature urban mothers often openly lamented the changes that were occurring with the sudden explosion of *ukuhlalisana* relationships, but they were also not about to let their families fall apart. In fact, they engaged in all kinds of strategies to keep their families together. This often meant continuing to interfere in their domestic and family lives of their children even after they had left home. Without control of their children women could become very vulnerable. In fact, in instances where the male household had died, there was a tendency for senior women to attempt to rebuild matrifocal families by turning to their daughters and other female kin. The problem was that senior women had little power and wealth and thus had little to off those who followed them. They also found it difficult to establish successful businesses of the kind that their sisters had created in the 1950s. One of the key economic differences between the 1990s and the 1950s was the absence of a large earning migrant population in the township, to whom could be sold sex, liquor and lodging and left wondering where all their wages had gone. The new immigrants into Duncan Village were generally unemployed and came with their partners and brought material to build their own houses. They brought food, liquor and paraffin, which did create options for women to re-enter the informal trading, but the opportunities for serious money making were much more restricted than in the 1950s, when female property owners held all the cards.

The tendency towards household fragmentation in Duncan Village in the 1980s and 1990s was exaggerated by very high incidents of shack fires which broke out in the township, especially during the winter months. By razing free-standing and backyard shack areas to the ground, fire stimulated processes of fission and fragmentation in household units. Young adults, in particular, used the opportunities provided by fire to break away from their parental homes. Under normal circumstances, they would have found it difficult to set up their own places, especially given the cost of building material. However, in the wake of fire, when building materials provided by donors agencies, churches, and local businesses youth took hold of these resources to realize their desire to create their own residential spaces. Some parents encouraged their sons to move away: 'It is not good for my son to live here anymore. He is old enough to work now and support himself. There is also the problem of privacy and it is better that he takes his girlfriends to his own place.' In observing this process of settlement and resettlement, I did notice how the interests of young men usually got precedence over those of young women. The street committees like the municipal officials that preceded them were champions of patriarchy and they generally attended to the interests of men before seeing what could be done for female-headed households. Civic structures in the townships did acknowledge the rights of women. However, they just did not always act in a way that supported a commitment to gender equality. For one thing, all the street committees were run by men. Many young men I interviewed believed that the main role of women in the struggle was to make babies for the revolution.

In 2005, research in Duncan Village revealed that the movement of young men out of the municipal houses and into the free-standing shack areas had left a vacuum in the yards of the municipal houses which women took advantage of. Single women preferred to rent a shack in the backyard of a municipal dwelling than stay in the free-standing shack because the yard environment offered more protection to them and their children. The desire for young men to move away from their parental home also left opportunities in the yards for other to take. In 2005 it was generally single women or migrant who took up lodging in the yards. 60% of tenants households in our 2005 survey were female-headed, about half of these were units that were made up of the daughters (and children) of landlords and ladies. Generally speaking, we found that while men moved away daughters tended to stay behind, especially if their mother was a widow and the main household was female headed. Amongst the municipal tenants, who were now owners of their government houses, almost half were landladies rather than land-lords. 30% were widows who had taken over the house on their husband's death. The other 15% had acquired control of the property in others ways. The reality in 2005 was that quite a large property of both the new 'owners' were landladies and a majority of tenants were female-headed households. This created an environment, as I have recently argued (cf. Bank 2008), where social reproduction was highly feminized. Bonds of sisterhood emerged in the yards as women shared domestic tasks and shared food and child-care arrangements. The evidence revealed that women were rebuilding social networks in the heart of the city's townships, but not in the way they did in the 1950s.

My ethnographic research in 2005 showed little of the entrepreneurial spirit of the previous, nor of the operation of a feminized 'house economy,' where younger women worked for and supported senior matriarchs. The power relations in the yards were very different, with many older women feeling poor, vulnerable and fragile, open to abuse and exploitation from both young men and even their own daughters who sometime pilfered their pension money and often undermined their authority. The close bonds of loyalty and respect between women of different generation seem to have been missing from many of the yards, and this is one of the reasons why the strongly corporate and tight-knit matrifocal family of an earlier era was unable to re-emerged in Duncan Village in the 1990s and 2000s, after apartheid restructuring had been dissolved and women (at least in principle) could once again compete on an equal footing for resources and opportunities (Bank 2006, 2008).

FACTORY GIRLS AND DE-INDUSTRIALIZATION IN MDANTSANE

In Mdantsane, relocation in the 1960s brought enormous hardship as nearly 8,000 households were relocated from East London's old locations into the new homeland township. In the early 1970s, Philip Mayer wrote about the social and economic impact of relocation to Mdantsane. He spoke of the high levels of unemployment that prevailed in the satellite township and the absence of adequate public transport to ferry commuter workers to and from East London. He acknowledged that the township offered 'spaciousness and greater privacy' than the East Bank and that the houses were 'decent and solid,' even allowing families to start small gardens in their backyards. But, on the other hand, his interviewees complained that, "here we are without employment"; "we are starving here" (Mayer 1971: 302). Behind the new façade of suburban respectability, he noted, there lay real hardship and poverty, which many complained was far greater than that they had encountered in the old East Bank location. One of the consequences of this situation was that the level of crime and violence was high. Gangs of unemployed youths roamed the streets: "the *tsotsi* element after nightfall is generally more frightening than it ever was in Duncan Village" and "even vigorous men rarely dare to venture out at night" (Mayer 1971: 298). The levels of poverty in Mdantsane in the early 1970s were compounded by the absence of significant local job opportunities and the need for residents to commute to east London to find employment. In 1975, two thirds of the cities industrial and commercial workforce was still drawn from Mdantsane (Matravers 1980: 32).

This dependence on the East London job market diminished from the mid-1970s when large numbers of factories started to move to the Ciskei to take advantage of generous state subsidies for industrial relocation. According to Black et al. (1986) explains:

> During the 1980s the manufacturing sector of Ciskei grew at a quite remarkable rate. While an average of 1200 manufacturing jobs was created each year between 1976 and 1981, the corresponding figure for the period 1982 to March 1986 came to 4516. By May 1986 the Ciskei Peoples Development Bank had assisted with the establishment of 124 manufacturing industries in the Ciskei, representing a total investment of R268, 1 m. This expansion is, of course, in addition to the growth that has taken place in the border towns of East London and King William Town where many Ciskeians live.

Between 1976 and 1986, then more than 25,000 industrial jobs were reported to have been created in the Ciskei alone as a result of the industrial decentralization programmed. Several thousand of these jobs were located in industrial parks on the outskirts of Mdantsane. They were mainly in the textile, furniture and foot-ware sectors and offered opportunities for young women to work for low wages in sweat shops. Because labor unions were banned in the homelands and because many of the firms were marginal concerns anyway, representing the last frontier of racial Fordism, women in these factories earned very little. But it was still something that helped to make ends meet at home, especially when combined with the wages and earnings of others. For almost 20 years from the mid-1970s to the mid-1990s, the industrial decentralization scheme threw out a lifeline to female-headed households in Mdantsane. It offered low wage employment to women, especially young women with little education, who could help their mothers survive. However, the kind of employment that was created in the Ciskei could not be sustained after democracy and the removal of government subsidies to homeland industrialists. Faced with the pressures of globalization and competition, the burgeoning homeland industrialization programmed simply collapsed like a pack of cards.

In the case studies below I explore the impact of this process on female headed households from Mdantsane. In all the other cases the key informants are members of matrifocal families from the old East London locations, who were forcibly removed from the city in the 1960s and have attempted to adapt to conditions in Mdantsane since then. All the cases show the critical role that factory employment played in women in the survival struggles. It is only Nomdakazana (in the last case) who is never able to re-enter wage employment after losing her job as the Jones pineapple factory in East London in the 1960s. She survives off her meat business that moves from the old locations to Mdantsane with some success. In all the cases, we come to appreciate the profound impact of de-industrialization in the late 1990s and 2000s:

CASE 1: 'WAVERLY BLANKETS WAS OUR LIFE'

Lungiswa Mde is a female household head and is 54 years old. Lungiswa currently lives with her 3 children (1 male and 2 younger females), 4 grandchildren and Nontsikelelo. The only source of income currently is social grants. Three of her grandchildren receive foster care grants. Lungiswa's family was removed from East Bank on the 11 November 1965 and was allocated a 4-room house in Zone 1 Mdantsane. Both her parents were working at the time. Her parents were Mhambi and Nofezekile Mde. In the late 1930s, her father came from the small town of Alice and was the first one to black men to work at the new Waverly blanket factory in East London. Her mother worked as a domestic worker for a white family in the Amalinda suburb of East London. In the 1970s, after being relocated to Mdantsane, Lungiswa was still entirely dependent on her father's salary because her mother could not afford to keep her job because of the huge cost of daily transport to and from Mdantsane.

In 1975, Lungiswa's father passed away in 1975, ushering in a period of great hardship for the family. The household was now headed by Nofezekile. Luckily, Lungiswa also got a job at Waverly blankets in 1979, which was now employing women rather than men. In the 1980s, her mother also worked as a domestic, but lost her job as a domestic worker in 1987. Lungiswa admitted that it now became very difficult for her to support the whole family. Her sister, Nontsikelelo (now 50 years) was lucky to get temporary employment in a Fort Jackson textile factory. *"She was employed because she was familiar with knitting."* Her younger brother, Madoda (now 52 years) received part-time employment at Waverly blankets. *"This came as such a relief to me, even though they were not permanently employed. We wanted to extend the house, because we had a large family but could not afford it."*

In the 1990s, Lungiswa was being paid R350 per week at Waverly blankets. Her siblings were also contributing to the family through their involvement in the textile industry. In the years since their relocation to Mdantsane, the Mpe family had survived off employment in the textile industry and through domestic work. The collapse of the textile industry and eventual closure of Waverley blankets in East London in 2000 proved to be decisive and dramatic moment for this female-headed household. Lungiswa was lucky enough to find alternative part-time employment with Metro-rail, as a cleaner, earning R700 per month. *"But After that contract expired, I didn't know what to do. Nonstikelelo also lost her job during this period."* She said: *"Look at my family now. We have served the blanket and textile factories since my father came here in the 1930s and all we to show for it now are three foster grants, which cannot keep us alive."* Lungiswa said that her only option of starting a business is to buy clothes from Durban and re-sell them to make profit. *"I don't have any special skills to start my own business."*

Case 2: 'The Factories Gave Us Life'

Before being moved to Mdantsane in 1965, Nini Jack stayed in Westbank location with her sister and worked as a domestic worker in a local suburb, the Quigney. She recalls that when she arrived in Mdantsane with her two children, she was horrified with the quality of the house they received. She said it was half finished: *"There were no ceilings, windows and doors. We had to install these by ourselves."* Luckily, she managed to retain her employment by 'sleeping-in' as a domestic worker during the week. Her sister looked after the children while she was away at work.

In the early 1970s she recalls her excitement at being offered a job in a new textile factory in Wilsonia on the outskirts of Mdantsane. The factory made shirts, ties and trousers. She got a job as a packer there. She said that the job was better paid than her domestic job and that it was close enough to her house for her to go home everyday. In 1977, Nini had a personal tragedy when her second-born died under mysterious circumstances. This was obviously a huge blow to her and I noticed that her facial expression changed when we discussed the topic. While struggling to recover from her son's death, she lost her job at the factory in 1984. She said that the factory which was now under new ownership now focused on employing younger women. She said 'they chose younger people because they were desperate and could be manipulated to work for less.

In 1985, Nini got a job in another textile factory, which was responsible for making nightdresses for young and old. She worked there until 1986. In mid-1986 she joined another firm that made socks and she worked there up until 1994, when the firm closed down and she was left unemployed. I asked her if she received any kind of compensation in the form of packages and she said that they were not compensated." *There were no packages in the factories. We were only compensated in the form of Unemployment Insurance Fund."* Since democracy Nini has struggled to keep her household running. As she explained: *"Since then it has been hard going because my only son is not working, he only earns little money from casual labor and that is not enough. I have to buy groceries and pay for electricity out of my own old age pension.*" She said that she now sells "boompies" and her son does a little bit of gardening.

Case 3: 'In and Out of Employment'

Nomdakazana Menzeleleli was born 24 January 1947. Nomdakazana currently stays with her 3 children and 8 grandchildren in Mdanstane, she is currently unemployed. *"You tell me how we are supposed to survive when there is no one working in this house."* The only sources of income are social grants: one of her children and 4 grandchildren receive a social grant. She feels that the only solution to her predicament is for her to secure employment. *"I've never thought of starting my own business. I'm a bit skeptical to sell things like sweets and fat cakes because my grand children would abuse them. I'm saying this, I don't care what kind of work it is, and I'll do it. I've never had happiness since coming to Mdantsane, I'm still struggling know."*

Nomdakazana was forcibly removed from Westbank in 1965. Her mother at the time was earning less than the required rent amount in Mdantsane. *"My mother phoned me and I had to come from work to explain that I would also contribute my own money in order fulfill the rent required."* The following year, Nomdakazana decided not to continue with her studies to complete her schooling. In the late 1960s, she worked at Cerelort Factory in East London, earning R7 per week. She complained that the household income was very little and did not cover all their expenses. Her mother also stopped working at this time, which further crippled the family. Nomdakazana became the sole provider for the family. At this time there were 6 people living in this house. One of her brothers managed to secure employment at a pineapple factory, called Jones on the West Bank.

In the early 1980's, Nomdakazana managed to secure employment at both SA Druggist and Polse Grill. In 1988 she was the employed at Nkqubela Chest Hospital in Mdantsane, earning just over R1000 per month. During this period she was still the only bread-winner in her family. *"I used to borrow money from people in order to survive."* At about this point, she stated to me that it did not matter what kind of job I could offer her, she would take it. *"Even if you say I must clean dirt or scrub floors, I need money know."* Nomdakazana was still working at Nkqubela Chest Hospital. She was still the only bread-winner for the family. In the late 1990's she claims she lost her job due to jealousy amongst one of her co-workers. She claims that while on leave and when she returned back, she was told her services were no longer needed. *"I was always the first one to arrive at work. Even if you say I must be at your house at 8:00 am, I'll be there at 7:30 am."* Nomdakazana is now unemployed and is desperate to get some form of employment to tide her over the next three years, when she qualifies for a pensions.

The collapse of factory employment for women in Mdantsane and East London from the mid-1990s has had a profound effect on struggling female-headed households. Recent research conducted in Mdantsane in 2005 revealed that there were essentially three economic strata in the former Ciskei township (Bank 2005). The first and best off were the minority of households with members in stable employment in the Eastern Cape government bureaucracy. Many of these households earned monthly incomes in excess of R7500 or a $1000 a month. Below this category were a large number of nuclear and extended families with a collective household income or around R2500-R3000 a month (about $400). Typically one of the members of these households had a secure blue-collar job, while others in the household contributed small amount through causal work or petty trade. Often there was also a welfare grant of one kind or another collected by a household member. The third and poorest category of households we found was the two generational female-headed households. The levels of unemployment in these units had increased as a result of de-industrialization and other job losses in the formal economy. Most of these households were heavily dependent on the welfare system for support. The increasing poverty of these units undermined co-operation between women of different generation and placed many household under social and economic stress.

Conclusion

In this paper, I have documented the rise and demise of the multigenerational, matrifocal family in the city of East London in South Africa. I have suggested that prior to the advent of apartheid there were large numbers of matrifocal families in the South African cities, many of which owned property and were strong social and economic units. Female-headed households grew up in the city because of increasing female migration into the urban areas from the 1930s onwards. Women left the rural areas because of poverty and proletarianization, but also to escape unwanted marriages and patriarchal violence and discrimination. Once they had set themselves up in the city, they either found work as domestic servants or started small businesses in the informal sector. They sold beer, food and even sex for survival. In these endeavors, single women relied on family labor (matrikin) and parsimony (thrift) to turn a profit. The key to making something more substantial of their enterprises was access to residential property. If women could acquire 'site permits' or even control urban property as 'substitute owner' (looking after someone else's property), they were in an excellent position to convert small profits into larger ones. In this paper, I have argued that multigenerational, property owning matrifocal families were a dominant force in the urban locations of East London in the 1950s. These families did not conform to the norms and expectation of the state, or the local black elite, but they were nevertheless played a key role in advancing the interests of women in a hostile urban environment

In the 1960s and beyond, the fortunes of matrifocal families changed dramatically. These units were now excluded from the city on the grounds that new municipal houses in East London were only available to the male heads of nuclear families. Matriarchs were given the choice of either becoming housewives in town or accepting relocation to Mdantsane and elsewhere in the homelands. I argue that former East Bank matriarchs moved to the Mdantsane in their droves in the 1960s and 1970s, where they were thrust into a life of poverty with few social resources and economic opportunities. They could no longer earn a living off the wages of migrants, who now lived in single sex hostels. There was also no rental market in the township to exploit because backyard shack erection was illegal and the Ciskei government owned all the houses. This meant that most female household heads had to either re-enter domestic service, or try to find factory work in textile and furniture factories. These factories offered jobs to the daughters of East Bank matriarchs and provided some basis for the reconstruction and maintenance of two- and three-generation female-headed households in the Ciskei in the 1980s. Access to industrial jobs thus elongated the life of the matrifocal families in Mdantsane but, when globalization and de-industrialization destroyed the local industrial economy, thousands of working women became unemployed in the East London area. Without access to low-wage industrial jobs, the latter households became increasingly vulnerable to poverty and, by 2005, they were located firmly on the bottom of the socio-economic ladder, with an average income of just over $200 a month.

In East London itself, political mobilization and social upheaval in the 1980s had placed youth on a collision course with both their parents and the state. The most conflicted relationships in families were between fathers and sons, and it did not take long before young men were leaving the parents (male-headed) homes for the shack areas, where they set up their own 'living together' households with their 'girlfriends.' The dominate trend in town after 1980 was therefore one of domestic fragmentation and decompression. However, as sons moved out of the house, daughters generally stayed behind at home and tended instead to build shacks for themselves in the yard of the main house. When male household heads died, the house was passed on their widows and there was once again some potential for the re-emergence of entrepreneurial matrifocal households similar to those documented in the East Bank. However, the problem in the yards was that we found limited economic co-operation between mothers and daughters. The structure of hierarchy, respect and obedience that had been in place in the 1950s could no longer be counted on in the 2000s. Instead of using property to embark on new accumulation strategies, urban matriarchs were seen to be struggling to survive, finding them-selves vulnerable to exploitation from other their daughters and their male tenants (who often physically threatened them). Many said that, if they had somewhere peaceful to retire to in the countryside, they would leave the city as soon as possible.

My main conclusion is that remnants or traces of the matrifocal family are still visible in East London in the 2000s, but it would be a mistake to assume that these units are able to operate with the same power and confidence of the predecessor from the 1950s. Globalization has stripped urban women of access to factory jobs and also exposed them competition in the informal sector. Social networks are wider than before, but the relationships between mothers and daughters are no longer underpinned by the same levels of obedience and respect. This has inhibited family co-operation and entrepreneurial success. To conclude on a more general note, I would suggest that the weakness and fragmentary nature of urban households in poor neighborhood in east London and other South African cities is one of the major barriers to local economic and social development in these areas.

References

Bank, L. 2001. Living Together, Moving Apart: Homemade Agendas, Identity Politics and Urban-Rural Linkages in the Eastern Cape, South Africa. *Journal of Contemporary African Studies* 19(1).

_____. 2002. Beyond Red and School: Gender, Tradition and Identity in the Rural Eastern Cape. *Journal of Southern African Studies* 28(3).

_____. 2006. *The Rhythm of the Yards.* FHISER Research Series No. 1. East London: University of Fort Hare Press.

_____. 2008. Beyond Yard Socialism. In *State of the Nation 2007/8*, ed. Ntsebeza et al. Pretoria: HSRC Press.

Bank, L. and L. Makubalo. 2005. *Urban Renewal in Mdantsane: Livelihoods, Civil Society and Social Capital.* FHISER Research Series No. 1. East London: University of Fort Hare Press.

Beall, J., O. Crankshaw, and S. Parnell. 2002. *Uniting a Divided City: Governance and Social Exclusion in Johannesburg.* London: Earthscan.

Black, J., and B. Davies. 1986. *Industrial Decentralisation in the Ciskei.* ISER Development Studies Report. Grahamstown: Rhodes University.

Bozzoli, B. 1983. Marxism, Feminism and Southern African Studies. *Journal of Southern African Studies* 9(2).

_____. 2003. *Theatres of Struggle and the End of Apartheid.* Edinburgh: IAL.

Burke, T. 1996. *Lifebouy Men, Lux Women: Commodification, Consumption and Cleanliness in Modern Zimbabwe.* Durham: Duke University Press.

Butler, J. 1990. *Gender Troubles: Feminism and Subversion of Identity.* New York: Routledge.

Chapman, M., ed. 2001. *The Drum Decade: Stories from the 1950s.* Pietermaritzburg: University of Natal Press.

Clovers, L. 2005. To be a Man: Changing Constructions of Manhood in *Drum* Magazine, 1951-65. In *African Masculinities*, ed. L. Ouzgane and R. Morrel. New York: Palgrave.

Cook, G., and J. Opland, ed. 1980. *Mdantsane: Transitional City.* Grahamstown: ISER.

Dubow, S. 2005. Introduction. In *South Africa's 1940s: Worlds of Possibilities*, ed. S. Dubow and A. Jeeves. Cape Town: Double Storey.

Ferguson, J. 1999. *Expectations of Modernity: Myths and Meanings of Urban Life on the Zambian Copperbelt*. Berkeley: University of California Press.

Glaser, C. 2000. *Bo-Tsotsi: The Youth Gangs of Soweto, 1935-1976*. Cape Town: David Philip Publishers.

Hannerz, U. 1997. Sophiatown: The View from Afar. In *Readings in African Popular Culture*, ed. K. Barber. London: James Currey.

Hellman, E. 1948. *Rooiyard: A Sociological Survey of an Urban Native Slumyard*. Rhodes Livingston Institute Papers (13). Cape Town: Oxford University Press.

Hindson, D., and J. McCarthy, ed. 1994. *Here to Stay: Informal Settlements in KwaZulu-Natal*. Durban: Indicator Press.

Hooper, B. 1995. The Poem of Male Desires: Female Bodies, Modernity. *Planning Theory* 13.

_____. 1995. Paris: Capital of the Nineteenth Century. *Planning Theory* 13.

Mabin, A., and D. Smit. 1997. Reconstructing South Africa's Cities: The making of urban planning 1900—2000. *Planning Perspectives* 12: 193-223.

Mager, A. 1999. *Gender and the Making of a South African Bantustan: A Social History of the Ciskei, 1945-1959*. Oxford: James Currey.

Mamdani, M. 1996. *Citizen and Subject*. Princeton: Princeton University Press.

Mayekiso, M. 1996. *Township Politics: Civic Struggles for a New South Africa*. New York: Monthly Review Press.

Mayer, P. 1971. *Townsmen or Tribesmen: Conservatism and the Process of Urbanization in a South African City*. Cape Town: Oxford University Press.

McAllister, P. 2001. *Building the Homestead: Agriculture, Labour and Beer in South Africa's Transkei*. Aldershot: Ashgate Press.

Minkley, G. 1996. I Shall Die Married to Beer: Gender, Family and Space in East London's Locations. *Kronos: The Journal of Cape History* 23.

Pauw, B. A. 1973. *The Second Generation: A Study of the Family among Urbanised Bantu in East London*. Cape Town: Oxford University Press.

Rabinow, P. 1989. *French Modern: Norms and Forms of the Social Environment*. Chicago: University of Chicago Press.

Reader, D. 1960. *The Black Man's Portion: History, Demography and Living Conditions of East London*. Cape Town: Oxford University Press.

Robinson, J. 1998. *The Power of Apartheid*. London: Routledge.

Ross, F. 1996. Diffusing Domesticity: Domestic Fluidity in Die Bos. *Social Dynamics* 22(1).

Sandecock, L. 2000. *Towards Cosmopolis*. New York: Wiley.

Seekings, J. 1993. *Heroes or Villains: Youth Politics in the 1980s*. Johannesburg: Ravan.

Smith, R. 1988. *Kinship and Class in the West Indies*. Cambridge: Cambridge University Press.

_____. 1996. *The Matrifocal Family*. London: Routledge.

Taylor, N. 1999. *Urban Planning Theory Since 1945*. London: SAGE Publications.

White, L. 1990. *The Comforts of Home: Prostitution in Colonial Nairobi*. Chicago: University of Chicago Press.

Wilson, E. 2001. *The Contradictions of Culture: Cities, Culture and Women*. London: Sage.

Chapter 7

Towards a Different Kind of Freedom: Notes on Historicizing Globalization and Women in Africa

Abena Busia

This chapter is structured in three parts: I will open with a section discussing the concept of globalization and glossing the differences between its use as a technical concept, and one which recognizes the politics of its supposed neutral economic underpinnings. The burden of this section will also be to raise questions about the politics of knowledge-making, asking the question when, why, and under what conditions terms gain global currency and to what ends. From then I go on to argue that, given the politics of the term, African women, whose bodies have long been subjected to the impact of slavery and the empires and colonies that followed in its wake, have long negotiated, in overt and subtle ways, the impact of globalization on their societies and social conditions.

The second section of this chapter will then illustrate this contention with reference to a wide assortment of literature about women's life experiences across the continent from the mid eighteenth century to the closing years of the twentieth. Based on my nearly two decades of work on the *Women Writing Africa* project I will demonstrate that African women's lives have always been affected by aspects of the global economy. These women are usually not acknowledged as being integrated into this type of economy nor are they accounted for in the theorizing and policy-making process. In a variety of media, from their songs to their legal petitions, the texts of this project reveal the women's constant awareness and negotiations of being impacted by a globalized economy, whether in its guise of slavery or in the guise of the consumer market economies through which it is acknowledged today.

Finally, I will read Chimamanda Ngozi Adichie's award winning novel *Purple Hibiscus* as a way of illustrating the impact of globalization on the family through contemporary literature. Through its storytelling techniques, Adichie theorizes the complexities and inadequacies of the interaction between capitalist consumer economies and liberal democratic ideals through the way these forces play out in an intimate family drama. I hope to show how these texts work together to reveal the many ways in which a consciousness of their subject positions is reflected in their cultural production as the authors reveal the legacy of long centuries of the forces of globalization on the ways in which social orders and the roles of women within them are impacted by the demands of a changing economy.

Situated Knowledge

> Manifest or latent hierarchies obstruct the advancement of an international and transcultural feminist discourse. As the basis of this discourse, a mutual understanding of social and cultural reading is crucial. It is also necessary to clarify underlying theoretical perspectives and acknowledge that knowledge is situated (Potts and Wenk 2002: 460).

On the day I finish this essay, I take a group of my students, freshman and graduates, to the African Burial Ground Historic Monument in Lower Manhattan. I come back and re-write this preface. The trip has helped me clarify what it is I want to emphasize from the start, and to focus on why it is important that any discussion of globalization and Africa be grounded in the history of the Trans-Atlantic slave trade in order to make any ethical sense at all.

The Colonial era African burial ground, its existence, its forgotten history, and the politics of making it a research, artistic, cultural and historical project is a vital symbol of the fate of Africans in history in the New World. It has become a large reminder of "the politics of omission and the distortion of history." There were enslaved peoples in New York; they were amongst the earliest inhabitants of the city, in fact the city was built on the backs of their labor, and by the middle of the seventeenth century, Africans comprised 40% of the population. They fought for their liberty, they fought for their dignity, and they fought for a place in the city they built. What today takes up some of the most valuable real estate in Manhattan; Wall Street, Washington Square Park, Greenwich Village and more, was given them as wasteland outside the city limits to make a life for themselves, and bury their dead when the churches started refusing them permission to bury them in already consecrated ground.

The original eleven petitioners were denied the right to pass on their land to descendants and over the years it had all been taken away from them. Worse, the large tract of land that on eighteenth century maps is clearly and unequivocally marked "Negros Burial Ground" was filled in, desecrated, built over, and erased from public consciousness. It proved possible to wipe out the memory of several generations of hard labor, perhaps twenty thousand graves, and the legacy those lives represented. During the following centuries, the history of New York, and thus the history of the making of the Americas was systematically compromised and we told ourselves lies about the foundation of this new World:

> The distortions of history are not simply academic. All of what a people knows itself to be is historic. The future is an ideal, and the present is a fleeting moment that becomes the past in an instant. We know ourselves to be what we are according to what we have been. The distortion of African American history is a distortion of the identity of each and every person who is a member of that ethnic group (Blakey 2001: 224).

More egregious, as we know, when the remains were uncovered as a result of excavations to build the New Federal building, the sanctity of the place was not the primary interest of the people in authority over that building project. As our subject here is "globalization" it is a suitably symbolic irony that we are talking about a site near Wall Street, (after a city wall built by slaves), which probably became the site of the commercial heart of the city and the new country *because* it was a slave market. Those commercial and fiscal concerns remained paramount and it took years of community organizing and protest on the part of coalitions, led by African American leaders from all walks of life, to wrest control of the site and the restoration projects, and re-invest the site with dignity and meaning. Today a monument stands there and efforts are ongoing to ensure that we take the pains to piece together the history contained beneath it, and that that history will never again be forgotten.

That history, however, is being painfully pieced together not through the histories we already have on record, but through what those histories leave out, and more crucially, through the evidence we Africans left behind, in our bones and the fragments of our lives we left in our graves; for this truly is an *African* burial site, and it speaks volumes. Centuries after, we can do forensic scientific and cultural history that gives testimony to lives of hard labor; a woman with a shattered face and a musket bullet in her ribs, men with muscles torn and women with fractured neck vertebrae, all from carrying too heavy a load in the arms or on the head. But we also see an Africa remembered; sculpted teeth as sign of beautification, worn teeth which once lodged a clay pipe; glass beads as a flash of the spirit: symbolic signs of African ethnic identity and affiliation abound, making Akan, Fon, Mende, peoples identifiable. And for those interested in family structure, children, children, more children, and a mother buried with her baby in her arms.

This is not where, when I accepted to write this paper, I thought I would begin, but it is clear to me that it is the best place to do so, for my concerns have always had to do with the twin issues of the authority others accord to our lives as Africans, (and for me here, as African women), and equally as urgent, the authority we grant ourselves as witnesses to our own lives. To do either of these things, first our stories must be acknowledged, and acknowledged as authoritative. Yet our fate as a people has too often suffered what Carole Boyce Davies and 'Molara Ogundipe-Leslie isolate as the fate of Black women:

> Historically there have been few avenues for the full hearing of black women's testimonies. Instead there have been systematic attempts to discredit us as credible representatives of ourselves. These attempts have ranged from the larger institutional structures where black women's voices are often absent to the local levels of women's communities where black women's voices are often dismissed as irrelevant (Davies and Ogundipe-Leslie 1995: 4).

In approaching this subject of "Frontiers of Globalization" I am concerned first with the inter-related questions of knowledge production, language use and the according of power and privilege. That is, I believe we must remain conscious and vigilant about structures of power even in knowledge production and dissemination and ask ourselves constantly, whose experiences become the defining ones around which concerns are raised and policies driven? As Nkiru Nzegwu so cogently reminds us, "Imperialism thrives on knowledge racialization" (Nzegwu 2003: 116).[1]

To begin with the term that vexes we; "globalization." As Ali Mazrui says quite succinctly, "it consists of processes that lead towards global interdependence and increasing rapidity of exchange across vast distances. The word "globalization" is itself quite new, but the central processes towards global interdependence and exchange started centuries ago" (Mazrui 2001: 97). If this is so, why then is the term itself new? Why, after centuries of a process of increasing interdependence, is that process only now being named? I live with the unease, (perhaps unjustifiable), that "globalization" was not an issue when it only, or at least predominantly adversely impacted "other" bodies, black females in particular. Then something happened in the closing years of the twentieth century that made the West feel the process more acutely and start articulating concerns that had impacted the lives and bodies of "the rest of us" for centuries; only then was the process named.

In an address to the African Studies Association a few years ago I had occasion to observe:

I am concerned also, (as are all of us in this room), with the larger context in which we recognize that very often African knowledge is surreptitious knowledge as far as the western world is concerned. The history of power and imperialism and colonialism has given rise to a world in which it is not possible to be in African [and Diaspora] Studies and be unaware of the questions and problems posed by the seeming contradictions between western cultural and economic imperialism and Black/African cultural identities, but the reverse is not true. There are two things I wish to stress about that sentence. The first is that indeed the reverse is *not* true. We have not reversed the power differentials between the "West and the Rest of Us," and in the immediate centuries that shape the lives we live today, that struggle for power has been an unequal one at every level (Busia 2006: 18).

The point I am making is that when speaking of issues that concern the "global village" that the world has become, the power to define still lies with the hegemonic West (Mazrui 2001: 98). And this despite the fact that around the world we have been negotiating, and through many and various means, the impact that centuries of this process we did not name, has had upon us. Those negotiations are instructive, if we could but learn to learn from them, and they continue to shape the way we live on a daily basis, in the most unexpected ways (Walker 2001). Thus I would like to continue in this paper, as I did then, by simply offering what I call "exemplary moments," the words of African women, to see if we can find our way clear to the answers we are seeking by understanding the complexity of the worlds they represent in miniature. Certainly I am not alone in this call. I am one in a large community of people who work "in love and struggle as we continue to make meaning."[2]

The Long Duree

From the mid fifteenth to the late nineteenth century, about 11 million people born in Africa were carried across the ocean.

Thousands of men participated directly in the transatlantic slave trade, traveling far from their homes in order to do so. But many other men, women, and children, Europeans,

Africans, Americans, and Asians, were indirectly employed near where they lived, in making the building materials for the castles and forts, in designing and constructing the specialized sailing vessels, in manufacturing the armaments, chains, and instruments of coercion, in providing the financial capital, the credit, the insurance, the foreign exchange, and the other complex services that were essential to the operation of the trade. Many thousands more were employed in spinning, weaving, dyeing, and packing the fabrics, in casting and forging the metalwares, in distilling the brandy and the rum, and in the manufacture and processing of the many other goods and commodities that were taken to Africa to be exchanged for slaves. Even the peoples of North America who traded deerskins to the incoming European settlers were drawn in to the oceanic economy.

Among those who received dividends from the slave trade were the British royal family, the British aristocracy, the English Church, and many institutions, families, and individuals. Plantation owners in the West Indies and North America prospered from the sale of commodities produced by slave labor, as did some of their employees and business partners, and profits remitted to Britain supported others who never left home. A similar reckoning could be made for the other slaving nations. But it is scarcely an exaggeration to say that every person in the Europeanised world who put sugar in their tea or coffee, spread jam on their bread, who ate sweets, cakes, or ice-cream, who smoked or chewed tobacco, took snuff, drank rum or corn brandy, or wore coloured cotton clothes, also benefited from, and participated in, a globalised economy of tropical plantations worked by slaves forcibly brought from Africa (St. Clair 2006: 4-5).

In the light of this reality, to accept the identification of African countries as "developing economies" is not the place to start. What made that status a given? How did they become, and remain, in a seeming state of perpetual "developing?" I begin with this extended quote about the impact of the slave trade on the world economy to emphasize the obvious point that a globalized economy is not a new thing, and that African slaves were at the epicenter of the making of the modern world (Inikori 2001; Harris 2001; Dodson 2001).

In grappling not only with the question of Africa but with the question of gender and globalization, the presenters at AWID's Ninth International Forum on "Reinventing Globalization" in Mexico in 2002, for all their diversity, were in agreement on one central issue:

> Globalization processes, in their current form, are a threat to the gains women have made over the past three decades, in struggling for an end to poverty and equal status and rights with men: in their families, and community and the state. [....] [R]adical action is needed if globalization is to be re-routed down a just and sustainable path (Kerr and Sweetman 2003: 3).

Clearly "globalization" is not a neutral term. Though there are those who struggle to keep it a definition of a technical term used for transnational influences on economic systems, culture, and political systems that transcend national borders, for others, the reality is that it is:

> The effort to standardize consumer habits, values, and ways of thinking that contributes to the development of global markets, greater efficiencies and profits; politically, it is based on neo-liberal values and assumptions that justify this latest expression of Western colonization; undermines local economies, traditions of self-sufficiency, and the non-monetized aspects of local cultures; a source of poverty as it requires participating in a money economy even when automation makes work even more scarce; [www.centerforecojustice education.org].

That is to say, it is an inherently political process, dominated by the predominantly Western-based companies which have replaced the slave-trading companies of old, promoting a "Western-dominated culture of consumerism and capitalist development" which, as the editors of the AWID 2002 papers make clear, is also inherently connected to gender inequality. For them, as for many organizations which focus on centralizing the role of women in development economics, the reality that financial institutions have become the main political actors on the global stage is a threat to democracy in general, and to women in particular, requiring a challenge to the ways they create and maintain inequalities through their ties to the way society is organized. (Randriamaro 2008: 46) In this regard, I also need to centralize the question of feminist studies, in particular in Africa. Practically everywhere in the world feminist studies has its roots in feminist praxis. The relationship between ideology and strategy has always been strong and an integral part of the woman's movement. In Africa in particular there has always been a conscious linking of feminist ideologies to African realities. Bisi Adeleye-Fayemi the Executive Director of the African Women's Development Fund, in a lecture on "Creating and Sustaining Feminist Space in Africa" reminds us that:

> Feminism in Africa is located in the continent's historical realities of marginalization, oppression, and domination brought about by slavery, colonialism, racism, neo-colonialism, and globalization. It also places the inter-connectedness of gender, women's oppression, race, ethnicity, poverty, and class at the centre of the discourse. It is therefore impractical to talk about a feminist theory in Africa without an understanding of how these issues have shaped African women's lives and world view in historical terms. African feminist thought, by implication, is anti-imperialist, socialist-oriented, and keenly aware of the implications of social injustices on society as a whole. It is also anti-racist because it challenges the institutional racism of global and regional structures, which exploit the continent and undermine its progress (Adeleye-Fayemi 2000).

That is African feminism has to be political at every level, and is rooted in a recognition of a deep need for transformational practices in every aspect of our lives. In this context the significance of what globalization looks like and what it has meant to African women (as the legacy of a new kind of slavery) is very important. Bisi Adeleye-Fayemi very succinctly articulates it as a recognition of the deregulation of markets, free trade and privatization, which in the last decades of the twentieth century has meant, for Africans in general and African women in particular, being structurally adjusted downwards into increasing infrastructural insecurity, spiraling indebtedness and accelerating poverty. So globalization, which theoretically, was meant to mean equal access to resources and the eradication of poverty has come to mean a greater control of resources by the rich and greater insecurity on every level for the poor both inside the domestic economies of the rich countries as well as the global south, an insecurity that has become political insecurity and, military insecurity, going right down to food and water insecurity for the poor.

Make no mistake, when you are on the margins, what is said in one place today can literally translate into whether you live or die in another place tomorrow, and we all know this. The recent economic instability in the world money markets caused by the fragility of the US sub-prime mortgage markets and the weakness of the banking sector has made this all too clear. But this is the concern; globalization seems to have become a central concern for academic debate when it begun to affect the lives of those in the global north as dramatically as it has always affected the lives of those in the global south.

I'm conscious of the fact that when I first started living and teaching in the United States twenty years ago I found myself in the peculiar position of becoming overnight an "expert" in multicultural practices because I was born in Ghana, raised in England, and living in the United States teaching Americans about their own literature. The dual process of working on multicultural education and the transformation of the curriculum for gender as well as race, has made me conscious of a shift in the academy of the terms in which we speak–from a sense of the "multicultural" in the early 1980s to a sense of the "global" in the late1990s. This has happened in many sophisticated ways, but I see it, in a sense, as a shift from theorizing about the "barbarians at the gate," in the case of multicultural education to having to theorize about strategies for being "at the gate of the barbarians" in the case of globalization. And whatever way you look at it, we Africans are counted among "the barbarians."

Being Witness to Ourselves

> By deepening our understanding of violence against women during the epoch of imperialism, we will be better able to comprehend and so to counteract the multiple forms of violence meted out against women in postcolonial African states today. Imperialism is the major trope of this analysis because it is the common historical force that makes it possible to consider an area as large and diverse as the African continent as having general features that transcend the boundaries of nation, culture and geography. This collective African experience-

> *being conquered by the colonizing powers; being culturally*
> *and materially subjected to a nineteenth-century European*
> *racial hierarchy and its gender politics; being indoctrinated*
> *into all-male European administrative systems; and facing*
> *the continuous flow of material and human resources from*
> *Africa to Europe- has persistently affected all aspects of social,*
> *cultural, political, and economic life in post-colonial African*
> *states* (Mama 1996: 47).

One small response to this inequality of power is the *Women Writing Africa* project my colleagues and I have been engaged in for almost two decades. *Women Writing Africa* (WWA) is a project of cultural restoration which hopes to restore African women's voices, including the stories of dispossession that mark the harrowing start of the slave routes, to the public sphere. The several volumes document the history of self-conscious literary expression by African women throughout the continent. This expression is for us both oral and written, ritual and quotidian, sacred and profane. Our hope is to allow new readings of Africa's history by shedding light on the things that women do and say, for in doing this, we hope to find where the fault lines of memory lie and so change our assumptions of how knowledge has been shaped by bringing to a broad public the hitherto obscured history, culture, and thought, of African women, as we have lived and worked within our families, societies, and nations. I begin by using these texts to discuss the issue of the impact of globalization through the words of African women in the global economy in the making of the modern world.

One of the earliest letters in the West Africa/Sahel volume is a letter written in 1739 by one Madlena Van Poppos. I begin with this letter to establish how early African women began to articulate the impact of global economic movements on their lives.

The eldest [sic] of the community of the Negroes in St. Thomas write [sic] to the Queen of Denmark in 1739.

> Great Queen:
> At the time I lived in Poppo in Africa, I served the
> Lord Mau. Now that I have come to the Land of Whites
> I don't want to serve that Lord. I do not have reason to
> serve that Lord; my heart is saddened, because Negro
> woman cannot serve the Lord Jesus on St. Thomas. If the

Whites do not want to serve the Lord, be that as it may. But if the poor Black brethren and sisters want to serve the Lord, they have to behave as if they were Maroons. If it pleases you Great Queen, you have to pray to the Lord Jesus for us, and also pray A Niba, the Master of the Earth, to let Brother Martinus remain and preach the word of the Lord, because we have to learn to know the Lord, and also to baptize us Negroes, in the name of the Father, the Son, and the Holy Ghost. May the Lord keep and bless sons and daughters, and the whole family, and I shall pray to the Lord Jesus for them. In the name of more than 250 Negro women who love the Lord Jesus, written by Marotta, now Madlena from Poppo in Africa (Sutherland-Addy and Diaw 2005: 122).

The letter seems occasioned by a condition confirmed elsewhere in the church history, as well as in other sources; that the condition under which the slaves were living in St. Thomas was wretched. The Moravian mission to St. Thomas had been inspired by a chance encounter at the Court of King Christian VI of Denmark in 1731 between Count Zinzendorf and a West Indian Negro slave named Anthony Ulrich, who pleaded for someone to come to St. Thomas to preach the Gospel to the suffering slaves. One significant factor about this letter is the language in which it was written. In 1739, St. Thomas was a Danish colony, the Danes having established a trading post there since 1666.

By all expert accounts, that Madlena and her fellow slaves were speaking Dutch rather than Danish was only to be expected, that there is a written record of this Dutch is what is exceptionally rare. During the period in question, though St. Thomas was a Danish Colony, Dutch entrepreneurship in the region was such that the majority of the planters were Dutch. Thus Dutch was the lingua franca and the language that the slaves adapted. However, Danish remained the official language and all official records, documents and public signs were written in Danish, and official historiography can barely find traces of the Dutch language. The language of the slaves, Dutch Creole, was preserved in oral form in the lore of folk tales originating in West Africa, and in written form in missionary translations of the bible, and in liturgical texts. However, it would be a full twenty years or so after this letter was written that the first of these liturgical texts, a translation of the Psalms and a religious Primer, would be published. The significance of this letter is reflects the state of flux not only on the island, but also in the part of Africa where Madlena identifies herself as coming from. My point is Madlena Van Poppos a seemingly insignificant figure in the annals of world history, yet in trying to find out about her and the occasion for her letter a complex history of state, social and ecclesiastical relations is laid bare. This letter of petition also represents the earliest diplomatic embassy written in Dutch creole. Madlena Van Poppos' text thus reflects the way in which the nature of the slave economy disrupted and scattered people's lives. It affected where they went, how they learned to read and write and, in its reference to "the Lord Mau," to negotiate the distinction between their own systems of knowledge and the new systems of knowledge that being part of the slave economy brought upon them. Her words, if we take what she says and how she says it seriously, have much to teach us. And this is true whether the words were written, spoken, or sung.

Two laments in this same volume, one from Senegal and one from Ghana, illustrate this intimate connection. The Ghanaian lament whose refrain I translate as "the warring hosts have destroyed my most precious treasure,"[3] is sung by the group which claims to be the oldest of the Adzewa groups found amongst the Fante people in the Central Region whose most important town is Cape Coast. Every Fanti community in Ghana has at least one militia or Asafo group, which once defended the community. Today Asafo remains a strong ritual institution, with every man automatically a member of his father's Asafo, and with women taking charge of the ritual and celebratory occasions. The Adzewa group, an association of women, learn about and pass on the history of the Asafo, particularly through a sacred core of texts, always sung first during formal performances. The Adzewa group also has the license to compose songs expressing frank opinions on current events. "The Warring Hosts" forms part of the sacred core of texts from the Bentsir Adzewa group of Cape Coast. This piece, one of the most significant in the group's canon, is exemplary of the way in which significant historical events were, and continue to be chronicled, by women in song: it is in effect a "call and response" in which the poignant response "the warring hosts have destroyed everything I treasure" carries in its simplicity the horror and the poignancy of a great devastation (Sutherland-Addy 1998).

The Warring Hosts

Call	In this situation, what am I to do?
	The warring hosts have destroyed my most precious treasure.
	Ayee.
	Adwoa, daughter of Asebu ancestors.
Response	The warring hosts have destroyed my most precious treasure.
	Ayee.
Call	Adwoa, Daughter-of-Kwesi-the-Whiteman.
Response	The warring hosts have destroyed my most precious treasure.
	Ayee.
Call	Adwoa, daughter of Kofi Dadzie.
Response	The warring hosts have destroyed my most precious treasure.
	Ayee.
Call	Know that however pale your skin
	You can be to the whiteman no closer kin
	Than Adwoa, daughter of the whiteman.
Response	The warring hosts have destroyed my most precious treasure.
	Ayee.
Call	Ayee! Pitiable one.
Response	Pity, <u>enyaado,</u> ee.
	The whiteman says, "What a pity."
	Pity, <u>enyaado,</u> ee.
	The warring hosts have destroyed my most precious treasure.
	Ayee.
Call	What is it? Aaaahhhh! It is my most precious treasure,
	Adwoa, Daughter-of-Kwesi-the-Whiteman.
Response	The warring hosts have destroyed my most precious treasure.
	Ayee.
Ensemble	Ayee! Pitiable one.
	Pity, <u>enyaado,</u> ee, such a pity.
	The whiteman says, "What a pity."

Pity, enyaado, ee,
The warring hosts have destroyed my most precious
treasure.

(Sutherland-Addy and Diaw 2005: 133)

The song was composed in honor of Adwoa Kwadua, best known for responding bravely to the wartime death of her husband and the 99 men of his Asafo company. In an alliance with the British Governor Charles MacCarthy, they had lost a campaign against the Asante kingdom. Adwoa Kwadua assumed the onerous burden of redeeming the lives of these dead men by paying each of the surviving families a measure of gold dust. News of this brave act reached the Governor who personally offered his condolences.

Governor MacCarthy is the "White-man" in the song, given the Fanti name "Kwesi," thus acknowledging the family bond between him and Adwoa, as father and daughter. The word *"enyaado"* is a gracious greeting of respect offered to Adwoa Kwadua by the Governor.

Thus in this seemingly simple song, we have a complexity of allusions recording a complex historical situation. Part of the trauma we live with, is this dilemma of the bitterness of choices. For the Fante rulers, the known Asante empire was no more palliative a solution than the British. And what matters to us is that in the end, *all* "warring hosts" indiscriminately, are responsible for the destruction of the precious things, the death of the 99 lives. What is memorialized is the nobility of the survivors, the women left behind who have to make choices about how to resolve the immediate situation. This honorific song has now been sung continuously by the descendants of those 100 warriors for almost two hundred years.

We find a parallel situation, from the same time period, amongst the women of Nder, Senegal, with even more dramatic results. Again, there are two "warring hosts" in the form of French penetration and Islamic expansion to parallel the British penetration and Asante expansion. And once again it is the women who are caught in the vice. The abolition of the slave trade at the Congress of Vienna in 1815 ushered in an era of economic transformation for France's African colonial possessions. When the French took back the colony of Senegal in 1817, which they had lost to the English, they began agricultural colonization in order to transform international trade. France gained land for agricultural experimentation through the Treaty of Ndaw, signed in May 1819 with the dignitaries from Waalo. Waalo thus became a center for colonial agriculture, a testing ground for France's new economic policies. The ruling class of Waalo hoped to benefit from this new situation to free themselves from the pressure that the Trazza Moors were putting on their kingdom by refusing to pay them tribute. This provoked a conflict between Waalo and the Trazza Moors. The situation became even more complicated when the Tukuler ruler of Fuuta started making claims on Dagana, a village that sheltered the agricultural buildings. Due to the covetousness of its neighbors, Waalo was confronted by a vast coalition, resulting in a battle that took place in its capital, Nder. When the Moors and the Tukuler made their offensive, the ruler was absent and it was the young heir to the throne and the *lingeer* (the King's first wife) who were responsible for the defense of Nder. Faced with the inevitable fatal outcome of the combat, the first wife asked all of the woman, except one, to meet in a large hut which they set on fire, preferring death to certain captivity. (We know about this example of bravery thanks to the only woman from the group who escaped death.) By allowing one woman to survive to recount their bravery, the women of Nder showed that they did not want their sacrifice to be in vain: it would serve as an example of courage and patriotism. In early 19th century Senegal, the women chose to immolate themselves and burn rather than submit to Moorish incursion or rely, as their male rulers had done, on the protection of the French who were bartering their lands and lives:

> The Moors entered Nder.
> At that time,
> Some of the men
> Had left for the fields.
> Still others had gone elsewhere.
> All the men were absent from the village.
> Only the women were present.
> The Moors attacked them.
> Among the women was Lingeer Mbarka Dia
> Who was very close to Fati Yamar,
> The Lingeer of Nder
> And wife of Amar Fatim Borso,

Brak of Waalo.

Armed with their pestles,
The women rushed into battle in the middle of the Moors.
Fighting against them
They struggled and managed to kill
Three hundred and eleven.
Then they withdrew and said to themselves:
If the Moors are victorious
They will take us to Mauritania
And if they lead us there,
They will make us slaves

So they chose among themselves one named
Seydani Ma Fatim.
Seydami Ma Fatim had first refused
When the women asked her:
"Agree to leave with the Moors.
We will burn ourselves in the tata.
For if the Moors take us
They will turn us into slaves

The women attempted to convince Seydami Ma Fatim.
They reasoned so well with her
That in the end
She agreed to leave with the Moors.
And when she arrived in Rosso,
Relatives there helped her settle
In their home near Garak.
She even had children there.

But the true glorious event
Was the women's act of bravery and valor.
They sacrificed themselves by fire in the tata,
A building which corresponds today
To the National Assembly [sic].
It is this Assembly that the women entered
And, with their belongings,
They lit the fire.
Lingeer Mbraka Dia said:
"Never will we follow the Moors
Who want to reduce us to slavery.

Better to all perish in the flaming tata!
Better to die here than tomorrow be slaves of the Moors"
And, while entering the flaming room,
They began to sing.
What were they singing?
They sang:
"Today Waalo crumbles
But what a great realm it was!
Today Waalo crumbles
But what a great realm it was!
What a dark day is today!
The whole of Waalo has crumbled.
It is today that Waalo falls
But what a great realm it was!"
They sang
And sang some more
Until the building was totally reduced to ashes.
Everything inside burned.

When these events took place,
Amar Fatim Borso, away in Saint Louis,
Was informed of them.

We know this story because the women who chose to die, chose someone to live to tell that story. The houses burn, but even ashes can be memorials. *Talatay* Nder, or Nder Tuesday, is sacralized today in the collective memory of contemporary Senegal as emblematic of the refusal to submit.

Some women could resist more actively: on November 18th 1929, a mission school teacher Mark Emeruwa, acting as a census taker on behalf of his local warrant chief Okugo, walked into the compound of a woman named Nwanyeruwa wife of a man named Ojim, in Oloko, Bende Division, Owerri province in Eastern Nigeria, and insisted on counting the wives and livestock in the compound. The rest, really is, history. The ensuing demonstrations sparked off by Nwanyeruwa's resistance to this request spread throughout Owerri and Calabar Provinces and lasted approximately six weeks until the end of December when British troops restored order. By that time fifty-five women had been killed, ten native courts destroyed and several others damaged, and the houses of court personnel attacked, a half a dozen factories attacked, and chief Okugo tried, convicted of corruption, and dismissed from office. The incidents were so severe a Commission of Inquiry was held in the months following.

Though the Aba Women's war has rightly become one of the most celebrated moments of West African Women's Collective Action, it should best be seen in a larger context of Women's ability to mobilize for the purpose of collective civil protest which predated this celebrated instance, and can be seen in continuing actions such as the contemporary demonstration held by Ogoni women in defense of themselves and their communities in their resistance to the policies of Shell Oil company in Nigeria.

The immediate context of these disturbances is the complex situation in Iboland in the 1920s that resulted from an unstable combination of the rise of colonial administrations in that area, the economic situation in Eastern Nigeria of the late 1920s and the impact both of these had had on local issues including governance and local and household management. In their attempts to "pacify" the peoples of the Lower Niger, the British had attempted to replicate their form of indirect rule of governance through local authorities such as the Emirs, which had been quite successful in Northern Nigeria. However, in Southern Nigeria, especially in Iboland where systems of autocratic chieftaincy did not exist, in their attempt to address the situation through the imposition of the system of warrant chiefs, caused a great deal of unrest. In some cases there had been no chiefs at all, in others where there had been, the British had chosen their warrant chiefs from outside the customary families, thus in almost all cases, these chiefs were seen as illegitimate. In the particular case of Okugo the warrant chief in the locality where the disturbances first broke out, court testimony reveals the number of autocratic impositions he had made on women and their labor which underlay their objections to his in his rule. If there were anxieties that the "native authorities" were becoming simply British administrative agents in traditional disguise, Okugo seems to have been a case in point, in Nwanyeruwa's words, before being appointed by the British "he was an ordinary man."

In many places it was the extra powers given to the warrant chiefs, in particular the economic powers of tax raising and impress, that were the source of the problem. Nwanyeruwa's testimony before the courts of inquiry make it very clear what Okugo's abuses were thought to be.

In fact it is believed that the rumor of the suggestion to tax women came not from the government, but by the warrant chiefs. And they were already angry about the taxation of their men.

The conflation between census counting and the imposition of taxes had its source in the taxes imposed in 1926, which had been preceded by a census of male heads of household. These taxes had already proved burdensome. Then, in addition to this, it was a period of rapid inflation and there had been a sharp and rapid decline in the price of palm oil. Nwanyeruwa, like many of the women of her area, was a small farmer, specializing in palm oil trading which had been introduced as a cash crop by the British after the abolition on the Trans-Atlantic Slave Trade. She is preparing palm oil when the census taker enters her compound. The indignation of the chief concerning the attack on his messenger has as much to do with gender and status politics as it has to do with the horrible mess that red palm oil makes on the body and clothes. It stains and is most difficult to remove. As many of these women were also farmers, it meant that much of the economic health of the communities were regulated and governed by women in the time and area under discussion, in particular the palm oil trading. Thus at heart the economic threat of the taxation of women was a real issue. That the British may not actually have been about to impose a tax on women in the end is a moot point. The point is that the behavior of their warrant chiefs and a combination of other local factors led the women to believe a tax was imminent, and the behavior of those chiefs did nothing to allay their fears.

In addition to this combination of administrative abuse and confusion, the process of census taking itself violated many taboos. Through the region of West Africa and the Sahel there is resistance to the counting of people, especially of women, which is considered particularly abhorrent. Animals can be counted, but not fruit bearing trees, or women. There were two issues, the counting itself, and the rumors about the purposes for which the counting was being done, which in retrospect some feel was instigated by the warrant chiefs. Thus insult was being added to injury.

There can be no doubt about the specifically feminist nature of the strategy in that it was femaleness and women's agency and power that were on display through their symbols of war. "This affair does not concern men"; the choice of dress, the use of body language the "sing and dance" all drew attention to their role and status as women, in particular as women acting in protection of the "good of the land." This protective role demonstrated the power their society accorded them in defense of all that was sacred. In addition, among the Igbo traditional social structures led to the forming of associations of wives and daughters in the regulation of affairs, and these associations also governed issues of trade. The sacred and the secular roles were not distinct but interdependent.

The evidence shows that Nwanyeruwa was an elderly woman at the time of the war, with one grown son whose wife had died the year before, some sources say she was not a Christian, though her own evidence explains that she took her oath on the sword and not the bible because as an unlettered woman she could not be baptized as an ability to read the bible was a pre-requisite for baptism. Other evidence suggests she was a traditional nurse and circumciser. It was her activities and travels as a circumciser that made her privy to the rumors about the pending taxation of women. It seems clear that the action that followed Nwayeruwa's protest was collective action and when spokespersons and coordinators were required there were three other, younger women, all farmers and petty traders who took up the role.

Although it took a long time, in those places where women objected to warrant chiefs on the bases of oppression and corruption, the government acceded to their demands, dismissed the chiefs, and institutionalized mechanisms for getting the women involved in the selection of chiefs. They also for the first time appointed women to the Native courts. The testimony appended is Nwanyeruwa's opening testimony given before the commission of inquiry sitting at Umudike, on Wednesday March 12th 1930. She is responding after being sworn in by the sword, to the question from the chairman "Will you tell us what you know about these occurrences at Oloko?"

In French West Africa, parallel processes were taking place. In the concluding years of the nineteenth century French colonization of Black West Africa opened the conquered countries up to grand projects aimed at creating the infrastructure necessary to their exploitation. The dearth of labor forced the colonial administration to take a certain number of measures. One was to inaugurate obligatory public service or forced labor; the law put into effect on 25 November 1912. It took the form of a financial obligation which could be paid by laboring on any number of public projects. The work was varied and took place over the vast territory which was the French West Africa.

Included in Volume Two of *Women Writing Africa* is a series of popular songs found which, according to their collector all date from the colonial period "because they are born of colonization and oppose it." All the songs share a principal theme, colonial exaction, and deal specifically with forced labor, military recruitment, and sexual abuse, and offer a critique of French colonial history filtered through a woman's eyes. These songs express how women lived through [or experienced] this period of their country's history.

The first song recalls this forced labor whose conditions had been fixed by governmental decree of the French Sudan on 30 October 1930; the law aimed at construction of roads, marketplaces, camps, and wells. The work could as easily encompass clearing land, building irrigation ditches, etc. within the territory of each county. Everyone between 18 and 60 owed either ten days of forced labor each year, or had to pay the equivalent value in cash. But in fact, this quota was never realized. The songs denounce the rigors of the work imposed by the "whites."

The White Folk Have Come

> The White folk have come
> A basket for each woman
> The lady is transformed into a an early rising rooster
> The White folk have come
>
> The White man has come to Yako
> A basket for each woman
> Here she is, the ever ready tool when the rooster sings
> Here is a stone suspended
> If you don't know the suspended stone
> You do not know the White man

The next two songs both make mention of Bamako. For the people of Upper Volta during colonial times, Bamako was a symbol of hell. The city symbolized hard labor, separation, suffering and the dehumanizing work associated with three harsh realities: the construction of the Dakar-Niger railway; the Niger Administrative Office, and military recruiting in Kati, a city in Mali. The movement of bodies in service of others far away is critiqued in these songs, however obliquely. The women focus on the affective, the impact of these harsh realities on them, their lives, the lives of their loved ones:

I still crave my lover

I still crave my lover
I still crave my lover
And there he goes, off to Bamako
Off to work there for three months.

Bamako

Bamako! I don't have the blues about my mother
Bamako! I don't have the blues about my father
I'm singing about my lover who has no clothes
To go to Bamako, that's tough!
I'm singing about my lover who has no clothes
To go to Bamako.

In resistance to forced military recruiting, the fourth song presents physical infirmity as attractive, because that exempted the sufferer from military duty, while in contrast having a healthy child is lamented as bringing the suffering of the draft:

Nasaara

Here comes the White man!
If you have a feeble child, be happy
But if you have a robust child,
Get ready to leave for Kati tomorrow.

The last song in the series alludes to a practice which affected mainly girls, preferably young and pretty ones, ("Pogo" and "Pogbi" are the names given to twin girls among the Mossi).

Most colonial administrators came without their wives. As a result, they "requisitioned" young girls--ostensibly to teach them language and culture, but in reality for sex. The women had to be coerced; some were already engaged, all knew their futures would be compromised. And as soon as they became pregnant they were sent back, to be replaced by some other person, the victim now forced to lead a marginal life even among her own who now refused to recognize her as one of theirs:

Poko

Poko! Oh! Oh!
What has become of Pogbi?
Pogbi ! Oh! Oh!
What has become of Poko?
Pogbi is the mistress of the White man
Poko's hair is nuzzling the White man

Thus these anti-colonial work songs (Sutherland-Addy and Diaw 2005: 163) show how in the 1920s, the economic structure set up by the French had a pervasive impact on women's lives. In particular these last songs speak to the degradation of African women's status under colonialism, and the long schizophrenic notions colonialists had towards interracial unions, alternating between desire and contempt, indulged in on the one hand, prohibited by law on the other, always denigrated (Busia 1986; Mama 1996: 50).

The continuities of impact is made more emphatically clear when we consider that the research on current globalization strategies show that a key survival strategy, on which whole families depend, is women migrating for work as domestic or sex workers. "For women from poor backgrounds who are uneducated, it can often only take place illegally, via a globalized network of traffickers in human beings. Desperate for a livelihood, some travel in full or partial awareness of the dangers they face, yet they take the gamble in the hope of bridging the extraordinary gap between their lives of poverty and the affluence of life in the US and Europe" (Kerr and Sweetman 2003: 10). This is a reflection on the situation in the 1980s, but like much else, this was not new, but an exacerbation of a long standing state of affairs, in contexts in which African women in urban spaces were frequently cast as prostitutes, thereby justifying their continued harassment (Mama 1996).

Yet, as this 1950 letter from a group of Tanzanian women accused of being prostitutes, shows, such decisions could be quite strategic:

Sir,

We women are human beings like the men. God created us all to assist each other, men and women. Now for about two years we see that we women are returning to slavery. You Europeans came to help us to completely finish slavery so everybody could get freedom.

When the men instituted the laws to forbid us to go abroad to find work to help ourselves and our parents, the law was brought to you and to our rulers to be accepted. But we are not called to any meeting to be asked why we go abroad rather than staying at home, and what problems sent us there. We hear our opponents saying that we go because of prostitution (Umalaya). This word is an insult to us. If we are called prostitutes, can a woman make herself a prostitute on her own? First of all, is not a prostitute the man who gave us the money?...They do not think of that.

It would be better to forbid the men to travel, because they let their coffee plantations fall into decay or they sell the plantations which they have been entrusted by their fathers and go and make mischief. When we return home we buy the plantations of those scoundrels. The drunkards do not know how to take care of the plantations they have gotten from their fathers. The men do not know how to treat their wives well. When a man sells coffee he divides up the shilling in two parts—to get drunk and to give someone who has done nothing for the money he gives away for fornication. Perhaps, he sends you, his wife, to bring him his money order; if you refuse you will be beaten and chased away, because you do not follow orders. It is difficult to talk about our lives together with our men. We endure for the sake of our children.

Now we ask you, sir, to give the order to our council that we may discuss with our husbands and parents. The person whom it is necessary to forbid traveling may be stopped. The one who has the right to go may be allowed, but do not despise us because we are women. Even if we are women, our fathers and our husbands ought to thank us, because the plantations we have bought would have been taken by foreigners like the Rwandese and tribes outside Bukoba.

We ask for your mercy to meet with you, since we are beaten and chased away at the harbor, as if we are animals.

We are sorry when we see that women do not get the protection of our sacred government.

We are humble and obedient Z and G, your children from Kiziba (Lihamba and Moyo 2007: 164).

This rich text reveals a clear and sophisticated analysis of familial, local, national and international political and economic contexts and imbrications. "Sex roles are never simply 'cultural' but are affected by any number of factors such as whether a woman can or cannot own land, manage her own income, absent herself from her husband's home, be received in her natal home in case of divorce and so on' (Green 1999: 21). Written on behalf of a large group by two women who sign themselves "Z and G" they make such inter-connections so very clear. The first is, that large scale professionalized prostitution began in the region at the turn of the nineteenth century, following the establishment of colonial rule and its accompanying commercialization. As in other parts of Africa, Colonial politics and economic policies created large informal homesteads predominantly populated by the single men doing the petty labor of colonial service, casual and domestic workers, porters, soldiers and policemen, which offered ripe opportunity for sex work. By the 1940s, Bahaya women such as those who write the petition could be found in all large cities of East Africa not only Dar es Salaam but Kampala, Nairobi, and Mombasa as well (Lihamba and Moyo 2007).

Secondly (in a reality which parallels the behaviors of "new Diaspora" Africans today with remittances home via Western Union as well as the monies amassed to build retirement homes in natal countries), many of these women, too many in the eyes of indigenous male authorities, returned annually bearing lavish gifts for family members, and even with enough money to afford their siblings and offspring an education they had never had, buy plots of land, and build houses; that is, to acquire the trappings of authority and the success of upward mobility in a context in which customs and laws prohibited women from inheriting or owning clan land. Again as in other parts of the continent facing the same shifts in the structures of family power, widows and divorced women made destitute by such customs, with little option but prostitution in the absence of yet another husband and male "protector," could through such means over-turn established order.

Finally, there were specific localized constraints; this petition was written after a protracted two-year smear campaign against Bahaya women by the male council of chiefs who charged that the women were harming the good name of the community. To frustrate the literal mobility which enabled the symbolic one, in the late 1940s the authorities had brought measures prohibiting their movement, including prohibiting them from leaving the district, and from using the major means of transportation, the steamer across Lake Victoria. Women who tried to resist were frequently abused. These measures were initially supported by the local district commissioners. However, the women organized, and mobilized regionally, hiring lawyers to defend their rights, and eventually, in 1950, sending this petition. They were ultimately successful. The Provincial Commissioner eventually agreed with them, and had the orders against them rescinded in 1951.

It is important to acknowledge the clear-sighted way in which they marshal their arguments. They are resisting several sets of legal structures; indigenous laws that discriminate against them as single women and a civic set up in the context of a global economy that has exacerbated the patriarchal structures which disposes them. At the same time their strategy is important because they appeal to those very colonial authorities on the basis of the abolition of slavery, a move which has given rise to a new human rights ethic that those colonial authorities are supposed to represent. In claiming their right to mobility they challenge the economic order that constrained them and assert their right to acquire wealth. That is to say, the money from their sex work enables them to have access to real estate hitherto denied them. They have empowered themselves to reenter their communities as property owners, and resist the laws by which the male authorities are trying to frustrate them, on two counts, one "traditional" and the other in the new possibilities for economic transformation.

This possibility for economic transformation is always a two edged sword. Ama Ata Aidoo in her story "In the Cutting of a Drink" from her collection *No Sweetness Here* (published in the 1960's but referring back to the same period of the1950s as the Tanzanian letter) highlights through the very structure of the story the importance to, and of, family in the face of such powerful social change. The story integrates into its very form a traditional way of reporting back to the elders. The speaker, a young man who has clearly been sent to the capitol city in search of a disappeared sister, has returned and we hear him in the process of giving his report. The structure of the text is under-girded by the formal structures which order communal speaking and assume a kinship unit concerned about the welfare of all its members, as audience. Aidoo brilliantly shapes the story of the form used for the kind of consultation that requires collective reporting and decision-making. In this instance what is cleverly done is the way she indicates the difficulty of the news being broken, that the missing kinswoman has become a prostitute without ever using the painful word itself. This story not only reflects the tension shown in the Tanzanian letter between city life and country life, but through the use of the emotively haunting phrase "any kind of work is work" also highlights the way access to a cash economy makes the resultant mobility hard for their communities to negotiate at critical moments.

Purple Hibiscus

> *We have to reflect on the distinction between physical, structural and symbolic violence as well as consider the interconnection and relations among them. Recent developments underscore the importance of addressing these issues from a feminist perspective.*
>
> (Potts and Wenk 2002: 460)

There is much that can be said about Adichie's novel *Purple Hibiscus* which brings our illustrations to the present day, but I will focus only on the two central issues about which we are concerned, "family structures" and "globalization," for which it is admirably suited as it is a novel set in very contemporary context, taking on the issues of modernity in the globalized world of today, looking at those issues squarely in the context of gender and the family. The brilliance of the novel is the way Adichie negotiates both literal and symbolic readings of the state of the household and its relationship, ideologically, with the state of the nation. In doing this she has dramatized a central concern of many feminists, "for the need for women in Africa and beyond to speak against the way in which human security concerns are currently being equated with the security of states and corporations, at the expense of the security of individuals" (Kerr and Sweetman 2003: 8).

Adichie's masterstroke is the way in which she splits the public and the private, in order to underscore the untenability of the world order which relies on such a split. That is to say, the public face of the powerful father who rules the household is so exemplary, even the character most critical of the status quo, the narrator's cousin Amaka, says of him "Uncle Eugene is not a bad man really." The novel is set in the Nigeria of a repressive political regime with the patriarch of the family representing everything supposedly good about western liberal democracy and capitalist possibility. He is a manufacturer, owning and running a company which processes food and makes soft drinks; he owns and bank rolls the only progressive newspaper in the country, radically opposed to military rule; he is a staunch supporter of democratic ideals, who has amassed great wealth which he uses generously to supports a large community of people, in addition to his nuclear family; he is a devout Catholic who really does help widows and the poor, and bail people out of jail.

It is only in private, in the confines of the house, that we see his unacceptable dark side; he is a man, violently abusive in the domestic context—both psychologically and physically, in a clinically text book fashion:

> Efforts aimed at the control of wives may be carried out through a mix of obvious and more subtle violence. Control can be enforced through direct as well as insidious means. What is commonly referred to as wife battery may include isolation, arbitrary and unpredictable punishments, and intermittent rewards. Perhaps most startling, it often includes alternating periods of active and passive brutality with periods of kindness. These acts of kindness serve to exhaust endurance and manipulate dependency. The most insidious forms of violence do not involve overt brutality but psychological cruelty that results in anguish and disintegration of the self (Green 1999: 26).

His wife and children live in terror and constant fear. And the mother is indeed virtually confined to the household:

> The confinement of women to the economically dependent role of housewife is a condition that has made it difficult for many women to leave otherwise unbearable violent situations. In other words, the domestication of

women is a precondition for the crime we define as domestic violence. Similarly, the power to coerce, intimidate, and harass that is wielded by officials and men in uniform in dictatorial societies is a condition for the widespread rape and abuse of women that occur under repressive regimes, since this power is sanctioned by military, religious, or other male-dominated authorities (Mama 1996: 52).

He controls the children's every hour, to the last minute, planning out not only when they should do their homework, but even their recreational times during term, as well as during the vacations, until they fear their very thoughts and every action. In particular Kambili, the stammering daughter who struggles to find her voice, speak clear, and learn to laugh, monitors herself to be always approved of her father "failing" frequently in ways which convince of the rightness of his autocracy. Domestic violence is presented as the necessary discipline of love and care. While championing democracy in the state the father creates a society composed of satellites of dependent individuals in the home. The household structure thus reminds us of the unwilling sacrifice women have made to make to create the noble "universal" ideals the father's public life represents. The price of being "appropriate victims" of violence, of reinforcing gender roles and relations remains very high (Green 1999: 23).

The parents—father and mother—represent the ideal type of the impact of the long process of globalization on the family, without ever degenerating into stereotypes. The mother is the very emblem of woman that colonial enterprise and education wanted to create; she is schooled enough herself to values and appreciates education, and to be supportive of her husband, but is herself confined to the domestic an ideal housewife supposedly in charge of the operations of the house (Gadzekpo 2001). She is perfectly dutiful and completely concentrated on the needs of her husband, ceding authority over every aspect of her life to that husband. Her interactions are only with the children and "that girl," Sisi the maid. She exemplifies perfect refinement in confinement and domesticity, handling the planning of the meals, the setting of the table, and the color of the curtains.

The mother is deftly symbolized by a glass étagère with "finger-sized ceramic figurines of ballet dancers in various contorted postures" (7) which she polishes often. In what has been called "the Politics of Disengagement" (Green 1999) this polishing is a survival strategy, a ritual she creates to protect herself. We learn to piece together, the way she pieces together the pieces when they break, that she polishes the étagère and its contents after each time she has been violently beaten. This family is the perfect representation of the split between the public male and the private female --except for the fact that it is the husband who defines the limits of that private.

Structurally and ideologically speaking the household which provides the counter narrative in the novel is that of Aunty Ifeoma, the father's sister, from whose garden they receive the flourishing experimental hybrid "purple hibiscus" of the title. Aunty Ifeoma is a widowed university professor, with free spirits and the same politically democratic ideals as her brother, but her house is a very different space. In the contrasting households of the brother and sister we see the upper end and the struggling end of the current Nigerian middle class. Though the sister has a roof over her head, she lives on campus in an environment where electricity and water are in short and intermittent supply. She seldom has enough gas, either for her car or her cooker, and while her brother's family has meat, and in abundance, for her children, chicken cut into small finger sized pieces, is for special occasions. She faces deprivation but not destitution, the condition of so many African universities in the late twentieth century, but there is laughter in her household.

It is also in Aunty Ifeoma's household that we are made to take stock of the materiality of contemporary manifestations of globalization. That is to say, luxury is normative in the father's Enugu household. It is the absence of those luxuries in Aunty Ifeoma's Nsukka household which bring into sharp relief the burden of desire. The one element critics agree on about globalization in its current manifestations is the volume and rapidity of exchange in the circulation of material goods, including monetary transfers. It is in Aunty Ifeoma's household that we see material goods from soft drinks to satellite television as the underpinning of globalized desire. These references also make clear, despite the homogenization of those desires, that desire is still uni-directional in ways that validate the hegemony of "the West" and the assumed desirability of gross material circulation (Mazrui 2001). These desires exist even in the presence of a character like Amaka, who fiercely astute about and resistant to the legacy cultural legacy of colonialism, fails to investigate the ideological underpinnings of the price of access to CNN and stereophonic sound (Maloba 2007).

It must be stated however, that the split is not quite so neat; this is not a novel built on binaries. There is a third shared space which makes clear how complex the issue of family structure is in a contemporary context. It is almost a cliché to state it, but to the extent it remains true, it remains crucial to remember the radically different meanings the words "family structures" can have, both within Africa, and above all when speaking in comparative contexts in which African experiences are being viewed alongside practices elsewhere, "the West" in particular. Although there are many variations on the identification of family, there is almost universal agreement that to most Africans, and even, some of us would argue, peoples of African descent, the notion of family is not nuclear, but based on some form of organization of kinship group made up of several generations of the living, and frequently embracing, to this day, the ancestors and the yet to be born. Marriage is a union of two such sets of kin, and households, even when in practice comprised in contemporary urban spaces of a nuclear family, are seldom conceptualized as autonomous units independent of kin.

However we must acknowledge the tension today between the idea of family as nuclear and the idea of family as kin, in particular when placed in the context of current economic forces. Much work has been done by scholars looking at these competing strains, as for instance, when adjudicating the estate of propertied men; who inherits, the wife and children or the natal family (Cohen and Odhiambo 1992; Appiah 1992)? These are not easy questions, so in considering the impact of globalization on family structures in Africa, it is vital to acknowledge that the late twentieth century formulation of globalization is impacting an Africa in which family structures have already been influenced and put under strain by the layering of colonial systems over indigenous structures (Kuenyehia 1998; Dowuona-Hammond 1998).

The idea of family as nuclear and the idea of family as kin both coalesce and fracture in the compound of their house in Abba, the father and Auntie Ifeoma's natal home. The father's notion of himself in his larger world is very real traditional, and very patriarchal. We see this in the ways people respond to him; the scenes in his home during festival time dramatize the regard in which he is held, and the responsibilities that come with that regard. He is "the big man" and he seems to have few equals—in one glaring indication that things are definitely changing—even the traditional rulers pick themselves up and come to him.

His community is dependent on his beneficence and largess indicated in ways that are orchestrated around conventional forms of address and exchange, with one glaring exception—his relationship with his father.

The father's unbending fundamentalist Catholicism makes him declare a prohibition on intercourse with his own father who has remained "a traditionalist" true to his own native ways of worship. The children are allowed only once, on arrival, to go to the old man to greet him, and that for not more than fifteen minutes. They are interdicted from eating food prepared by "pagans" and are not even allowed to drink store bought 'fanta' in their grandfather's house. Any infractions of these injunctions are met with terrifying disapproval and physical violence. This behavior brings censure, articulated through the old men of his father's age group and is another signal that reminds us where the tensions lie between form and essence, an index to the limitations of the father's spirit in sharp contrast to that of his pocket.

It is in Aunty Ifeoma's presence whether in her home or her car that restitution between the generations can begin to be made. She with her slender means offers an inclusive spiritual largess that her brother's affluence fails to provide. In her presence the children learn to embrace both a joyful Catholicism allowed to express itself through vernacular song, and an appreciation of cultural rites, whether private, as performed by the grandfather each morning, or collective, in the communal festivals and masquerades. Under the shelter of her roof the three generations begin to share a communion that empowers the children to begin to question their father's vision of his world.

It is the disastrous consequences of this questioning, particularly on the part of Jaja the elder brother, that frames the telling of the story which opens with the words "Things started to fall apart at home when my brother Jaja, did not go to communion and Papa flung his heavy missal across the room and broke the figurines on the étagère" (3). The story is then told in retrospect, going back through the previous year. By the time we return to this moment after Church on Palm Sunday, we understand why "things fall apart." The "holy week" that is ushered in by this Palm Sunday is ushering in a terrible liberation; the father dies.

The father dies at the slow hand of the mother, and her choice of weapon is pertinent, for true to herself, she chooses a passive one; small sips of poison. It is also important that the choice of the slow poison resorts indigenous ways of knowledge: "I started putting the poison in his tea before I came to Nsukka. Sisi got it for me; her uncle is a powerful witch doctor"; indigenous knowledge acquired through the seemingly obeisant household maid whose name the father never learned, becomes the silent source of insurrectionary resistance and action.

The death of the father is not a celebration of indigeneity and romanticized poverty. Neither do we have an unequivocal endorsement of the trappings that wealth brings. The novel serves as a critique on the uses of wealth and power, and the need for a transformation in society for the just uses of both wealth and power. I want to argue that the death of the father is indicative and symbolic; a declaration of the need for a change in attitudes towards gender, gender practices, and agency, if the promises of progress that are said to support liberal democratic processes are really to work and flourish. And they must flourish in the household if they are to be upheld in the state otherwise, as here, the disorder in the household is replicated by the disorder in the state; and the role of the father in the house becomes representative of the role of the leader in the state.

The changes the father is striving for cannot come about unless he too changes. Adichie reminds of the inadequacy, or insufficiency of gender analysis when thinking of processes of liberalization and the global economy. Whether or not they had access to the goods of that economy, women's lives in Africa have always negotiated the impact of being a part of that economy; at one point they *were* the goods being traded before they started being producers of goods for a market which they continue to have limited real access to. We can no longer afford further intellectual "African Burial Grounds." Adichie's work, and the voices of the women who have spoken through the centuries before her, remind us of the ways in which such gendered revaluations must also be inclusive of the strategies and world views, the knowledge of women whose bodies have been on the frontlines of the globalizing economics of the making of the modern world since that modern world first began to take shape. Or, to paraphrase Kambili's words: "[Their] defiance seems to me like Aunty Ifeoma's experimental purple hibiscus: rare, fragrant, with undertones of freedom, a different kind of freedom... a freedom to be, to do (16)."

Notes

1. For a collection of important, provocative essays raising full discussions on the authority of African women and African women's work, see Oyěwùmúmí, Oyèrónké 2003, and Davies and Ogundipe-Leslie 1995.

2. The inscription on the title page of my personal copy of *Moving Beyond Boundaries*, given me by the editor, my friend Carole Boyce Davies.

3. Though all the poems cited in this paper appear in Volume 2 of *Women Writing Africa*, the versions here are my own.

References

Adeleye-Fayemi, Bisi. 2000. Creating and Sustaining Feminist Space in Africa: Local-Global Challenges in the 21st Century. Paper presented at the Ontario Institute for Studies in Education by the Dame Nita Barrow Distinguished Visitor Lecture, November 30, at the University of Toronto, in Toronto Ontario.

Adichie, Chimamanda Ngozi. 2003. *Purple Hibiscus*. Chapel Hill: Algonquin Books.

Appiah, Kwame Anthony. 1992. *In My Father's House*. Oxford and New York: Oxford University Press.

Blakey, Michael L. 2001. The Study of New York's African Burial Ground: Biocultural and Engaged. In *African Roots/American Cultures*, ed. Sheila Walker, 222-231. Laham: Rowman & Littlefield.

Busia, Abena P. A. 2006. What Is Africa to Me?: Knowledge Possession, Knowledge Production, and the Health of Our Bodies Politic in Africa and the Africa Diaspora. *African Studies Review* 49(1): 15-30.

_____. 1986. Miscegenation as Metonymy: Sexuality and Power in the Colonial Novel. *The Journal of Ethnic and Racial Studies* 9(3).

Cohen, David William, and E. S. Atieno Odhiambo. 1992. *Burying SM: The Politics of Knowledge and the Sociology of Power in Africa*. Portsmouth: Heinemann.

Davies, Carol Boyce, and 'Molara Ogundipe-Leslie, ed. 1995. *Moving Beyond Boundaries: International Dimensions of Black Women's Writing*. New York: New York University Press.

Daymond, M. J., and Dorothy Driver. 2003. *Women Writing Africa, vol. 1: Southern Region*. New York: Feminist Press.

Dodson, Howard. 2001. The Trans-Atlantic Slave Trade and the Making of the Modern World. In *African Roots / American Cultures*, ed. Sheila Walker, 118-122. Laham: Rowman & Littlefield.

Dowuona-Hammond, Christine. 1998. Women and Inheritance in Ghana. In *Women and Law in West Africa*, ed. Akua Kuenyehia, 132-168. Ghana: WLWA.

Gadzekpo, Audrey. 2001. Gender Discourses and Representational Practices in Gold Coast Newspapers. *Jenda: A Journal of Culture and African Women's Studies* 1(2). http://www.jendajournal.com/jendavol1.2/gadzekpo.html.

Green, December. 1999. *Gender Violence in Africa*. New York: St. Martin's Press.

Harris, Joseph. 2001. The African Diaspora in World History and Politics. In *African Roots / American Cultures*, ed. Sheila Walker, 104-117. Laham: Rowman & Littlefield.

Inikori, Joseph E. 2001. Africans and Economic Development in the Atlantic World, 1500-1870. In *African Roots / American Cultures*, ed. Sheila Walker, 123-138. Laham: Rowman & Littlefield.

Kerr, Joanna and Caroline Sweetman. 2003. Editorial. *Gender and Development* 11(1): 3-14.

Kuenyehia, Akua. 1998. Family Law in Ghana and its Implications for Women. In *Women and Law in West Africa*, ed. Akua Kueyehia, 23-61. Ghana: WLWA.

Lihamba, Amandina, and Fulata Moyo. 2007. *Women Writing Africa, vol. 3: Eastern Region*. New York: Feminist Press.

Maloba, W. O. 2007. *African Women in Revolution*. Trenton: Africa World Press.

Mama, Amina. 1996. Sheores and Villains: Conceptualizing Colonial and Contemporary Violence Against Women in Africa. In *Feminist Genealogies, Colonial Legacies, Democratic Futures*, ed. Janqui M. Alexander and Chandra T. Mohanty, 46-62. New York and London: Routledge.

Mazrui, Ali. 2001. Pretender to Universalism: Western Culture in a Globalizing Age. In *Unpacking Europe: Towards a Critical Reading*, ed. Salah Hassan and Iftikhar Dadi, 96-111. Rotterdam: Museum Boijmans Van Beuningen.

Nwanyeruwa, Testimony Before The Commission Of Inquiry, *Report of the Aba Commission of Inquiry* Lagos, Nigeria, 1930, pp. 24-26.

Nzegwu, Nkiru. 2003. Gender Imperialism in Academia. In *African Women and Feminism*, ed. Oyeronke Oyewumi, 99-158. Trenton: Africa World Press.

Oyĕwumùmí, Oyèrónké, ed. 2005. *African Gender Studies: A Reader*. New York: Palgrave Macmillan.

———. 2003. *African Women and Feminism*. Trenton: Africa World Press.

Potts, Lydia, and Silke Wenk. 2002. Gender Constructions and Violence-Ambivalences of Modernity in the Process of Globalization: Towards an Interdisciplinary and International Research Network. *Signs: Journal of Women in Culture and Society* 28(1): 459-461.

Randriamaro, Zo. 2008. African Women Challenging Neo-Liberal Economic Orthodoxy. AWID Publications. http://awid.org/publications/gen_dev/randriamaro.pdf.

St. Clair, William. 2006. *Grand Slave Emporium: Cape Coast Castle and the British Slave Trade*. London: Profile Books.

Sow, Fatou. 2008. Fundamentalisms, Globalization, and Women's Human Rights in Senegal. AWID Publications. http://awid.org/publications/gen_dev/sow.pdf.

Sutherland-Addy, Esi. 1998. Women and the Verbal Arts in the Oguaa-Edina Traditional Area. *Institute of African Studies Research Review* 14(1).

———, and Aminata Diaw. 2005. *Women Writing Africa, vol. 2: West Africa and the Sahel*. New York: Feminist Press.

Walker, Sheila, ed. 2001. *African Roots / American Cultures*. Laham: Rowman & Littlefield.

Walker, Sheila, ed. 2001. Everyday Africa in New Jersey: Wonderings and Wanderings in the African Diaspora. In *African Roots / American Cultures*, ed. Sheila Walker, 45-80. Laham: Rowman & Littlefield.

Chapter 8

AFRICAN MASCULINITIES, RELATIONSHIPS, AND SEXUALITIES

Victor Seidler

When deeply rooted, one is prepared for every opening; or, as Aime Cesaire expresses it, 'Porous to all the breathings of the world'.

– Joseph Ki-Zerbo

LEARNINGS

Within an increasingly globalized world it can be difficult to listen and to learn from different cultural histories and traditions and the kind of intellectual and emotional challenges that they offer. European modernities have helped to shape colonial relationships of domination between the West and Africa that still echo in the present where we see Africa as a space of poverty, hardship and the scourge of AIDS on the global media. The West has long assumed that it has everything to teach and little to learn because it alone could take reason, science and modernity for granted. Supposedly it was only through accepting subordination to colonial powers that Africa would be able to make a transition from nature to culture, from tradition to modernity. Often colonial power was framed as the 'white man's burden' and legitimated as a civilizing mission as if Africa did not have its own rituals, traditions, histories and cultures. Rather Africa became known through an anthropological gaze as an object of anthropological researches into the 'primitive' and un/civilized. It was partly through the work of Christian missionaries that the civilizing mission would be achieved and people would learn shame in relation to their bodies.[1]

Within a postcolonial world after years of struggles for independence against colonial rule often people are wary of recalling how histories of colonial oppression still work to shape the present. Aware that a focus upon the past can feel like an attempt to erase responsibilities that African states have for what is happening in the present, it can be difficult to find a balance between the injustices of the past and the inequalities, corruptions and injustices in the present. We need to be careful about how development discourses in the present inherit and sustain certain assumptions about the superiority of the West as providing a universal model of modernity that others will want to emulate as they eventually make a transition from tradition towards modernity. There are different paths towards development and African countries will have to find their own way as they negotiate terms with NGOs and Aid agencies to produce more just international terms of trade. As we are forced to rethink global priorities in the face of global warming and so have to learn to live with a different relationship with nature so that West has to be ready to rethink its own philosophical assumptions and the readiness with which it identified progress with the control and domination of nature. We need a new ecological philosophy and social theory that will help sustain a respect for nature while appreciating the need for a different vision of global justice. Talking back to the West, Cheikh Hamidou Kane recognizes:

> Evidence is a quality of the surface. Your science is the triumph of evidence, a proliferation of the surface. It makes you master of the external, but at the same time it exiles you there, more and more.

This sentiment is echoed in the wisdom offered by Alassane Ndaw:

> To know something is to be in union with it, to be within
> it, to approach it internally. Remaining on the outside, you
> can never know something in its essence. To know things,
> you have not to dissect them but rather to link them with
> something else.[2]

Often we learn from those we are close too which is why the family in its diverse forms remains such a vital institution within a globalised world. Charles, a young university educated father from northern Uganda was interviewed for the project 'Young Men and the Construction of Masculinity in Sub-Saharan Africa' by Gary Barker and Christine Ricardo and described his interactions with his wife, saying he believes it is important for her to work, although he admits their relationship would be strained if she was working and he was not. He said he did not believe in violence against women and also did not plan to take a second wife though this was encouraged within his culture. As he explains, "Actually, I plan to inherit my father's experience, actually, my father's behavior. He didn't beat my mother. And I do not want ever to beat my wife. We can settle the differences between us, within the two of us. And that's the way my father was handling my mom. If they quarreled, he would keep quiet, wait, and...they would settle their difference. He has really been a role model for me as far as relationship is concerned. And he had only one wife. For me, I will not have more than one wife." Through the positive example of his father, Charles was able to reflect on the value and importance of not using violence against women (p.52).[3]

In a focus group discussion with Christian and Muslim young men, all enrolled in secondary school in Kaduna, Nigeria, the prevailing discourse was that girls and women were not equal to men and that men should work while women should care for the home and children. Most of the young questioned the importance of education for girls arguing that it might only be useful because "educated mothers can educate sons better," as one said (p.52). However, one Muslim young man disagreed. He said that girls and women were equal and deserved equal education. In a subsequent individual interview Ali said he had seen in his family how women's education is important. A female cousin had a PHD. He also described how his father had used violence against his mother, but was challenged by male friends and colleagues and so changed his behavior. All these things, Ali said, had led him to change his views on girls and women. These positive experiences with his own family had provided him with opportunities to reflect upon the workings of gender roles.[4]

A diversity of projects in different parts of Africa had shown the importance of both learning in the families and in the wider networks within which they could interact with peers who were committed to gender equality. This suggests the importance both of self-reflection and also the need to create 'safe spaces' in which young men can try new behaviors without being ridiculed, as is often the case, in their male peer groups. Some young fathers have been encouraged to change their behaviors, in terms of caring for their own health, practicing safer sex and supporting their partners because of the high value they place on their children. This is to draw upon traditional beliefs in diverse cultures about the responsibilities of fathering. In South Africa, one program engaged low-income, urban based youth in an updated, traditional initiation program 'in the bush' in which elder men taught values of responsibility, non-violence, sexual restrain and respect for elders. This was in sharp contrast to the sexually violent versions of manhood prominent in townships. As Wood and Jewkes reported, in the long-run some of these young men revert to the masculinities their peers adhere too. But in different contexts the family has been key in helping keeping sons out of ongoing sectarian violence.[5]

CHANGING GENDER ECONOMIES

In their final reflections on pathways to change, Gary Barker and Christine Ricardo recognize:

> Change is happening, and it is happening even without program and policy initiatives to promote it. The educational attainment of girls and women, which has increased in the region, is clearly changing gender norms. Changes in economies mean that the economic advantages of men compared to women have eroded in some settings. Young men interviewed in diverse settings in Nigeria, South Africa and Uganda confirm the importance of young women's education and women's income and perceive that these are good for families. Some men and boys are changing how they view women. Nonetheless, this change goes hand in

hand with traditional gender hierarchies. Young men accept change, but also hang on to traditional views. (p.54)

We need to explore some of the issues that this raises about how we understand change while recognizing, as Barker and Ricardo acknowledge: "To be sure, some program initiatives and research on HIV/AIDS is prescriptive and represent outside-in approaches in which foreigners are attempting to change African men and cast them in a negative light. Some of these efforts have only generated defensiveness (p.54)."

But 'defensiveness' can often be justified if these agencies draw upon Anglophone models that are often implicitly taken for granted within the universalism of social-scientific methodologies. Not only are these methodologies often presented as 'objective' and 'neutral,' but they are often blind to the assumptions they make about the processes of change. While we might agree with their conclusion that "The challenge to promote changes in gender norms is to tap into the voices of change and pathways to change that exist in the context of Africa," we need to be careful how this is to be interpreted and the kind of assumptions that inform their own study when they talk the processes "to change gender norms." We need to be able to listen to what African men are saying about their own priorities and values and their own images of change. This means questioning the cultural individualism that are so often assumed within research models and the deafness that they can produce about the importance of familial relationships and responsibilities. Identities are shaped through a sense of responsibilities to others so that people belong to their families but also to their ancestral connections. Even if these are breaking down in urban areas we need to grasp the processes of urbanization and ways that help produce complex loyalties and affiliations.[6]

VOICES

'Though you know not whither you are bound, may you know whence you came.'

Serere oral tradition.

'Listen to the ancestors, to spirit, to the trees, to the animals. Listen to all those forces that come and speak to us.'

Sobonfu Some

'Every time you speak from the heart, invoking or telling a
being from the other world that something is going on in
this world, you are in ritual.'

Sobonfu Some.

'Every birth is the rebirth of an ancestor.'

African oral tradition.

Often it can be difficult for men to share themselves, especially
if they are concerned to present themselves in ways that will bring
honor to themselves and their families. A man who has grown up in
Burkina Faso shared that he will rarely talk personally or emotionally
with people from his own generation. These are conversations that
he will only have with men in an older generation. He acknowledges
the difficulties that he has in sharing himself more personally, recognizing how he has grown up not to think of himself individually as
Western psychologies so often assume, but through the position and
responsibilities he has within his family and the wider community.
Working within the terms of international organizations, he has learnt
to present himself through the values of his organization, through its
institutional rhetoric. He knows that people expect him to be positive
and clear about his goals and he has learnt to identify with the organizational mission. He finds it hard to reveal himself more personally.
He exists as a son, as a brother and as a man with the responsibilities
towards others that define his position.

But as he feels more trust and can relax in a men's group he begins
to appreciate how he has held a very idealized image of his childhood
as a way of blocking and holding in check some of the pain and hurt
he carries in his relationship with his father. He feels obliged to show
respect that is owed to a father by his son and this makes it difficult for
him to recall disturbing and threatening memories of having been hit
by his father. For years, he recognizes, these memories had been suppressed because he felt they reflected a lack of respect that was owed to
his father. He wanted to forget these memories that he thought about
as 'bad' or 'negative' since they seemed to reflect badly on his own
character suggesting that he was not a 'good' son because a good son is
one who respects his father. But at the same time his refusal to feel the
violence he suffered at his father's hand 'holds him' into a particular
position with his father where he is still seeking his father's valida-

tion. He constantly feels that he has to achieve more and that he is not 'doing enough' to make his father proud of him. This shapes a particular emotional economy between fathers and sons. This can make a transition from boyhood to manhood more difficult because you can feel locked into needing a father's approval. It can make it harder to shape a separation if you have felt obliged to suppress feelings you had when you were young.[7]

INTERGENERATIONAL TENSIONS

Historically, diverse tribal societies have been organized around the authority and manhood of the chiefs. References to the 'big man' and to community and tribal hierarchies often leave young men waiting to become men. In parts of Namibia for example, as Linday and Miescher argue, "...male power was equated with men who had their own livestock, houses, wives, and juvenile dependents—men who were 'senior' and who performed the social role of 'fathers.' Such power was reproduced through their ability to determine the criteria and candidates for becoming 'real men' by getting married and setting up their own households (p. 10)."[8]

But this is where colonial histories also make themselves felt. Colonialism undermined and often upset some of the traditional big men, or created new big men backed by colonial powers. Europeans used their colonial power to construct African masculinities in relation to notions of European manhood. For example, historically the term 'boy' has meant maleness, but also social immaturity and inferiority before adult men, particularly white men. European colonial powers framed their own distinctions between 'boy' and 'man' so shaping a radicalized hierarchy of masculinities that the European colonizers sought to control for their own purposes. As Lindsay and Miescher argue in their introduction to their edited *Men and Masculinities in Modern Africa* the word 'boy' was used as an insult by European men towards African men but also by African elders to keep the younger generation of men "in their place" (p.5). The discourse around masculinities became encoded in European colonial relations of power which served to question and undermine the masculinities of the colonizers. This has also meant the reshaping of masculinities that played a critical role in wars of independence against colonial power and remain issues within post-colonial states where it has often been difficult to question traditional masculinities. Through acknowledging the influence of unspoken histories and the traumatic effect of colonial pasts we can begin to listen to silences in the present.

Older men, whether as fathers, chiefs or elders, determine when young men can own land, have access to family goods or wealth and marry. The institutionalized stratification of age groups puts younger men at the service of elders. The control of property and women by older men creates a structural conflict between younger and older generations of men. In much of Africa, adolescent women often marry older men in part because they have the resources to pay bride wealth or bride-price. This intergenerational tension manifests itself in different ways in contemporary Africa. In South Africa, according to Carton in 'Locusts fall from the Sky: Manhood and Migrants in Kwazulu' there have been conflicts between rural-based older men who think these urban-based young men who have migrated to cities for work are not respectful of traditional customs and hierarchies. These migrant workers send income to their families, thereby maintaining a status as men even if not physically present. Migration to cities and modernization has become a way for young men to challenge and usurp the power of elders. Migration to cities, in other words, has become part of a new rite of passage. By moving to the city, young men escape rural power hierarchies and can earn money that allows some independence and access to women.[9]

In the case of Nigeria, young men interviewed in Kaduna showed anger towards Al-Hajis, Islamic men who had made the pilgrimage to Mecca and thus had some money and other men who had wealth:

> Ali: "In our communities, there is plenty of work for us.... they exploit us and want us to do the hard work (like lifting and building things).
> Khaled: "We become men when we think about being on our own. It depends upon when you get a lot of money to be free. Then you can do what you want.
> Muhamed: "Nobody will help us if we do not look for work and money. The government doesn't care about us... and helping us find work. We have to care for ourselves. The elites only look out for their own children.

In some parts of Nigeria men up to the age of 40 are considered to be youth since they are not married. One man who was 39 when he finally acquired a civil service job, a job for which he said he had to pay a bribe and years of itinerant work to acquire, expressed rage at older men for the challenges he faced in acquiring employment:

> The leaders (referring to older men) are the ones who make the Muslims and Christians go to the streets and loot houses and shops. They are the ones behind it. They should know that as soon as we have the chance, we will kill them all (says this with visible anger on his face). (p.13)

INITIATIONS

A common factor in the initiations that serve as rites of passage is the reinforcement of a clear separation between boys and men, between men and women. In many settings, there are expectations that boys must be separated from their mothers—that is from the female confines and spaces. Boys are often taken to live in a special compound for boys when they reach puberty and as they prepare for ritual initiations. Boys learn to live together and support each other as they listen to older men sharing their experiences of manhood. There are rituals of abandoning boyhood and assuming the responsibilities of adult manhood. These initiation rituals are often seen as central to personal development. Some of the rites involve a cathartic moment of being out of control, or drunk or under the control of evil spirits before achieving a defined adult identity as a man.[10]

Manhood is something that is not fully achieved through initiation and young men in diverse social settings frequently report a sense of being observed and watched to see if they measure up to culturally framed visions of manhood. Through jokes, social ridicule and insinuation young men are made aware of what society expects of them as men. Young men often receive multiple and conflicting ideas about what it means to be 'man enough.' Though there is research on land use and work there is much less research on men as fathers and partners and traditional gender analysis has often focused exclusively on condemning men's behavior, emphasizing accounts of men's alcohol use and violence against women and children. Often there is a failure to probe for underlying factors that lead men towards such behaviors or to explore tensions between men and prevailing cultural masculinities. This is partly because of the limits of role theory within gender analysis or the assumption that masculinities can be defined exclusively as relationships of power within traditions of hegemonic masculinity. This tends to set the discussion of masculinities within Western Anglophone traditions that are set within universal terms that fail to fully appreciate, as I argue in *Transforming Masculinities: Men, Cultures, Bodies, Power, Sex, and Love,* the significance of cultural masculinities. Rather than reproduce assumptions drawn from modernization theory that assume that post-colonial societies will follow in the Northern path towards freedom and progress, we need to engage with the diversity of African cultural traditions and the particular tensions it can produce for more equal gender relations within the family and larger society.

Doudou Diene, Director of Intercultural Dialogue, UNESCO, reminds us of the African proverb "In the forest, when the branches quarrel, the roots embrace" as a plea for "a return to the sources that feed, invigorate, unite and give sense to the world's diversity." At the same time he recognizes "The prevailing clamor would have us hear only the siren voices that speak the language of power, the end of history, materialism, and the struggle for domination. These are the criteria by which Africa tends to be viewed and described. But as Africa's venerable sages observed of the colonial visitor, "The white man (the European) see only what he already knows."[11]

Sobonfu Some reminds us "The family in Africa is always extended. You never refer to your cousin as 'cousin,' because that would be an insult. So your cousins are your sisters and brothers. Your nieces are your children. Your uncles are your fathers. Your aunts are your mothers. Children are also encouraged to call other people outside the family mothers and fathers, sisters and brothers." This helps to understand the inadequacy of importing distinctions between the 'nuclear' and 'extended' families as they have been framed to illuminate changes in family relationships within Western societies. Rather we need to recognize how identities are framed through relationships of responsibility to the group so that you exist 'as an individual' through your obligations to the group. As Seydou Badian expresses it, "The group is the reality, the sovereign good, the refuge, the citadel without which the individual would be at risk. Man moves, evolves, actualizes himself within the group. Absolute refusal—schismatic refusal—is heresy. It fragments the group, undermining and damning the individual: it is a sort of suicide."

We need to grasp a different relational and emotional logic that recognizes the breaks wrought by urbanization as young people have migrated to the cities to make their lives and the complex loyalties that a younger generation inherits. Sometimes this involves a break with traditional moralities that can create traumatic feelings of unease as people attempt to define themselves within these new environments. At issues are different senses of belonging that often cross the boundaries between nature and culture that have framed Enlightenment modernities. Within the West, secular modernities have been largely shaped around visions of progress as the control and domination of nature. It is through notions of 'possessive individualism' that we often frame questions about the relationship between 'individuals' and 'society' and think about the family as an institution that 'socializes' individuals through 'passing on' the norms and values of the larger society.

But this is already to assume a radical separation between 'nature' and 'culture' whereby within contemporary post-structuralist theories identities are framed through language within the sphere of culture alone. With the disenchantment of nature, as Max Weber explores it, there is a disconnection with living nature and so with any sense of 'spirit' that crosses boundaries between 'nature' and 'culture.' Rather these become discrete realms that are framed through what Caroline Merchant identifies as the 'death of nature' marked through the 17th century Scientific Revolutions. This frames 'the human' in contrast to 'the animal' that has to be disdained and 'the human' is defined through a relationship of superiority to nature. 'Civilization' comes to be identified through the distance that can be established with nature. As modernity is framed through the secularization of a dominant Christian tradition this encodes a disdain for the body that is framed as 'animal' and identified with the 'sins of the flesh.' The projects of European colonization are partly legitimated through missionary activities of the Churches while nature becomes a resource that needs to be exploited. The traditional language of 'spirit' that crossed the boundaries of nature and culture was to be replaced by an internalized notion.[12]

According to Dagara oral tradition "In initiation, one important lesson is learning how to build an intimate connection with spirit, the self, and others, where the question is usually, "How do you build a relationship with yourself, with another, or with spirit, for that matter?" This is a sentiment that is well understood by Sobonfu Some when he warns: "We must try not to educate our children away from the spirit, so that they don't have to work so hard trying to reconnect when they grow up. When they know they already have spirit, then everything else becomes understood. And it makes life easier for them." It can be difficult to understand what is being suggested within the secular materialism of the West that always assumes in its discourses of 'development' that it has everything to teach and little to learn. But possibly an ecological awareness that is developing as a response to the planetary crisis of global warming makes it possibly to listen to the challenges to Western conceptions of 'progress' and 'civilization.' This is not to devalue the advances of Western technologies and global communications but it is to place them in a different context of inter-cultural listening.

Transitions to Manhood

To be able to achieve manhood in diverse African states and cultures often involves some level of financial independence, employment or income and subsequently starting a family. Since bride-price is commonplace, marriage and family formation are therefore tied to having income or access to property. A young man interviewed in Lira in northern Uganda expresses the dilemma so many young men face: "To call oneself a man it is simpler after (one is) married with children. No children and you are still a boy." Barker and Ricardo also quote a study from Nigeria that confirms the importance of marriage in achieving manhood:

> A mature, but unmarried man is viewed with suspicion and often precluded from occupying certain social positions. He is also viewed as irresponsible as perhaps even as a 'homosexual'...In the Eastern zone the consequences of not marrying are very serious for a man. He is forbidden to hold certain titles and in the event of his death, he cannot be buried like a married man. (Social Sciences and Reproductive Health Research Network 2001: 102)

A focus group discussion carried out with out-of-school mostly unemployed young men in Kaduma, Nigeria, confirms an association between work, marriage and manhood:

> Ali: I have proposed to a girl. The problem is there is traditionally a lot involved to get married. It all depends on what I can buy or pay for my wife.
> Adenyi: I can't get married now because I can only get married when I have money. The moment I get money, I will get married. I have a girlfriend and I share money with her. Something might come of it, since I have some money. We might have sex, since I have some money and she loves me. But I do not have enough money to get married. (p.6)

As Barker and Ricardo report "Many of these young men described themselves as being trapped as 'youth.' Because they could not acquire employment, they were not socially recognized as adult men and thus could not get married. Some of the young men in Kaduna (the site of recent clashes between Christian and Muslim youth) said that being employed also brought social recognition beyond their family. Unemployed young men were frequently harassed by military forces or soldiers who were sent to areas where riots had taken place. Thus, having stable work—which might be identified by having a uniform or identity card—was also coveted for the protection it offered. Police and soldiers respect young men with stable employment. In contrast, they expect that 'idle' and unemployed young men will be troublemakers or 'hooligans,' and treat them as such (p.6)."

Townsend in 'Men, Migration and Households in Botswana: An Exploration of Connections over Time and Space' (Journal of Southern African Studies 23(3): 405-420 1997) finds that because of migration in Bostwana men may support two or more households, depending on their age and role in the extended family. They may also be supporting their parents. Men in this setting rarely establish their own households before they are 40. Indeed, the fact that younger, unmarried men have to contribute to their parents' households often delays the formation of their families. The social norm is for young men to care for the livestock of their families. Among ethnic groups that rely upon cattle herding for subsistence, manhood begins when the father bestows land and cattle or other livestock to the son which can either serve as a bride-price, or enable him to achieve the status of manhood and form a family. In this way, achieving manhood often depends on an older man who holds more power deciding when a younger man is able to achieve manhood. Younger men resent this dependency and the power older men have over their lives and status as men.

Relationships between couples can also be stressed if a man does not have secure employment. If a man cannot provide financially for his family he can feel threatened and open to ridicule by his wife. Cornwall in 'To Be a Man is more than a Day's Work: Shifting Ideals of Masculinity in Adodo, Southwestern Nigeria' reports how some young married women keep their possessions in their father's house as a precaution in the case of having an "economically unviable" husband.[13] Accounts from out-of-work men in Tanzania and South Africa suggest that some compensate this feeling of emasculation by taking on outside sexual partners, or drinking. Masculinity is something that men feel they have to continually affirm and it is often open to threat so they can feel vulnerable about it. It is not something that can be taken for granted and if people cannot affirm it through work, they seek other means to affirm it. A young man interviewed in Uganda reports:

> Interviewer: What happens when a man is not working?
> Charles: Life becomes difficult. Because the wife will be asking for you for money and other things.... You don't have food. We don't have salt. You feel like you were better (off) not (having been) born. That is the summary. You were better (off) not being married. (p.7)

Sometimes it is not enough simply to have a job. An adult man interviewed in Nigeria confirmed the importance of having stable employment to be publicly recognized as a man when he said:

> Yusef: Most of all, if you are a civil servant, society will recognize you. If you are a casual worker, they will not recognize you (as a man)....If you are a civil servant, everyone relies on you. Even after you are civil servant, there is pressure, because even more people come to you for help, wanting your money. (p.7)

As Barker and Ricardo point out "These limited examples confirm the importance of work in achieving manhood. This issue is important to highlight precisely because the connection between work and achieving a socially recognized manhood has seldom been examined in economic policies...affirms the need to take into account employment and job creation beyond their instrumental or income-producing purposes. Young men who do not achieve a sense of socially respected manhood seem more likely to engage in violence; they are precisely the young men drawn into ethnic clashes in Nigeria, and in conflicts in Liberia and Sierre Leone, or to gang-related activity in townships in South Africa (p.7-8)."

Most young men affirm that intermittent low-paying employment is not adequate to achieve a socially recognized manhood and to form a family. But as Barker and Ricardo remind us "the informal sector is, for millions of young men in Africa, an intermediate or only survival option; it is a coping mechanism rather than a long-term solution (p.8)." A group of weakly-employed young men in Kaduna, Nigeria, support this conclusion:

> Interviewer: How is finding work for you?
> Halim: When I left school, I was an apprentice (unpaid), and I learned. I was not idle. I found work fast, but it is very difficult and offers meager pay.
> Ali: My father was a painter and used to go with him to his work. When he died, I followed my father's friends (also painters) and on some odd jobs. But I have had not job since 2000. When not working, I do small work, bricklaying, building and digging. Sometimes I have work, other times not.
> Omar: Sometimes I work. When I don't work, I play football. The bad part is, sometimes the police harass us, (Why?) Because we have no work and think we are hooligans. (p.8)

MASCULINITIES

Masculinities in Africa must also be studied in the context of urbanization and changing political and economic regimes within post-colonial states that have struggled for independence and can be divided by ethnic conflicts and competition for state resources. Different masculinities were formed and shaped through these conflicts.

In South Africa there were versions of 'struggle masculinity' that were shaped by constant confrontations with the police and the apartheid-era military that sustained white minority rule. Yet while black men were subordinated to whites within a white racist regime, they still maintained gender privileges over women in the homelands. As Morell has explored in 'Men, Movements and Gender Transformation in South Africa' (The Journal of Men's Studies 10 (3): 309, 2002), "Where black men resisted class and race oppression, they were also simultaneously, defending their masculinity. This often involved efforts to re-establish or perpetuate power over women."

Often young men who have moved to cities in different parts of Africa lose connection with their rural roots and so may feel also distant from the positive forms of social control that was sometimes exercised by clans and elders. But at the same time, cities may expose young men to more gender-equal notions of masculinity or force them to question their own stereotypes as they mix with people from different groups. The expansion of formal education in different countries and the increased enrolment of girls in public education also shifts the terms of gender relations and can encourage men to feel they have to behave differently and question traditional patterns of male behavior. They might also question ideas about other ethnic groups as they live in closer proximity within urban spaces. As Sommers notes: "In Africa and elsewhere, cities force people to mix and become familiar with members of groups whose paths might never cross in rural areas (2003:7)."[14] While cities can sometimes become spaces of ethnic and tribal conflict they can also become spaces "where rival groups come to see each other as 'human,' struggling for the same things—to achieve an education, to find work and to maintain their families (p.14)."

In cities young men can have more opportunities to escape the gaze of people they know and so form sexual experiences that are frequently associated with initiation into manhood. This fosters a perception of sex as performance that is somehow separated from intimacy, specifically as a means to prove masculine prowess. Young men often experience pressure from peers to be sexually active and have multiple partners in order to be seen as men. But often there is a gap between the language that young men will use with their peers and the feelings they might express in intimate relationships. We have to be careful about assuming too clear a distinction between sexual experiences viewed as displays of sexual competence or achievement and as acts of intimacy. We need to draw upon narrative methodologies that allow us to hear different levels of experience and which allow us to establish relationships of trust with young men that enable them to share the contradictory feelings they have. Often men will conceal their insecurities and uncertainties and do their utmost to be convincing in their performative accounts so as not to threaten their male identities. Since emotions are so easily interpreted as signs of weakness, we need to analyze the particular cultural codes that express themselves at different levels of male experience.

The status that a sexually active young man might attain among his peers can be sometimes more important than the intimacy that comes from their sexual relationships. But we need to be careful in the ways we analyze data and question whether research methods that tend to take what people say at face value, need to be reconsidered when researching complex relationships between men and masculinity. We need to consider how social pressures govern young men's sexual behaviors and choices and recognize how patterns of sexual bravado as a means of peer acceptance often works with particular audiences. There can also be a fear of intimacy that helps shape not only the relationships young men can establish with themselves but also the ways they want to appear to others. This helps to make more complex the recognition by Barker and Ricardo "that changing sexual behavior among young men must consider how sexual behavior is linked to the sense of self and desire to achieve a socially recognized version of manhood (p.17)."

M. Silberschmidt in 'Disempowerment of Men in Rural and Urban East Africa: Implications for Male Identity, Sexuality and Sexual Behaviour' (World Development 29 (4): 657-671, 2001) explores how the notion that young men have a right to multiple partners is reinforced in numerous ways. Throughout the region, the tradition of polygamy, he argues, is closely linked to the norm by which masculinity is expressed as sexual conquest and prowess, particularly as represented by fertility. These links have implications for sexual behaviors and choices in relation to number of partners and use of condoms. While the tradition of polygamy tends to place men in a position of power over their wives, in its traditional form it also worked to restrict extra-marital affairs. But in some settings, particularly urban settings, the tradition has become more informally interpreted as a man's right to have as many sexual partners as he wishes. While the tradition has been dismantled by various social and economic factors and limited by law in some countries, it has often mutated into the normative discourse that a man needs more than one partner.

For example, a group of young men in Mbale, Uganda responded to the question of whether it is ok to have many wives and partners by saying:

> Patrick: Depends. For example my father married 10 wives. It depends on income. Some marry because of desire. Others because they have the resources.
> Eddie: 10 or more (wives) in those days. These days because of poverty and sickness just one (wife), real one, and perhaps an additional one.
> Interviewer: Why an additional one?
> Eddie: From time immemorial, the grandparents, they have said you even need two walking sticks. Same with wives. A person with one wife is like a person with one eye. (p.17)

This social sanctioning of multiple partners can be linked to expectations that men should have sexual relations with a number of women by the time he gets married. But as Barker and Ricardo recognize "Although peer and traditional norms frame sexual activity as a defining issue in achieving and maintaining a socially recognized manhood, pre-marital sexual relations are still generally viewed as taboo in many if not most settings in sub-Saharan Africa (p.17)." This explains how young men "face conflicting pressures in terms of sexual behavior." Exploring issues around sex before marriage with university students in Nigeria, Alfred recognizes "The African tradition doesn't support sex before marriage...both of our major religions do not support this... however (all laugh) it depends on the individual to obey or disobey... so you have youths involved (and having sex) and so you have covering it up." Samuel agrees when he says "It is not good (sex before marriage) but all of us are involved (having sex), or the majority of us. They may be some good men among us, but the majority of us are (having sex)." (More laughter). (p. 18).

The laughter is always revealing. It can show the cultural unease of talking about sex and sexuality at the same time as prevailing norms somehow expect young men to be knowledgeable and experienced regarding sexuality and reproductive health issues. Often this means that young men in different cultures can feel obliged to cover up their ignorance and so pretend to know more than they do. They can feel haunted by their own uncertainties in relationship to the working of women's bodies and their own. As Rivers and Aggleton have explored though, young men often have a disproportionate share of the power and voice in intimate relationships with women, young men often have little accurate information and fear admitting their ignorance, which may lead them to engage in unsafe sexual behaviors that put both them and their partners at risk. Tensions can develop between the emotional vulnerabilities that young men feel they have to conceal and the behaviors they are expected to adopt in order to be accepted as masculine in society. While on the surface many young men may feel obliged to perform bravado identities, this may in fact be a compensation for insecurities or doubts about their sexualities. Often young men have misconceptions about what their partners want, which in the context of poor communication, can have serious implications for HIV risk. Young men feel isolated and lonely in their ignorance, unsure of what they have picked up from their peers.[15]

If we are to understand these complex processes of identification and performance we need to develop research methodologies that recognize the different layers of experience and the pressures upon men to present themselves in a particular light to interviewers. We have to be careful how we interpret what young men are saying about themselves and so recognize tensions between language and experience that post-structuralist research traditions often foreclose. Despite the strong social and peer pressures to engage in sexual activities as a way of proving their masculinity, it is often only through relationships of trust built over time with young men that we can learn to question the 'front' they feel obliged to present to learn about the companionship, intimacy and pleasure they are also exploring within their sexual relationships.

Often there is an uneasy tension between how young men feel obliged to speak about their relationship with peers and the vulnerabilities they can allow themselves to express in intimate spaces with their partners. As Barker and Ricardo acknowledge "...most of the research has focused on quantitative indicators of young men's sexual behaviors, including age of sexual debut, number of partners, and frequency of encounters and the links between social norms and pressures and sexual activities. Less is known about the nature of young men's sexual relationships, including types of partners, sexual practices, desires and sexual pleasure (p.19)."

CATEGORIZING

A common practice among young men in Africa and globally is that of categorizing women. These practices are culturally framed and they reveal different conceptions of gender and sexual differences. Young men often reflect views within their families that distinguish between girls they view as suitable for longer-term relationships, including marriage and girls with whom they had short-term sexual relationships. Young women who had sex before marriage either to earn income or because they wanted too, in Nigeria, were often classified as 'harlots.' Gordon's study in Zimbabwean schools, 'Girls cannot think as Boys do: Socialising Children through the Zimbabwean School System' (Gender and Development 62): 53-58, 1998) found that schools reinforced traditional roles while also promoting a discourse of equal rights of girls in education. Teachers along with male students reinforced a discourse that women were sexual instigators and temptresses, while girls described themselves as victims of sexual harassment and violence. It was also widely felt that women should become nurses or be in caring professions while boys and men should be in technical professions. Often young men have been groomed to take their superiority for granted and to reach aggressively and violently or risk being seen as 'un-masculine.' Male teachers often set the tone for how boys treat girls and they often propositioned female students, thus undermining moves towards greater gender-equality in schools. Casting girls and women as 'sexual temptresses' works as a cover, in effect blaming young women for any sexual transgressions that teachers and young men carry out.

Heterosexual masculinities are often constructed in Europe, North America and Latin America through a fear of emotions that are regarded as 'feminine' and so as a sign of weakness and threat to masculine identities. Homophobia is often part of the socialization of boys as they fear being stigmatized as gay when emotional vulnerabilities are experienced as dangerous signs of queer.[16] As Barker and Ricardo note, while homophobia is often used as a way of reinforcing prevailing gender norms and behaviors, "this appears to be somewhat less an issue in Africa in that being a 'real man' is not being not-gay, but more about being not-woman, not-girl, not-child. In some cultural groups in parts of Africa, a culturally recognized concept of same-sex attraction does not exist, is denied or repressed to the extent that the problem is not so much homophobia as it is denial and lack of familiarity with same-sex attraction."(p.21) With the notable exception of South Africa, there is still a widespread denial and stigmatization of homosexuality that is often referred to as 'un-African' with many countries still classifying sexual relations between men as illegal. As Barker and Ricardo suggest "There may in fact be significant same-sex sexual attraction and sexual encounters in Africa that are invisible or hidden precisely for this reason."

Kiama's study 'Men who Have Sex with Men in Kenya' shows that when sex between males is acknowledged, it is often in the context of 'special circumstances' where men might be separated from regular partners and women, such as prisons, boarding schools or the military. But the study shows that male-to-male sex is more common than assumed and that often, young men might have sexual experiences with other men without necessarily considering themselves of a non-heterosexual orientation. In this context of fear and social ostracism, there are many men in Africa, as in many parts of the world, who live 'constitutionally homosexual and socially heterosexual'[17]. For example, a study in Senegal with men who have sex with men showed that the vast majority also had sex with women. In some cases, men who have sex with men and who live a visible lifestyle as gay have suffered violence and social ostracism. In Kenya, nearly 40 percent of men who had sex with men reported having been raped outside their home and 13 percent reported having been assaulted by the police (Niang et al, 2002).[18]

Some young men make efforts to understand the difficulties that young women face and some men are keenly aware of the harassment and negative treatment they often receive. Some traditions hold women to be inferior and morally weak and in some cases women are seen as property to be given to the husband's family. A group of Christian and Muslim young men interviewed in a secondary school in Kaduna, Nigeria, reflected these views of girls:

> Salim: A girl's burden is different. In my village (he is from a rural area outside of Kaduna), I am from a family of four.

The burden on the girl is greater. God created women to help. She is expected to do that. Here in Africa we care much for boys than girls. Because boys remember their families, but the girl leaves (for her husband's family). If there is any inconvenience for a girl, they become harlots and get what they need (they sell or trade sex for money).
Edward: Yes, girls may need material things more than boys and they capitalize on that (selling sex) and get what they need.
Godfried: Those girls are harlots. If you are a good girl, you do not lay yourself out for any man. She can learn other things, like how to sew or press hair and continue her education, and give to a man at the proper time (after marriage). (p.20)

A group of adult men in Kaduna, while not entirely sympathetic, recognize that the sexual harassment women often experience at work is unjust:

Franklin: If a woman wants to get a job, she will have to give sex to get it. To become a civil servant like us, she will have to have sex.
Habib: Unless she is not pretty or she comes from a big (powerful) family. (The rest of the men laugh at this.)
Ayo: You can't let your daughter go to these places (where we work) because of these things, because you know this will happen.
Franklin: Nowadays, on the police force or in the military, a woman will get promoted if she has sex. It's the natural way they work. It's in the blood of the elites to do these things. (p.20)

TRANSFORMATIONS

Much of the literature on conflict in the region points to young unemployed men and their frustrations over corrupt post-colonial and often repressive regimes, whether as part of armed insurgencies or simply as social unrest. In addition to the intergenerational conflicts we have mentioned, the formation of specific youth cultures is also involved. In discussions of townships in South Africa, for example, it is commonly said that parents, teachers and religious leaders have lost their relevance and legitimacy for young people. In different cultural spaces young men are often presented as out of work, with free time and loosely connected to any social institution, creating their own urban languages and cultures. As Barker and Ricardo report, "It is often seen in a negative light, however, some reports suggest that unemployed young men in such settings are a major cultural voice for cultural expression, who are able to service through music and mingling of different tribal groups and their creative informal economic activity (p.34)."

Youths in urban areas have more free time and fewer social roles that constrain them. Some are also open to global media and the Internet and the global circulation of images of gender and sexual identities. Through popular cultures, different possibilities are made available and different spaces are opened up for reflection and engagement. Indeed, young men, who marry later than young women, particularly those in urban areas have a longer period when they are out of work and loosely connected to their families. They have fewer ties while at the same time are under pressures to acquire work and thus achieve manhood. But these are also times and spaces when young men can be looking to explore different ways of being and seeking out different forms of guidance about how to be men in more equal and loving relationships. They might be more curious about different ways of living that draw from traditional sources but allow for more equal gender and sexual relationships.

So often young men can feel that they need to be self-sufficient and that it can be a sign of weakness to acknowledge the support you need from others. But this is where traditional visions that recognize the need for community can be sustaining as young men shape different visions of leadership and possibilities for more equal gender relations. This can allow men to feel at ease with their masculinities as they recognize that gender equality does not mean 'sameness' even if it means learning to acknowledge and respect your own emotions and feelings as a man. Men have their own emotional and cultural histories to deal with in coming to terms with their inherited masculinities and challenging traditional gender hierarchies. They can also learn to draw support from other men to make changes in their intimate relationships and recognize they can get something different from their contact with men. Relating to feelings can be threatening as can sharing yourself more personally when you have grow up within an African culture that can leave you lonely in spirit when separated from traditional sources of support as you migrate to different regional and global cities.

If men are to learn to be more open in intimate and familial relationships they need to create spaces of reflection in which they can question aspects of their inherited masculinities and so shape different relationships between older and younger men. This involves a process of growth and development in which young men learn to listen and respect both their own emotional needs as well as those of their partners. Through projects that are focused upon working with young men in rural and urban areas they can learn from the mentoring of peers how to make changes in their lives that allow them to draw upon traditional cultures while navigating their lives in very different worlds than their fathers knew. Not only will they be enabled to create more equal gender relations in families, but provide more emotionally involved relationships with their children.

Notes

1. For a helpful discussion about the ways an Enlightenment vision of modernity has shaped relationships between Europe and its colonized visions of Africa see, for example D. Goldberg *Racist Culture* Oxford: Blackwell, 1998 and Paul Gilroy *Black Atlantic: Modernity and Double Consciousness* Cambridge: Harvard University Press, 1993.

2. The quotations that I have drawn upon from a variety of African sources, both traditional and modern are taken from Danielle and Olivier Folmi *African Wisdom 365 Days* London: Thames and Hudson 2000.

3. In this chapter I have drawn from numerous discussions and references made available in the study *Young Men and the Construction of Masculinity in Sub-Saharan Africa: Implications for HIV/AIDS, Conflict and Violence* by Gary Barker and Christine Ricardo Washington DC: The World Bank Social Development Papers Conflict Prevention and Reconstruction Paper 26/ June 2005.

4. For some helpful discussion drawing upon the experience in Brazil of the ways younger men can be set on a path of change through experiences they have witnessed in their families and the support they have received in challenging, for instance, violence towards their mothers, see Gary Barker *Dying to be a Man: Youth and Masculinity and Social Exclusion London*: Routledge Taylor and Francis Group, 2005.

5. For the work that K. Wood and R. Jewkes have done researching the experiences of young men in South African townships see 'Violence, Rape and Sexual Coercion: Everyday Love in a South African Township' *Gender and Development* 5(2): 41-46 1997 and 'Dangerous Love: Reflections on Violence among Xhosa Township Youth' in R. Morell ed. *Changing Men in Southern Africa* Durban: University of Natal Press/ London: Zed Books, 2001.

6. For a discussion of different methodologies for researching men and masculinities that recognize the significance of culture and history in inherited masculinities see, Victor J. Seidler *Transforming Masculinities: Men, Cultures, Bodies, Power, Sex, and Love* London: Routledge, 2006.

7. For an exploration of young men and masculinities in different historical and cultural settings see Victor J. Seidler *Young Men and Masculinities: Global Cultures and Intimate Lives* London: Zed Press, 2006.

8. For a fuller account of this work in Nambia and other discussions of men and masculinities in modern Africa see L. A Lindsay and S.F. Miescher eds *Men and Masculinities in Modern Africa* Portsmouth, NH: Heinemann 2003.

9. An exploration of the effects of migration to cities in Kwazulu is offered in B. Carton 'Locusts fall from the Sky: Manhood and Migrants in Kwazulu' in R. Morell ed *Changing Men in Southern Africa* Durban: University of Natal Press/ London: Zed Press, 2001.

10. For some discussions of the work into initiations in Western cultures that was initially raised by Robert Bly in *Iron John* New York: Addison-Wesley, 1990 see also Victor J. Seidler *Man Enough: Embodying Masculinities* London: Sage 1999.

11. Doudou Diene, Director of Intercultural Dialogue UNESCO shares these sentiments in the introduction to *African Wisdom 365 Days* London: Thames and Hudson, 2000.

12. Carolyn Merchant provides an important historical account of the transition from an organic towards a mechanistic relationship with nature that was signaled through the 17th century Scientific Revolutions in *The Death of Nature: Women, Ecology and the Scientific Revolution* London: Wildwood House, 1982.

13. Andrea Cornwall work on young men and masculinities in southwestern Nigeria 'To Be a Man Is More Than a Day's Work: Shifting Ideals of Manhood in Ado-Odo, Southwestern Nigeria' appears in L.A. Lindsay and S.F. Miescher eds *Men and Masculinities in Modern Africa* Portsmoth, NH: Heinemann, 2003.

14. See M. Sommers 'Urbanization, War and Africa's Youth at Risk: Towards Understanding and Addressing Future Challenges' Washington DC: USAID, 2003. See also M. Sommers paper 'Young, Male and Pentecostal: Urban Refugees in Dar Es Salaam, Tanzania' *Journal of Refugee Studies* 14 (4): 347-370.

15. Some of the research on young men and AIDS has been reported by K. Rivers and P. Aggleton *Gender and the HIV Epidemic: Men and the HIV Epidemic*' HIV and Development Programme, UNDP, 1998 and '*Gender and the HIV Epidemic: Adolescent Sexuality, Gender and the HIV Epidemic.*' HIV and Development Programme, UNDP, 1999.

16. For some theoretical discussions of cultural conceptions of masculinity see, for instance, D. Gilmore *Manhood in the Making: Cultural Concepts of Masculinity* New Haven, CT: Yale University Press, 1990 and Victor J. Seidler *Transforming Masculinities: Men, Cultures, Bodies, Power, Sex and Love* London: Routledge, 2006.

17. For some research on men who have sex with men in different African contexts see, for example, W. Kiama 'Men who have Sex with Men in Kenya' in M. Foreman ed *AIDS and Men Taking Risks or Taking Responsibility?* London Panos: Zed Books, 1999.

18. This research on the sexual health needs of men who have sex with men is reported in C. Niang, M Diagne, Y. Niang, A. Moreau, D. Gomis, M. Diouf, K. Seck, A. Wade, P. Tapsoba and C. Castle 'Meeting the Sexual Health Needs of Men who have Sex with Men in Senegal'. Washington DC: Horizons, 2002.

Chapter 9

RELIGION AND HIV RISK

Laurie F. DeRose

INTRODUCTION

The African continent has experienced three decades of economic hardship. Structural adjustment and globalization have contributed to both the rise of religious communities and the spread of HIV/AIDS in this economically disadvantaged context (Dilger 2007). The epidemic contributes to religious communities flourishing as people confront mortality, seek material help in the face of AIDS-related impoverishment, desire miraculous healing, and seek social support for chastity. How religious individuals and religious communities in turn respond to HIV/AIDS will help shape the future course of the epidemic.

This chapter has two goals: to review what is known about differences in HIV risk by religious affiliation, and also to review what is known about the effects of religion on abstinence, fidelity, and condom use—the most commonly recognized protective behaviors (referred to as the ABCs for Abstain, Be faithful, or use Condoms). As such this review is limited in that it does not include the effects of religion on other risk-reduction strategies like divorcing an adulterous spouse, judicious partner selection, reducing the number of partners, and shortening the duration of partner overlap. Nonetheless, because religion is so much a part of the dialogue about the ABCs of reducing HIV transmission, it is important to assess what we know and what we do not know about religion and the ABCs.

This literature has grown tremendously in recent years. In his 2003 publication, Takyi reported a MEDLINE search for religion and AIDS in Africa with few hits (Takyi 2003). Gray uncovered several studies on Islam and AIDS only a short time later using the same strategy (Gray 2004). When I repeated their searches, there were hundreds of hits, and these comprise the bulk of the evidence presented in this chapter. I also solicited additional references from some scholars actively publishing on the topic, and I followed up on leads from term papers submitted for the seminar I taught on African Demography and Development at Brown University during the spring of 2008. Despite the fact that this chapter thus contains more empirical evidence than previous reviews of the literature, I still find I must agree with Trinitapoli that "the role of religious organizations in HIV/AIDS risk in SSA [sub-Saharan Africa] has not yet been a topic of rigorous scholarly inquiry" (Trinitapoli 2006). Some analyses include religion in their description of study populations, but do not assess the effect of religion multivariate models (e.g., Rwenge 2000; Sa and Larsen 2008). Much of the literature I uncovered was suggestive, rather than empirically documenting effects of religion on HIV sero-status or behaviors related to HIV risk. I have privileged quantitative studies in my review: they are summarized in the text tables. I have also included insights from more qualitative work in the accompanying discussions.

OVERALL RISK

I first review empirical evidence on the relationship between religious affiliation and HIV sero-status. What this reveals is whether there are systematic differences in probability of being HIV positive for adherents of different faiths. For the most part, this literature provides few clues regarding the mechanisms for any significant differences; it therefore leaves open the question of whether individual behavior, community norms, or other unobserved community factors are responsible for religious differentials in HIV status. Studies providing empirical investigation of the relationship between religion and

HIV risk are nevertheless an appropriate starting point; these are summarized in Table 1 and discussed below.

Muslims compared to others

Often in simple descriptive statistics, HIV prevalence is lower among Muslims than others (Kagee, et al. 2005). Muslim advantage is sometimes attributed to protective factors outside of the ABC framework like circumcision (Bwayo, et al. 1994; Malamba, et al. 1994), less alcohol use (Mbulaiteye, et al. 2000), and polygyny (though the effect of polygyny on HIV risk is debated (Clark 2005; Gregson, et al. 1998; Kagimu, et al. 1995; Mbilinyi and Kaihula 2000; Oppong and Agyei-Mensah 2004; Takyi 2003; Trinitapoli 2006)). It also sometimes fails to emerge with controls for socioeconomic status (Allain, et al. 2004), particularly in communities where Muslims are less educated and less mobile and therefore may have been particularly protected early in the epidemic.

Regardless of the mechanisms, ecological studies provide mixed evidence regarding this Muslim advantage. Across 38 sub-Saharan countries, those with higher proportion of Muslims in their populations had lower national HIV prevalence rates (Gray 2004). In contrast, within the Kagera Region of Tanzania, wards with higher proportions of Muslims had *higher* HIV prevalence rates (Killewo, et al. 1994). Further work is needed to identify whether being Muslim matters differently according to social context or whether non-religious factors explain the opposite findings from these two ecological studies.

At the individual level, findings are also mixed. Muslims have lower rates of HIV infection than others in rural Uganda (Nunn, et al. 1994). They also have an advantage over Catholics and mainline Protestants in rural Uganda (Kiwanuka, et al. 1996) and suburban Kenya (Hawken, et al. 2002), and over Catholics and Pentecostals in Nigeria (Sagay, et al. 2005). Muslims who were sero-negative in baseline surveys had lower probability of acquiring HIV relative to non-Muslims in rural Uganda (Kengeya-Kayondo, et al. 1996), but sero-conversion rates in Kenya were not different among Muslims, Catholics, and Protestants (Rakwar, et al. 1999). Importantly, the Kenyan sample was a high-risk subpopulation (trucking company workers) whereas the Ugandan sample was representative of the district. It is possible that affiliation with Islam offers greater advantages to the general population than to high-risk subgroups. Nonetheless, a number of studies have shown no Muslim advantage in more representative samples (Allain, et al. 2004; Kongnyuy and Wiysonge 2007; Quigley, et al. 1997).

Christians compared to others

Some of the theoretical arguments why there should be a Muslim advantage apply to Christians as well: both Muslims and Christians could be protected from HIV by following their scriptural mandates for chastity. But like for Muslims, empirical evidence on the protection associated with Christian religious affiliation is mixed. In the study of Kenyan truckers mentioned above, both Muslims and mainline Christians had substantially (six times) lower risk of sero-conversion than others (Rakwar, et al. 1999). Among Nigerian women attending an antenatal clinic, Christian women also had lower rates of HIV than non-Christian women (Lawoyin and Adewole 2004). Being in a well-functioning church group in rural Zimbabwe reduced probability of being HIV positive by 25% (Gregson, et al. 2004). However in both Cameroon and rural Tanzania, neither Catholics nor Protestants differed from Muslims or others (Quigley, et al. 1997) (Kongnyuy and Wiysonge 2007).

Denominations compared

Important differences between adherents of major faiths might be captured by the subgroups to which they belong. My review of the literature found no studies that distinguished between different types of Muslim congregations on the African continent. Although this is unavoidable in those areas where Muslims are a small minority (because of small sample size or lack of diversity), it still represents an obstacle to understanding the relationship between religion and HIV risk. This point is underscored by the findings from studies that look at particular Christian denominations and find, not surprisingly, that they are not all the same with respect to the relationship between affiliation and HIV status.

There are two kinds of explanations for why some denominations have lower HIV rates that I shall term spiritual and sociological. Doing this carries disadvantages because the classification implies a dichotomy when the terms in fact overlap. For example, being a devout

Christian includes being involved with other believers for worship, prayer, and accountability to the church, so terming any protection offered by accountability as sociological implies that it is not spiritual even when it is.

Nonetheless, social scientists have identified various aspects of congregational life that may afford greater protection against HIV/AIDS than is found in most mainline congregations, and these can be understood from the outside without any reference to the spiritual experiences of the participants. Therefore, when I refer to sociological explanations of differences between congregations, I mean those that would pertain to any group with such practices regardless of the motivations or the experiences of the congregants. Sociological explanations were well summarized in Garner's article "Safe Sects?" Garner (2000) described how denominations in South Africa that did not differ with respect to what they taught about sexual purity still differed greatly in terms of how often the issue was systematically taught and how often the Bible was used in such teaching (indoctrination), opportunities within the group for spiritual expression ranging from personal prayer to exercise of ecstatic gifts like speaking in tongues (religious/subjective experience), group views on how separate the community was from outsiders (exclusion), and how much of everyday life overlapped with church life (socialization).

"Spiritual" explanations of differences instead emphasize factors like supernatural strength to overcome temptation, God leading accountability partners to inquire at needed times, repentance invoked by scripture, and the testimony or example of others. These spiritual explanations of why some Christians would have lower HIV risk than all Christians overlap with the sociological concept of exclusion as it includes the idea that some churchgoers are truly Christians and others remain outside Christian spiritual experience.

For social science researchers seeking empirical support for various hypotheses, differences between denominations do not reveal much about causation: it could be that particular denominations exercise greater social control, or that these same denominations are more likely to attract devout adherents than once-a-week participants. Nonetheless, denominational differences in HIV risk suggest an advantage for some groups.

In rural Uganda, those in Pentecostal churches or in other churches identified with the experience of being "saved" or "born again" have the same low rates of HIV as Muslims—statistically lower than among both Catholics and mainline Protestants (Kiwanuka, et al. 1996). A Ghanaian study found no denominational differences among Christians, but noted that while the effect of affiliation with Seventh-Day Adventism could not be measured given only 14 members in the sample, *none* of these were HIV positive (Allain, et al. 2004). Seventh-Day Adventists have been described in other literature as being particularly likely to excommunicate members who have been guilty of sexual sin (Agha, et al. 2006). Thus members would be under pressure to conform their sexual behavior to the expectations of the church. However, it is also worth noting that removing individuals engaged in high-risk behavior from congregations could decrease HIV prevalence within those congregations. Members also remove themselves from worshipping with highly religious groups because of feelings of guilt or hypocrisy (Sadgrove 2007). Conversely, denominations that proselytize could have higher rates of HIV than the general population (even if they do influence members toward safer sexual practices) because converts may be select on wanting lifestyle change, seeking support during AIDS-related illness, or seeking wives who would remain with them "in sickness or in health" (Mbilinyi and Kaihula 2000; Watkins and Chimbwete 2004). Converts have been shown to have higher HIV rates than those with the same affiliation as in their childhood (Allain, et al. 2004). Nonetheless, Pentecostals in Nigeria—a group well known for proselytizing— had lower rates of HIV infection than those from Orthodox churches (Akani, et al. 2005). Pentecostal men in rural Malawi were significantly less likely than Catholics to report ever having had a sexually transmitted infection; their advantage over Muslims and other Protestants was not significant when controls were employed (Trinitapoli and Regnerus 2006). Moreover, mortality trends in Zimbabwe are consistent with adherents of "Spirit-type" churches being less affected by the HIV/AIDS epidemic (Gregson, et al. 1999).

Effects of religiosity

For other behavioral outcomes like fertility, social scientists have found that religiosity explains more variation than religion does. That is, there is more variation within religious groups like Muslims and Christians than between devout Muslims and devout Christians or nominal Muslims and nominal Christians. It is easy to imagine that more religious adherents of either faith would be at lower risk of HIV than those who demonstrated less devotion.

But religiosity is harder to measure than religious affiliation. I located only two studies assessing the effect of religiosity on HIV risk. The first—the Ghanaian study that did not find effects of denomination—employed multiple measures of religious participation, and found that those with a formal church role had only one-third the probability of being HIV positive as others (Allain, et al. 2004). In rural Malawi where church attendance was used as a measure of religiosity, those who attended more frequently were less likely to report having sexually transmitted infections of any kind (Trinitapoli and Regnerus 2006). Although reported infections are a less reliable indicator of risk than sero-status, Trinitapoli and Regnerus's data are from the Malawi Diffusion and Ideological Change Project, a data collection effort that took social desirability bias in reporting seriously. Respondents' answers were adjusted by a factor corresponding to how many fictitious names the respondent claimed to be familiar with on a list that also included genuine public figures. This adjustment factor is of course imperfect, but does lessen concern that the results are driven by highly religious individuals also desiring to look good to survey takers. More generally, however, concern that religious individuals underreport religiously proscribed behavior seems to be overstated. Regnerus and Uecker's analysis of data from the United States found that religious adolescents did not give self-reports of sensitive behaviors that were less accurate than those of other youth (Regnerus and Uecker 2007). Similar validity checks are not possible with all data sets, but Regnerus and Uecker's review of the literature concluded that social desirability bias was not systematically related to religion or religiosity.

Perceived risk

Before turning to the ABCs of HIV transmission prevention, I also note that there have been four studies on the effect of religion on *perceived* risk of having or contracting HIV. These are summarized in table 2. The most notable feature from these studies is that Muslims do not perceive themselves to carry the advantage that some studies indicate they may have. Generally perceived risk includes how well the respondent adheres to the ABCs plus how much they trust any partner that they are faithful to. Protective factors such as circumcision may not figure into individual calculus of perceived risk because they have received less attention in the media and in public health campaigns.

Whether or not this is a correct or sufficient explanation for why Muslims do not report themselves at an advantage, it would not explain why Muslims perceive their HIV risk to be *higher*. Muslim women in Ghana (as well as women affiliating with African traditional religions) reported higher risk of HIV than Catholics or Protestants (Takyi 2003). The same pattern was found among Ghanaian men (Takyi 2001), though in the study of men statistical significance was ascertained only by a chi-square test of the relationship between affiliation and perceived risk categories whereas the study of women included numerous control variables (possibly because of greater sample size among women in the Demographic and Health Surveys). Similar findings emerged in rural Malawi where Muslim men were less confident than those from any other group that they were not currently infected with HIV, while men from Pentecostal churches had lower perceived risk than most other groups (Trinitapoli and Regnerus 2006).

Here again, religiosity may be more important than religious affiliation. For men, religiosity predicts lower perceived risk of HIV. Malawian men who attended services regularly were less likely to report a high chance of being currently infected with HIV. In heavily Muslim Senegal, men who considered religion to be very important were half as likely to consider themselves at risk of contracting HIV (Lagarde, et al. 2000).

However the same Senegalese study revealed that women who considered religion very important were over nine times *more* likely to feel at risk of HIV (Lagarde, et al. 2000). Because married women are less likely to be protected by their own fidelity than married men, the gender differences among highly religious respondents may reflect differences in how much control they feel they have over their own HIV status.

Summary: Religion and risk of HIV infection

Studies at the ecological level show both positive and negative effects of Islam on the HIV prevalence rate in communities. However, in individual-level studies Muslims have never been shown to be at higher risk of HIV compared to members of other religious groups. At worst, Muslims have the same HIV risk as those with other religious affiliations. The story for Christians is similar: although they have sometimes been shown to have no advantage with respect to HIV risk, they have never been shown to be at a disadvantage.

Attention to religiosity and denominational affiliation presents a more nuanced picture. More religious individuals within both Islam and Christianity have lower rates of HIV. No general conclusions can be drawn regarding denominational affiliation and HIV risk because the literature is so thin, but it may point to an advantage for adherents of stricter or "more spiritual" denominations. Evidence of denominational differences in abstinence, fidelity, and condom use is more extensive than for sero-status: I review literature on the effect of denominational affiliation on each of these protective behaviors below.

This picture of how religion affects sero-status obviously needs to be clarified by further research. In particular, gender differences in perceived risk need to be evaluated in multiple contexts. An important unanswered question is whether the *accuracy* of perceived risk differs between men and women by religion. That is, do affiliation and/or religiosity affect how accurate risk perceptions are for men and women differently? The accuracy of self-assessed risk of HIV is beginning to receive empirical attention (Bignami-Van Assche, et al. 2007), but to date these investigations do not include religion as a determinant of the accuracy of self-assessed risk.

ABSTINENCE

Abstinence can be a defense against AIDS at any point in an individual's life, but few will employ this strategy throughout their lives, and it is certainly incompatible with nearly all views of marriage. From a religious or moral perspective, premarital abstinence is usually the favored course. Public health literature usually puts more emphasis on delayed onset of sexual relations, whether marital or non-marital. As obvious as it is that later exposure to sex means shorter lifetime exposure to risk of a sexually transmitted infection, simulations show that this factor matters relatively little in lifetime chances of AIDS. This coupled with a common view that abstinence until marriage is unrealistic leads to much criticism of faith-based organizations that promote abstinence as a front line defense against AIDS.

However, much literature both in Africa and from other developed and developing countries shows that premarital sexual behavior is a strong predictor of later behavior (Hallett, et al. 2007). For instance, those who experience sexual debut within marriage are less likely to have affairs during marriage (White, et al. 2000). Women who have later sexual debut have fewer lifetime partners (Hallett, et al. 2007). Further, those whose first sex is early but within marriage do not carry forward the same risk of more lifetime partners as others with early first sex (Hallett, et al. 2007). Similarly, for men, later sexual debut is associated with lower odds of extramarital sex (Hill, et al. 2004; Mitsunaga, et al. 2005; White, et al. 2000). The number of sex partners men have before marriage is significantly associated marital fidelity in some study sites (White, et al. 2000). Delayed sexual debut also increases the probability of condom use at first sex (Agha, et al. 2006). Sexual socialization during adolescence is only one of the factors potentially contributing to these associations, but it nonetheless seems clear that if religious organizations can successfully promote premarital abstinence, the payoff may continue throughout an individual's lifetime.

Churches sometimes offer teaching for parents on how to approach issues of sexuality with their children (Adogame 2007). Perhaps more importantly, young people who are active in religious groups are more likely to meet both peers and adults who promote premarital abstinence (Odimegwu 2005), and supportive peers may be especially crucial for maintaining abstinence (Sadgrove 2007). Trinitapoli described a weekday service at a mission Protestant church attended by over 450 youth in Rumphi (Malawi) where skits were used to promote abstinence, including one that "illustrated a 'clever' and 'goal-oriented' young woman who tries negotiating with her boyfriend, who wants to have sex, but finally leaves him, saying 'Goodbye. I wish you all the best during your girl campaign. Sex can wait, but my future can't'"(Trinitapoli 2006). In contrast to these examples of ways that churches promote abstinence, all-night prayer meetings have been identified as risky places with respect to sexual behavior (Power, et al. 2007).

Here I examine the evidence of a relationship between religion and abstinence. Even though premarital abstinence is perhaps the most relevant dependent variable from both religious and public health perspectives given the associations with later fidelity, much of the literature either looks at age at sexual debut or whether unmarried individuals are currently sexually active. These are both measures of abstinence and are clearly related to premarital abstinence. Current sexual activity also combines both age at sexual debut and secondary abstinence—a strategy often advocated upon conversion or repentance. As such, if religious organizations are successful in promoting morality, there should be an association between religion and these outcomes as well as premarital sex per se. However, it has been suggested that emphasis on repentance undermines the potential for Christianity to promote abstinence, because repentance is always available for those who stray (Sadgrove 2007).

Religion and premarital sex

Three studies from the African continent use premarital sex as the dependent variable; they are summarized in Table 3. First, Muslim women in Nigeria were less likely to have premarital sex than their Catholic and other counterparts, but this was explained largely by age at marriage (Feyisetan and Pebley 1989). That is, when comparing rates of sexual activity among unmarried women of the same ages, the Muslim advantage became statistically insignificant. Other Christians were very similar to Muslims, though Catholics still had higher rates of premarital sex (Feyisetan and Pebley 1989). Second, Addai's (2000) work on Ghana found that married Muslim women were the least likely to report having had premarital sex. He also found that sectarian Christians were less likely to report having had premarital sex than Catholics and mainline Protestants, and that this advantage over major Christian denominations was also experienced by adherents of more conservative traditional religions as well as those with no religious affiliation (Addai 2000). It is difficult to evaluate the validity of Addai's findings, however, as he found no differences in reported sexual behavior among *unmarried* women in the same nationally representative sample. Selection bias and reporting bias could both lead to reports by married women not reflecting actual premarital experiences. Finally, Djamba found an effect of religiosity with those attending services more often being less likely to have premarital sex. His sample was from the Democratic Republic of the Congo, and most were either Catholic or Protestant; those with other or no affiliations had higher rates of premarital sex, but this relationship was only marginally significant ($p \leq .10$; Djamba 2003).

Religion and age at sexual debut

The literature on age at sexual debut also points to effects of religiosity in addition to (or perhaps more importantly than) religious affiliation. Among first-year university students in South Africa, those who scored high on the Rohrbaugh and Jessor religiosity scale experienced a later onset of sexual activity; the religious affiliation of the respondents was not given in the study (Nicholas and Durrheim 1995). In Nigeria, also in a campus-based sample, there were gender differences in how religiosity mattered, but it mattered for both men and women. Male students distributing tracts or engaging in other proselytizing had later sexual debut; for female students, Pentecostal affiliation, rating religion important, attending church regularly, praying and reading the Bible daily, and proselytizing were all associated with later sexual debut (Odimegwu 2005).

Gender differences also emerged in a representative sample of Manicaland Province, Zimbabwe where significantly earlier sexual debut was found among women who did not affiliate with a church and men who belonged to Catholic and mainline Protestant churches (in contrast to "Spirit-type" and other Apostolic churches; Hallett, et al. 2007). In Zambia, religion did not seem to matter for abstinence for most of the sample, but the exception was that those affiliating with denominations that excommunicated straying members were more likely to have later sexual debut (Agha, et al. 2006). All the young men in Campbell's South African mining area study who had delayed sexual debut were from church groups that forbade premarital sex (Campbell 2003).

Religion and current sexual activity

Very similar findings emerge when sexual activity is the dependent variable (Table 5). Religiosity matters. More religious individuals Nicholas and Durrheim's study of first-year university students were more likely to intend abstinence during their second year (Nicholas and Durrheim 1995). A study of Nigerian secondary school students that found no differences between Christians and Muslims in reported abstinence, but did find that those reporting that religion was very important to them were more likely to be abstaining at the time of the interview (Slap, et al. 2003). In Uganda there were higher rates of abstinence among those in "Saved" or Pentecostal sects than among Catholics, mainline Protestants, or Muslims (Kiwanuka, et al. 1996).

Semi-structured interview data from Mozambique found women from "healing" churches (Assemblies of God, Zionist, or Apostolic churches in this context) advantaged in the practice of abstinence relative to those from mainline denominations (Agadjanian 2005). There is also qualitative evidence that "born again" status can be used to resist sexual pressure. Among university students in Uganda where the born again movement is flourishing, Sadgrove described both discrepancies between public identities and private sexual practices (Christian hypocrisy), as well as public identities being a tool to help refuse sexual advances—thus giving born agains an advantage with respect to reducing or eliminating premarital sexual relations (Sadgrove 2007). Somewhat similarly, 30% of migrants aged 15-24 in two heavily Christian Nigerian cities had never had sex, and an additional minority were currently abstaining and intending to do so until marriage despite having previously initiated sexual activity; Smith described their discourse explaining this as involving "the intertwining of religion, sexual morality, and fears about AIDS" (Smith 2003).

Summary: Religion and abstinence

The existing literature from Africa indicates that more religious individuals are more likely to abstain. This is consistent with evidence from the United States, New Zealand, and Australia (Dunne, et al. 1994; Grunseit and Richters 2000; McCree, et al. 2003; Odimegwu 2005; Paul, et al. 2000; Rostosky, et al. 2003). Evidence from Africa also indicates that affiliation with less traditional Christian groups (that exhibit greater social control as well as more spiritual fervor) also predicts abstinence. However, there has been little empirical investigation of the effect of affiliating with Islam on premarital sexual activity. This does not seem to be a strategy where Muslims have an advantage, but with most of the studies focusing on Christians, such a conclusion would be quite premature.

FIDELITY

In nationally representative samples from twenty-three countries (not all in Africa), there were no significant differences by religious affiliation in proportions reporting that they were sticking to one partner in order to prevent AIDS (Snelling, et al. 2007). Although this does not mean that there are no significant differences by religious affiliation in the practice of fidelity for other motives, it nonetheless strongly indicates that religious communities have not differentiated themselves in promoting fidelity in response to the epidemic. Both "baseline" levels of fidelity and behavioral change contribute to the levels of fidelity reported in Table 6. Almost all of the studies rely on reported behavior, but again this may be less problematic for the examination of religious differences than sometimes suspected (Regnerus and Uecker 2007). In addition, some of the studies employed validity checks.

Religious groups can encourage fidelity by direct teaching as well as by providing accountability. Both Christian and Muslim leaders in Malawi reported a willingness to conduct home visits confronting individuals whose spouses suspected them of infidelity (Trinitapoli 2006).

Differences by religious affiliation

As with overall risk, there is some evidence of a Muslim advantage in fidelity. In contrast to overall risk, however, the mixed evidence includes some studies where Muslims are at a disadvantage, i.e., report lower levels of fidelity, rather than just being a mix of advantage and no advantage.

Starting first with studies finding Muslim men to be more faithful, they reported fewer sexual partners in the last year than other circumcised men in one Ugandan industrial borough (Bailey, et al. 1999), and they were less likely to report sex with a prostitute in Kenya (Rakwar, et al. 1999). Nationally representative data from Nigeria showed that Muslim men were less likely than Protestants and Catholics to report having an extramarital affair in the past year (Mitsunaga, et al. 2005). Also in rural Senegal, the proportion already being or intending to become faithful to protect themselves from AIDS was higher among Muslim men than Christian men (Lagarde, et al. 2000). The number of self-reported sexual partners among Muslim men under age 45 was significantly reduced following interventions where educators partnered with Imams and taught at Muslim religious gatherings (Kagimu, et al. 1995).

Two studies showed no Muslim advantage over traditional Christian denominations. In rural Malawi, both Protestants and Muslims had the same probability of an extramarital sexual partnership in the last year as Catholics (Clark 2005). Similarly, Muslims had the same probability of a recent affair as Protestants in five Nigerian towns (Isiugo-Abanihe 1994).

However certain Christian sects seem at an advantage in promoting fidelity. Saved and Pentecostal men and women were less likely to report two or more sexual partners than Catholics, Protestants, and Muslims in Uganda (Kiwanuka, et al. 1996). Pentecostal men in Malawi were also less likely than both Catholics and Muslims to report an extramarital sexual partner in the last year, an advantage they shared with mission Protestants and men affiliated with African Independent Churches (Trinitapoli and Regnerus 2006). This advantage among adherents of newer Protestant denominations was found using the same data set as the Malawian study showing no religious differences when all Protestants were lumped together (Clark 2005; Trinitapoli and Regnerus 2006). Clearly the finer divisions are relevant to practice of fidelity. Interviews from this study site:

> showed that for some, the dense and encompassing social networks of spirit-type denominations are perceived as supporting one's efforts to resist the temptations of multiple sexual partners, consistent with characterizations in the literature of born-again networks as providing a 'security circle,' a 'defensive "wall" against outside evil forces...' (Watkins 2004).

In Nigeria, other Christians (mostly Pentecostals and evangelicals) shared the Muslim advantage over Catholics and Protestants in affairs in the past year (Mitsunaga, et al. 2005). Also in Nigeria, Isiugo-Abanihe's descriptive statistics showed Pentecostal men and women had the lowest percentages ever having an affair as well as having an affair in the last week. All Protestants (Pentecostals and mainline Protestants) were combined for Isiugo-Abanihe's multivariate analysis, and they were no different from Muslims but less likely than Catholics and adherents of traditional religion to report a recent affair (Isiugo-Abanihe 1994). In Southwest Nigeria, a random sample of clients of sex workers was disproportionately Muslim and Catholic while Protestants were underrepresented (Messersmith, et al. 2000). In Mozambique, those from the more charismatic "healing" churches were more likely to practice fidelity than their counterparts in mainline denominations (Agadjanian 2005).

Only in Botswana did a "generic" Christian advantage emerge. Christians were less likely to report having concurrent sexual partners than adherents of traditional religion or those with no religious affiliation (Carter, et al. 2007).

Effects of religiosity

Data from the Malawi Diffusion and Ideological Change project show a 45 percent decline in the odds that men report having a recent extramarital sexual partner for each unit increase in service attendance (Trinitapoli and Regnerus 2006). In addition, respondents to semistructured interviews from the same project said they gave up extramarital sexual relations because of renewed religious commitment (Watkins and Chimbwete 2004), and one born-again male respondent "related several stories in which he chastised philandering male friends and admonished them to be faithful in the future" (Clark 2005). Kaler gives further qualitative evidence of Christian men in Malawi influencing each other toward chastity directly and through encouraging personal Bible study (Kaler 2004). Tanzanian men also tell stories of religious renewal supporting safer sexual behavior using fiery language (Pool, et al. 1996). In contrast, for some holding a position in the church may simply be a reason to be more discreet about affairs they do have (Smith 2007). And Senegalese considering religion to be very important were *not* more likely to report intending to or actually having become faithful to protect themselves from AIDS (Lagarde, et al. 2000).

For other outcomes religiosity matters more than religious affiliation, so these last findings seem somewhat confusing. Work from the

United States has also failed to show effects of religiosity on fidelity—going to church did not affect odds of extramarital relationships among Hispanic migrants in Durham, NC (Parrado, et al. 2004)—and it may be that effects of religiosity are highly context-dependent. Specifically, I mean that the effects of religiosity may depend on the religiousness of the community. In Malawi, personal religiosity and community religiosity were somewhat substitutable rather than being mutually reinforcing (Regnerus and Trinitapoli 2006). That is, personal devotion decreased the risk of extramarital partnerships more in more secular communities than in more religious ones, and less devout individuals were less at risk in more religious communities than they were in more secular ones. Most of the Senegalese sample considered religion to be very important, so this context was one where religiousness was more the rule than the exception, and as such might be expected to have less impact on behavior. In the Hispanic US sample, going to church may be normative.

A Comment on Polygyny

Although the ABC rhetoric usually references being faithful to one partner, it is nonetheless the case that faithful polygynous marriages can also be protective against HIV. In fact, it may be the case that in sub-Saharan Africa where long durations of postpartum abstinence are customary among a wide range of ethnic groups that polygyny affords some protection against HIV because husbands who are sexually active during the wife's postpartum abstinence are typically active with less risky partners if they are polygynously married (compared to an extramarital partner who may have other recent partners or concurrent partners). In heavily Muslim Senegal, polygyny is common but promiscuity is not and HIV rates are low (Oppong and Agyei-Mensah 2004). Co-wives have been known to help spy on their husband to keep him faithful (Mukiza-Gapere and Ntozi 1995), and to guard each other in an effort to prevent any one of them from introducing the HIV virus (Lugalla, et al. 2004).

However, the process of acquiring a new wife adds risk to existing marriages as men may have sex with prospective new brides before they marry (Clark 2005). Wives not receiving enough attention may also be particularly likely to have affairs themselves (Trinitapoli 2006), and young wives who married polygynous older men for economic stability might also have higher rates of infidelity with partners who are more their peers (Mbilinyi and Kaihula 2000). The balance of protective and risky factors associated with polygyny is unclear and has received little empirical investigation. As an exception, a study using nationally representative data from Nigeria found that men with two wives had the lowest rates of extramarital intercourse in the last year, but that men with three or more wives were even less faithful than their monogamous counterparts (Mitsunaga, et al. 2005).

Summary: Religion and Fidelity

Affiliation with major religions does not seem to consistently promote higher levels of fidelity, but there is more evidence that charismatic and born again movements within the Christian church are efficacious in promoting fidelity. Any link between Islam and lower HIV prevalence does not seem to be explained by greater fidelity (Gray 2004). Watkins and Chimbwete (2004) suggest that renewed religious commitment among Muslims may impact behavior less than among Christians because it is more private and less reinforced by group accountability than is becoming "born again."

The evidence on religiosity is suggestive of the hypothesis that communities that are more religious may increase overall levels of fidelity, but that personal devotion is especially important for those who are religious minorities within their communities. From a policy perspective, it would be useful to know whether more religious communities help reduce extramarital sex through influencing norms or restricting opportunities (e.g., fewer brothels and beer halls in more religious communities).

Muslims and Christians differ in the extent to which they practice polygyny. Typically African Christian churches tolerate existing polygynous marriages among their members, but strongly discourage the formation of new ones. The effect of polygyny on HIV risk is relevant to understanding religious differences, but remains understudied.

Finally, the relationship between religion and fidelity among unmarried people is understudied. The empirical studies of fidelity often combine marrieds and unmarrieds, but religion may affect each differently. An unmarried individual who is sexual active may not be motivated to avoid further violation of religious mandates because they are already transgressing, thus leading to disinhibition. Alternately, religious individuals may be particularly motivated to construe even their extramarital partnerships as moral—that is, leading to marriage (Smith 2004), and therefore maintain fidelity to a non-marital partner. Even among religious individuals who are more honest about the hypocrisy involved in premarital partnerships, religious identities can be used to avoid unwanted sex even while continuing wanted sex (Sadgrove 2007), thus still reducing HIV risk even while transgressing scriptural mandates.

For both married and unmarried individuals, the effect of religion on serial monogamy also needs to be understood. Construing premarital partnerships as permanent could lead to heightened risk relative to remaining abstinent if such behavior produces a series of premarital partners until plans for marriage are finally actualized. Feldman's work in Zambia concluded that the message of fidelity in marriage had ironically encouraged faithful premarital relations, thus leading to condomless sex in faithful relationships of only a few months' duration (Feldman, et al. 1997). Similarly, even perfect marital fidelity can coexist with higher HIV risk if there is higher marital turnover (divorce and remarriage).

CONDOM USE

Given the overwhelming anecdotal evidence that some religious organizations have actively denounced condom use or impeded it by promoting moral sexuality instead, it is surprising that empirical studies of religion and condom use are few (see Table 7). Cross-national data indicate that neither Islam nor Christianity impedes condom use relative to Buddhism or Hinduism; in fact Muslims and Christians are more likely to use condoms (Snelling, et al. 2007). However, it is still possible that within a given context that adherents of particular sects or the most religious individuals could be loathe to use condoms or be condemned by their communities if they did.

Some of the findings with respect to condom use could in fact represent a public health problem. For instance, Agha and her co-authors found that the same Christian groups that excommunicated errant members and thus promoted abstinence also had adherents who were less likely to have used a condom at first sex (Agha, et al. 2006). It is easy to imagine that those not planning to have sex (or not admitting to themselves or others that they were planning on doing so) would not carry condoms. Those affiliated with healing churches in Mozambique were also less likely to use condoms (Agadjanian 2005). Similarly, the Muslim men in the Ugandan industrial borough who had significantly fewer sexual partners in the last year were also less likely to have ever used a condom, and less likely to have used one at last sex (Bailey, et al. 1999).

It is important to note, however, that context matters even from solely a public health perspective. If first sex were more likely to be in marriage among the most conservative Christian groups, the lack of condom use at first sex is less problematic than in other kinds of partnerships. Or if the Muslim men who never used condoms had fewer partners because they had more wives and no outside partners, the lower rates of condom use are again of less concern.

Two other studies assessing the effects of religion on condom use also do not isolate non-marital sex. Nicholas and Durrheim found that more religious South African students were less likely to use condoms, but without conditioning on whether they were having sex at all (Nicholas and Durrheim 1995). Agadjanian showed that mainline church members in Mozambique were less likely to use condoms only if they attended services more frequently (Agadjanian 2005). In both highly religious subsamples, sexual mortality could be substituting for condom use. Granted this interpretation is charitable toward religious groups, but supporting a more damning interpretation would require better evidence.

Equally inconclusively, I located two other studies that found no differences in condom use by religious affiliation (Adetunji 2000; Takyi 2003). There are no studies showing difference by religion or religiosity in condom use during premarital or extramarital sex. Thus the case against religion in the fight against HIV/AIDS relies on descriptions of religious attitudes and propaganda against condoms as well as on arguments that religious groups influence whole societies in making condoms less available to religious and irreligious individuals alike.

To some it may be surprising that there is so little evidence regarding religion and condom use. But it has been observed in a variety of different contexts across the African continent that the abstinence-versus-condoms rhetoric seems more related to US culture wars than to African social reality (Green, et al. 2006; Gruénais 1999). In summarizing work on social change in response to the epidemic in Tanzania Pool notes:

> It is striking, and perhaps relevant from an intervention perspective, that a religious idiom was used to denounce sexual promiscuity and alcohol but not the use of condoms. Here there may be some resonance between the widespread activities of crusading 'born again' Protestant denominations preaching rebirth as a means to salvation, and AIDS interventions that also advocate change leading to salvation. The clinic, like the church, not only mediates between life and death, but also has the secret of who is saved and who is damned (Pool, et al. 1996).

Further, the apparent contradiction may not be experienced even in Western societies. More religious African American youth were more likely to use condoms when they did have sex (McCree, et al. 2003), and sexually active religious youth in Australia were also not less likely to use condoms (Dunne, et al. 1994). There is much evidence that Africans do not experience the contradiction. Informal conversion within congregations may help people reconcile official church teaches with practical concerns (Agadjanian and Menjívar 2008). Young Christian migrants in Nigeria did not generally use condoms in serious relationships, but were quite willing to utilize them in relationships they considered temporary (Smith 2003). Those with strong Christian beliefs in Tanzania still viewed condoms as supporting their children's survival (Bujra and Baylies 2000), and some pastors in Malawi have emphasized safety more than sin (Mbilinyi and Kaihula 2000). Other church leaders were also willing to support condom use with carefully prepared messages (Pfeiffer 2004; Trinitapoli 2006), as were a significant minority of Muslim leaders (Forster 2001; Trinitapoli 2006). As Agadjanian explained:

> No church is keen on promoting condoms. Yet the condom message makes its way into the teachings of even most conservative denominations—directly and especially indirectly. Church leaders and churchgoers alike use the expression "prevention" (or sometimes "protection")

as a euphemism for condom use; such condom-centered "prevention" becomes a standard—even if not explicitly articulated—addition to all churches' favorite repertoire of premarital chastity and marital fidelity (Agadjanian 2005).

Condom use increased significantly following HIV education that involved Muslim leaders (Kagimu, et al. 1995). Nonetheless it is also the case that Muslim (Trinitapoli 2006) and Christian (Pfeiffer 2004; Sadgrove 2007) leaders have explicitly denounced condoms. Rumors that condoms help spread HIV are thought to have originated with church leaders (Marindo, et al. 2003), and church "surveillance" has reportedly kept men from acquiring condoms (Mbilinyi and Kaihula 2000). I feel that Christian embracing and denouncing condoms simultaneous is well-captured in this quote from the Malawi Diffusion and Ideational Change project describing what a female church leader taught youth:

> There is no way for you to not be doing sex. So you are advised to be doing with condoms for the sake of early pregnant and catching HIV/AIDS. But let me warn you: you are not safe in the eyes of God because God hates pre-marital sex (Trinitapoli 2006).

DISCUSSION

The effect of religion on HIV is oversimplified in much of the discourse on the topic where the net effect of religion is treated as a trade-off between any benefits from promoting abstinence and fidelity against costs imposed by impeding condom use. This tension is often conceptualized at the individual level with, for example, religious individuals not having condoms because they do not view themselves as the kind of people who would need them. The tension is also well-recognized at the programmatic level where promoting abstinence has been criticized as an obstacle to promoting condom use; faith-based abstinence promotion may be even more problematic because it could reduce the perceived need for and acceptability of condoms within the community.

The empirical evidence on the relationship between religion and the ABCs of preventing HIV transmission does not answer all the relevant questions that emerge from even this oversimplified framework. Most notably, there has not been enough attention to community-level effects. For individuals, adhering to the ABCs as a set of options (if you do not abstain, be faithful; if you are not faithful, use condoms) can provide some protection regardless of which of the three strategies is chosen. But the broader literature on HIV risk commonly recognizes that an individual's ability to implement the ABCs depends upon community-level factors. The most commonly recognized of these is women's empowerment: where women are economically dependent on men, they often cannot refuse sex inside or outside marriage, and thus cannot practice abstinence or protect themselves from a partner who is not faithful to them. Where women are not empowered enough to refuse sex, it is hard to imagine them empowered enough to negotiate condom use. There is also a growing literature that gives attention to community norms expecting unsafe behavior from men, as well as economic situations that motivate economically frustrated men to reassert their masculinity through sexual practices that often carry HIV risk. The effects of religion may also operate at the community level, as much of the rhetoric against religion as a force inhibiting the spread of condom use implies. The relationship between religion and HIV needs to be understood in social context (Kalipeni, et al. 2004). However, almost all of the literature available on HIV and religion in Africa measures only individual religious affiliation. We do not know whether condom use among those not sticking to a single partner is lower in more religious communities.

Instead, much of what we know about the effect of religion on abstinence, fidelity, and condom use is at the individual level. And even at the individual level, there are serious gaps in our understanding. While we know that certain Christian groups promote abstinence and fidelity better than mainline congregations, we do not know whether affiliation with these groups is independently important or is a proxy for religiosity (or both). We also know very little about the effects of Islam on abstinence and fidelity. It seems that earlier marriage among Muslims may offer some protection where older husbands are likely to be HIV negative, but the effect of earlier marriage in areas of greater HIV prevalence is unknown. Whether polygyny affords protection or introduces risk is also an important, empirically answerable question.

There is no evidence that Islam promotes premarital abstinence for older individuals and little evidence that it helps promote fidelity, but this is in part because of a paucity of studies involving Muslims. It may also be attributable to a lack of distinction among Muslims (in contrast to studies that pay attention to different Christian denominations).

The summary of what we do know about religion and the ABCs of preventing HIV transmission indicates that certain Christian sects do promote abstinence and fidelity, and there is little evidence that they inhibit condom use (and none that they inhibit condom use among those with multiple partners). The same could be said of more religious individuals of any faith, though the evidence for that is thinner.

But what do these findings mean for overall risk? The evidence based on individual sero-status is largely consistent with this summary indicating that affiliation with Pentecostal or other vibrant and conservative congregations that emphasize spiritual experience reduces HIV risk through promoting safer sex. However, Muslims and Christians more generally also sometimes have lower rates of HIV than their neighbors. Whether this advantage emerges through the ABCs in ways yet undocumented or whether it derives from other sources deserves investigation. Lower HIV rates among Muslims have been explained by lower alcohol consumption (the Muslim advantage dropping to statistical insignificance when controls for frequency of drinking were introduced; Mbulaiteye, et al. 2000). If, however, Muslim advantage derived from greater sobriety leading to safer sexual choices, we would expect to see more abstinence and fidelity among Muslims, and the existing evidence does not show this.

Although the ABC framework has other serious shortcomings, I conclude by calling attention to a way that it could nonetheless be used to deepen our understanding of the relationship between religion and HIV risk. There may be religious differences—for men, women, or both—in the *efficacy* of fidelity as a risk-reduction strategy. Most women who are HIV positive acquired the virus from their spouse (UNAIDS 2000), and thus could be served by religious communities that helped them acquire and keep HIV negative partners (as well as providing alternatives for those in sero-discordant partnerships). There is very little literature on marital coping strategies like selecting less risky partners and divorcing adulterous partners, and to date this literature has not incorporated attention to religion (Reniers 2008;

Smith and Watkins 2005). It is likely that a mixed picture would again emerge as some Christian groups (e.g., some Charismatic churches in Nigeria) have taught women to eschew the cultural scripts of passive sexuality and to pursue and interest their husbands (Pearce 2002), while others have simply enjoined women to be good, clean submissive wives and trust God to protect them from their husband's infidelity or the consequences of it (Rankin, et al. 2005).

The study of religion and HIV risk also needs to assess whether risk differs between men and women within religious groups. It is easy to imagine that it may not because most marriages are religiously homogamous. But Muslim women might be protected more by their partners' circumcision than by their fidelity: even though circumcision does not reduce male to female transmission rates, it does reduce female to male transmission. Therefore, a faithful Muslim wife might be relatively safer with an adulterous husband than the wife of an uncircumcised man with an adulterous husband (because the circumcised man is less likely to acquire HIV from his affairs). Adultery may also have different consequences for men and women; numerous African Christian clergy are supportive of the double-standard that men's infidelity should be forgiven and women's infidelity penalized by divorce (Rankin, et al. 2005). Knowing differences in sources of infection would help us to understand how religion affects sources of risk and where interventions can be targeted to increase the safety of both relatively protected groups and higher risk groups.

Table 1: Religious affiliation and measured HIV sero-status

Authors	Location	Sample	Findings
Gray 2004	38 Sub-Saharan countries	National-level averages	Countries with higher proportion of Muslims had lower HIV prevalence
Killewo, Dahlgren et al. 1994	Tanzania (Kagera Region)	Random sample of 2475 aged 15-54	Wards with a higher proportion of Muslim had a higher prevalence of HIV
Nunn, Kengeya-Kayondo et al. 1994	Uganda (Rural: Masaka District)	3809 over 13 years; 72% of the adult population in 15 neighboring villages	Muslims had lower risk than non-Muslims
Kiwanuka, Gray et al. 1996	Uganda (Rural: Rakai District)	6366 females and 5148 males	Both Muslims and those in Saved/Pentecostal sects had lower risk than Catholics and Protestants
Hawken, Melis et al. 2002	Kenya (Mombassa)	Suburban random sample of 1497 consenting adults 15-49	Muslims lower risk than both Catholics and Protestants
Sagay, Kapiga et al. 2005	Nigeria (Jos, Plateau state)	2657 women receiving antenatal services	Muslims had lower risk than both Catholics and Pentecostals but not Protestants (traditional/other category too small for analysis)

Authors	Location	Sample	Findings
Malamba, Wagner et al. 1994	Uganda (Rural: Masaka District)	233 randomly selected HIV-1-positive cases and 233 negative controls matched on age and village of residence: 132 & 161 interviewed, respectively	Muslims had lower risk than non-Muslims
Kengeya-Kayondo, Kamali et al. 1996	Uganda (Rural: Masaka District)	12588.2 person-years of follow-up of sero-negative individuals	Muslims less likely to sero-convert than non-Muslims
Rakwar, Lavreys et al. 1999	Kenya	752 sero-negative male trucking company workers followed for three monthly intervals	Muslims less likely to sero-convert than adherents of other religions, but no advantage over Catholics or Protestants
Quigley, Munguti et al. 1997	Tanzania (Rural)	Alll HIV+ (338) and 1/8 of HIV- (1078) respondents from a baseline sample	Muslims had same risk as Catholics, Protestants, and Others
Allain, Anokwa et al. 2004	Ghana (Urban: Kumasi)	194: 64 HIV+ and 130 HIV-, age-matched potential blood donors	No Muslim/Christian differences or denominational differences among Christians (SDA category too small for analysis)
Kongnyuy and Wiysonge 2007	Cameroon	Nationally representative (DHS) sample of 2678 formally married or cohabiting men 15-59	No differences between Muslims, Christians, and others

Authors	Location	Sample	Findings
Bwayo, Plummer et al. 1994	Kenya	970 Truck drivers along the Mombasa-Nairobi highway	Muslim and Protestant advantage disappeared when controlling for circumcision
Lawoyin and Adewole 2004	Nigeria (inner city Ibadan)	342 consenting pregnant women attending a randomly selected primary health care clinic	Christians had lower risk than non-Christians
Duda, Darko et al. 2005	Ghana (Accra)	Random sample of 1,328 women 18 and older	No differences in HIV status by religious affiliation (categories not given)
Akani, Erhabor et al. 2005	Nigeria (Port Harcourt)	64 Prospective couples referred from Faith-Based Organisations	Pentecostals had a lower infection rate than those from Orthodox churches

TABLE 2: RELIGION AND PERCEIVED RISK OF HIV INFECTION

AUTHORS	LOCATION	SAMPLE	FINDINGS
Trinitapoli and Regnerus 2006	Rural Malawi	978 men; wave 2 of the MDICP in 3 regions	Men from Pentecostal churches had lower perceived risk; Muslim men had higher perceived risk. Men who attended services regularly had lower perceived risk.
Takyi 2003	Ghana	4843 women; Nationally representative (DHS) data	Muslims and adherents of African traditional religions reported higher risk than Catholics and Protestants
Takyi 2001	Ghana	1546 men; Nationally representative (DHS) data	Chi-square test for association between reported religion and reported risk significant. No and traditional religion 50.4% at risk, Muslim 48.7, Other Christian 42.8, Catholic 39.3, Protestant 38.7
Lagarde, Enel et al. 2000	Senegal (Rural: Central area)	Random sample of 858 adults aged 15-59 years	Men who considered religion to be very important were half as likely to feel at risk of getting HIV; such women were 9.3x more likely to feel at risk

TABLE 3: RELIGION AND PREMARITAL SEX

AUTHORS	LOCATION	SAMPLE	FINDINGS
Feyisetan and Pebley 1989	Nigeria (urban)	Random sample of every-married women in 9 major cities	Lower rates of premarital sex among Muslims explained by earlier marriage. When standardized for age, both Others and Muslims had lower rates than Catholics.
Addai 200	Ghana	Nationally representative sample of 4562 women	Married Muslim women least likely to report having had premarital sex; those from the more conservative Traditional religions, sectarian Christians, or women with No Religion less likely to report premarital sex than Catholics and Protestants
Djamba 2003	Democratic Republic of Congo (Kinshasa)	Random sample of 2,000 women aged 14–24	Those who attended services more often were less likely to have premarital sex

TABLE 4: RELIGION AND AGE AT SEXUAL DEBUT

AUTHORS	LOCATION	SAMPLE	FINDINGS
Nicholas and Durrheim 1995	South Africa	1817 first-year university students; selection procedures not given	Students who scored high on the Rohrbaugh and Jessor religiosity scale experienced a later onset of sexual activity
Odimegwu 2005	Nigeria	1,153 campus-based adolescents (at 2 national universities) aged 10-24	Male students distributing tracts or engaging in other proselytizing had later sexual debut; for female students, Pentecostal affiliation, rating religion important, attending church regularly, praying and reading the Bible daily, and proselytizing all associated with later sexual debut
Hallett, Lewis et al. 2007	Zimbabwe (rural Manicaland Province)	Random sample of 4,138 men and 4,948 women aged 15-44 (77% response)	Women not associated with a church had earlier sexual debut; Men belonging to traditional churches had earlier sexual debut
Agha, Hutchinson et al. 2006	Zambia	Representative probability sample of 5534 women aged 13–20	Young women affiliated with groups that excommunicate members had later sexual debut

TABLE 5: RELIGION AND CURRENT SEXUAL ACTIVITY

AUTHORS	LOCATION	SAMPLE	FINDINGS
Nicholas and Durrheim 1995	South Africa	1817 first-year university students; selection procedures not given	Students who scored high on the Rohrbaugh and Jessor religiosity scale more likely to intend secondary abstinence during the first year at university
Kiwanuka, Gray et al. 1996	Uganda (Rural)	6366 females and 5148 males	More abstinence among Saved/Pentecostal sects than Catholics, Protestants, or Muslims
Slap, Lot et al. 2003	Nigeria (Plateau state)	Students aged 12-21 attending 39 secondary schools	No Christian/Muslim differences in proportion of students reporting abstinence. Proportion of students reporting abstinence increased as reported religious importance increased

TABLE 6: RELIGION AND FIDELITY

AUTHORS	LOCATION	SAMPLE	FINDINGS
Snelling, Omariba et al. 2007	Twenty-three countries participating in DHS III	Nationally representative samples of women	No differences by religious affiliation in reporting sticking to one partner to prevent AIDS
Kiwanuka, Gray et al. 1996	Uganda (Rural)	6366 females and 5148 males	Saved/Pentecostal men and women were less likely to have two or more sexual partners than Catholics, Protestants, and Muslims
Bailey, Neema et al. 1999	Uganda (Industrial Borough, Mbale)	188 circumcised and 177 uncircumcised men aged 17 and older selected by single stage cluster sampling	Muslims had fewer sexual partners in the last year than other circumcised men
Trinitapoli and Regnerus 2006	Malawi (Rural areas in 3 districts)	Random sample of 978 men	Pentecostal, mission Protestant, and AIC men less likely than both Catholics and Muslims to report an extramarital sexual partner in the past year. 45 percent decline in the odds that men report having a recent extramarital sexual partner for each unit increase in service attendance
Clark 2005	Malawi (Rural areas in 3 districts)	Matched married couples 883 wives and 853 husbands in 1998; follow-up in 2001 re-interviewed about 80% of the women and 70% of the men as well as any different or additional marital partners of these individuals.	Both Protestants and Muslims had the same probability of an extramarital sexual partnership in the last year as Catholics

Authors	Location	Sample	Findings
Rakwar, Lavreys et al. 1999	Kenya	752 sero-negative male trucking company workers followed for three monthly intervals	Muslims less likely than other men to report sex with a prostitute
Carter, Kraft et al. 2007	Botswana	807 aged 15–49 years from 7 of the 11 most populous health districts	Christians less likely to report concurrency than those reporting no or traditional religions
Mitsunaga, Powell et al. 2005	Nigeria	Nationally representative sample of 1153 men and their wives	Muslims and "other Christian" (mostly Pentecostal or evangelical) men were less likely to report having an affair in the 12 months before survey than Catholic and Protestant men
Isiugo-Abanihe 1994	Nigeria (5 towns)	Random sample of 3,200 couples	In the descriptive statistics, Pentecostal men and women had the lowest percentages ever having an affair as well as having an affair in the last week. In the multivariate, Pentecostals were combined with Protestants and were no different from Muslim men in probability of recent affair, but adherents of indigenous religion and Catholics were more likely
Lagarde, Enel et al. 2000	Senegal (Rural Central area)	random sample of 858 aged 15-59	Those considering religion to be very important were not more likely to report intending to or actually having become faithful to protect themselves from AIDS. Proportion already being or who intending to become faithful to protect themselves from AIDS was higher among Muslim than Christian men

TABLE 7: RELIGION AND CONDOM USE

AUTHORS	LOCATION	SAMPLE	FINDINGS
Snelling, Omariba et al. 2007	Twenty-three countries participating in DHS III	Nationally representative samples of women	Women belonging to Christian and Islamic but not Buddhist/Hindu religions are more likely to report use of condoms
Nicholas and Durrheim 1995	South Africa	1817 first-year university students; selection procedures not given	Students who scored high on the Rohrbaugh and Jessor religiosity scale were less likely to use condoms
Agha, Hutchinson et al. 2006	Zambia (Lusaka)	Representative probability sample of 5534 women aged 13–20	Few differences in condom use by religious affiliation, but young women affiliated with groups that excommunicate members less likely to use condoms at first sex
Agadjanian 2005	Mozambique (peri-urban areas of Maputo, also rural Chibuto)	731 men and women; congregations selected randomly proportionate to presence in the population; respondents selected randomly within congregations (Zionists oversampled)	Frequency of church attendance significantly decreases the odds of condom use only among mainline church members
Adetunji 2000	Zimbabwe	2,141 men; Nationally representative (DHS) sample	No difference between spiritualist, Christian, traditional religion
Bailey, Neema et al. 1999	Uganda (Industrial Borough, Mbale)	188 circumcised and 177 uncircumcised men aged 17 and older selected by single stage cluster sampling	Muslims were less likely than other circumcised men to have ever used a condom or used one at last sex
Takyi 2003	Ghana	4843 women; Nationally representative (DHS) data	Religious affiliation not associated with condom use

Bibliography

Addai, Isaac. 2000. Religious Affiliation and Sexual Initiation among Ghanaian Women. *Review of Religious Research* 41 (3):328-343.

Adetunji, Jacob. 2000. Condom Use in Marital and Nonmarital Relationships in Zimbabwe. *International Family Planning Perspectives* 26 (4):196-200.

Adogame, Afe. 2007. HIV/AIDS Support and African Pentecostalism: The Case of the Redeemed Christian Church of God (RCCG). *Journal of Health Psychology* 12 (3):475-484.

Agadjanian, Victor. 2005. Gender, Religious Involvement, and HIV/AIDS Prevention in Mozambique. *Social Science & Medicine* 61 (7):1529-1539.

Agadjanian, Victor, and Cecilia Menjívar. 2008. Talking about the "Epidemic of the Millennium": Religion, Informal Communication, and HIV/AIDS in *Sub-Saharan Africa Social Problems* 55 (3):301-321.

Agha, Sohail, Paul Hutchinson, and Thankian Kusanthan. 2006. The effects of religious affiliation on sexual initiation and condom use in Zambia. *Journal of Adolescent Health* 38 (5):550-555.

Akani, C.I., O. Erhabor, and S. Babatunde. 2005. Pre-marital HIV testing in couples from faith-based organisations: experience in Port Harcourt, Nigeria. *Nigerian Journal of Medicine* 14 (1):39-44.

Allain, J.-P., M. Anokwa, A. Casbard, S. Owusu-Ofori, and J. Dennis-Antwi. 2004. Sociology and behaviour of West African blood donors: the impact of religion on human immunodeficiency virus infection. *Vox Sanguinis: International Journal of Transfusion Medicine* 87 (4):233-240.

Bailey, Robert C., Stella Neema, and Richard Othieno. 1999. Sexual behaviors and other HIV risk factors in circumcised and uncircumcised men in Uganda. *Journal of AIDS* 22 (3):294-301.

Bignami-Van Assche, Simona, L.-W. Chao, P. Anglewicz, D. Chilongozi, and A. Bula. 2007. The validity of self-reported likelihood of HIV infection among the general population in rural Malawi. *Sexually Transmitted Infections* 83:35-40.

Bujra, Janet, and Carolyn Baylies. 2000. Responses to the AIDS Epidemic in Tanzania and Zambia. In *AIDS, Sexuality and Gender in Africa: Collective Strategies and Struggles in Tanzania and Zambia*, edited by C.

Baylies, J. Bujra and with the Gender and AIDS Group. London and New York: Routledge.

Bwayo, J., F. Plummer, M. Omari, A. Mutere, S. Moses, J. Ndinya-Achola, P. Velentgas, and J. Kreiss. 1994. Human immunodeficiency virus infection in long-distance truck drivers in East Africa. *Archives of Internal Medicine* 154 (12):139.

Campbell, Catherine. 2003. 'Letting Them Die': Why HIV/AIDS Prevention Programmes Fail. London: James Currey.

Carter, Marion W., Joan Marie Kraft, Todd Koppenhaver, Christine Galavotti, Thierry H. Roels, Peter H. Kilmarx, and Boga Fidzani. 2007. "A Bull Cannot be Contained in a Single Kraal": Concurrent Sexual Partnerships in Botswana. *AIDS and Behavior* 11 (6):822-830.

Clark, Shelley. 2005. Social Networks, Extra-Marital Partnerships, and Suspicion Among Married Couples in Rural Malawi. Paper presented at the IUSSP Conference in Tours, France, July 2005.

Dilger, Hansjörg. 2007. Healing the Wounds of Modernity: Salvation, Community and Care in a Neo-Pentecostal Church in Dar Es Salaam, Tanzania. *Journal of Religion in Africa* 37 (1):59-83.

Djamba, Yanyi K. 2003. Social Capital and Premarital Sexual Activity in Africa: The Case of Kinshasa, Democratic Republic of Congo. *Archives of Sexual Behavior* 32 (4):327-337.

Dunne, M.P., R. Edwards, J. Lucke, M. Donald, and B. Raphael. 1994. Religiosity, sexual intercourse and condom use among university students. *Australian Journal Of Public Health* 18 (3):339-341.

Feldman, Douglas A., Peggy O'Hara, K.S. Baboo, N-i W. Chitalu, and Ying Lu. 1997. HIV prevention among Zambian adolescents Developing a value utilization/norm change model. *Social Science & Medicine* 44 (4):455–468.

Feyisetan, Bamikale, and Anne R. Pebley. 1989. Premarital Sexuality in Urban Nigeria. *Studies in Family Planning* 20 (6):343-354.

Forster, Peter G. 2001. AIDS in Malawi: Contemporary Discourse and Cultural Continuities. *African Studies* 60 (2):245-261.

Garner, R.C. 2000. "Safe Sects? Dynamic Religion and AIDS in South Africa." *The Journal of Modern African Studies* 38(1):41-69.

Gray, Peter B. 2004. HIV and Islam: is HIV prevalence lower among Muslims? *Social Science & Medicine* 58 (9):1751-1756.

Green, E.C., D.T. Halperin, V. Nantulya, and J.A. Hogle. 2006. Uganda's HIV prevention success: the role of sexual behavior change and the national response. *AIDS and Behavior* 10 (4):335-46; discussion 347-350.

Gregson, Simon, Nicola Terceira, Phyllis Mushati, Constance Nyamukapa, and Catherine Campbell. 2004. Community Group Participation: Can it Help Young Women to Avoid HIV? An Exploratory Study of Social Capital and School Education in Rural Zimbabwe. *Social Science & Medicine* 58 (11):2119–2132.

Gregson, Simon, Tom Zhuwau, Roy M. Anderson, and Stephen K. Chandiwana. 1999. Apostles and Zionists: The Influence of Religion on Demographic Change in Rural Zimbabwe. *Population Studies* 53:179-93.

Gregson, Simon, Tom Zhuwau, Roy M. Anderson, and Stephen K. Changiwana. 1998. Is There Evidence for Behaviour Change in Response to AIDS in Rural Zimbabwe? *Social Science & Medicine* 46 (3):321-333.

Gruénais, M.-É. 1999. Does religion protect from AIDS? Congolese religious congregations face pandemic HIV-infection. *Cahiers d'Etudes Africaines* 39 (2):253-270.

Grunseit, A.C., and J. Richters. 2000. Age at first intercourse in an Australian national sample of technical college students. *Australian And New Zealand Journal of Public Health* 24 (1):11-16.

Hallett, Timothy B., James J.C. Lewis, Ben A. Lopman, Constance A. Nyamukapa, Phyllis Mushati, Mainford Wambe, Geoff P. Garnett, and Simon Gregson. 2007. Age at first sex and HIV infection in rural Zimbabwe. *Studies in Family Planning* 38 (1):1-10.

Hawken, Mark P., Reinhilde D.J. Melis, Diana T. Ngombo, Kishorchandra N. Mandaliya, Lucy W. Ng'ang'a, Jessica Price, Gina Dallabetta, and Marleen Temmerman. 2002. Opportunity for prevention of HIV and sexually transmitted infections in Kenyan youth: results of a population-based survey. *Journal of Acquired Immune Deficiency Syndromes* 31 (5):529-535.

Hill, Zelee E., John Cleland, and Mohamad M. Ali. 2004. Religious Affiliation and Extramarital Sex Among Men in Brazil. *International Family Planning Perspectives* 30 (4):20-26.

Isiugo-Abanihe, Uche C. 1994. Extramarital relations and perceptions of HIV/AIDS in Nigeria. *Health Transition Review* 4:111-125.

Kagee, Ashraf, Yoesrie Toefy, Leickness Simbayi, and Seth Kalichman. 2005. HIV prevalence in three predominantly Muslim residential areas in the Cape Town metropole. *South African Medical Journal* 95 (7):512-516.

Kagimu, M., E. Marum, and D Serwadda. 1995. Planning and evaluating strategies for AIDS health education interventions in the Muslim community in Uganda. *AIDS Education and Prevention* 7 (1):10-21.

Kaler, Amy. 2004. AIDS-talk in everyday life: the presence of HIV/AIDS in men's informal conversation in Southern Malawi. *Social Science & Medicine* 59 (2):285-297.

Kalipeni, Ezekiel, Susan Craddock, Joseph R. Oppong, and Jayati Ghosh. 2004. Introduction to Part III: Understanding the Issues in Social Terms. In *HIV/AIDS in Africa: Beyond Epidemiology*, edited by E. Kalipeni, S. Craddock, J. R. Oppong and J. Ghosh. Malden, MA: Blackwell Publishing Ltd.

Kengeya-Kayondo, J.F., A. Kamali, A.J. Nunn, A. Ruberantwari, H.U. Wagner, and D.W. Mulder. 1996. Incidence of HIV-1 infection in adults and socio-demographic characteristics of seroconverters in a rural population in Uganda: 1990-1994. *International Journal Of Epidemiology* 25 (5):1077-1082.

Killewo, J., L. Dahlgren, and A. Sandstrom. 1994. Socio-geographical patterns of HIV-1 transmission in Kagera region, Tanzania. *Social Science & Medicine* 38 (1):129-134.

Kiwanuka, N., R. Gray, N.K. Sewankambo, D. Serwadda, M. Wawer, and C. Li. 1996. Religion, behaviours, and circumcision as determinants of HIV dynamics in rural Uganda. Paper presented at International Conference on AIDS, July 7-12, 1996.

Kongnyuy, E.J., and C.S. Wiysonge. 2007. Alcohol use and extramarital sex among men in Cameroon. *BMC International Health and Human Rights* 7:6.

Lagarde, Emmanuel, Catherine Enel, Karim Seck, Aissatou Gueye-Ndiaye, Jean-Pierre Piau, Gilles Pison, Valerie Delaunay, Ibrahima Ndoye, and Souleymane Mboup. 2000. Religion and Protective Behaviours Toward AIDS in Rural Senegal. *AIDS* 14:2027-2033.

Lawoyin, T.O., and D.A. Adewole. 2004. Predictors of maternal HIV infection at the primary care level in inner city Ibadan. *International Journal of STD & AIDS* 15 (3):165-168.

Lugalla, Joe, Maria Emmelin, Aldin Mutembei, Mwiru Sima, Gideon Kwesigabo, Japhet Killewo, and Lars Dahlgren. 2004. Social, cultural and sexual behavioral determinants of observed decline in HIV infection trends: lessons from the Kagera Region, Tanzania. *Social Science & Medicine* 59 (1):185-198.

Malamba, Samuel S., Hans-Ulrich Wagner, Gillian Maude, Martin Okongo, Andrew J. Nunn, Jane F. Kengeya-Kayondo, and Daan W. Mulder. 1994. Risk factors for HIV-1 infection in adults in a rural Ugandan community: A case-control study. *AIDS* 8 (2):253–257.

Marindo, R., S. Pearson, and J.B. Casterline. 2003. Condom use and abstinence among unmarried young people in Zimbabwe Which strategy, whose agenda? Policy Research Division Working paper No. 170. New York: Population Council.

Mbilinyi, Marjorie, and Naomi Kaihula. 2000. Sinners and Outsiders: The Drama of AIDS in Rungwe. In *AIDS, Sexuality and Gender in Africa: Collective Strategies and Struggles in Tanzania and Zambia*, edited by C. Baylies, J. Bujra and with the Gender and AIDS Group. London and New York: Routledge.

Mbulaiteye, S.M., i A. Ruberantwar, J.S. Nakiyingi, L.M. Carpenter, A. Kamali, and J.A. Whitworth. 2000. Alcohol and HIV: a study among sexually active adults in rural southwest Uganda. *International Journal of Epidemiology* 29 (5):911-915.

McCree, Donna Hubbard, Gina M. Wingood, Ralph DiClemente, Susan Davies, and Katherine F. Harrington. 2003. Religiosity and Risky Sexual Behavior in African-American Adolescent Females. *Journal of Adolescent Health* 33:2-8.

Messersmith, Lisa J., Thomas T. Kane, Adetanwa I. Odebiyi, and Alfred A. Adewuyi. 2000. Who's at Risk? Men's STD Experience and Condom Use in Southwest Nigeria. *Studies in Family Planning* 31 (3):203-216.

Mitsunaga, T.M., A.M. Powell, N.J. Heard, and U.M. Larsen. 2005. Extramarital sex among Nigerian men: polygyny and other risk factors. *Journal of Acquired Immune Deficiency Syndromes* 39 (4):478-488.

Mukiza-Gapere, Jackson, and James P. Ntozi. 1995. Impact of AIDS on Marriage Patterns, Customs and Practices in Uganda. *Health Transition Review* 5 (Supplement):201–208.

Nicholas, Lionel, and Kevin Durrheim. 1995. Religiosity, AIDS, and sexuality knowledge, attitudes, beliefs, and practices of black South-African first-year university students. *Psychological Reports* 77 (3, Pt. 2):1328–1330.

Nunn, A.J., J.F. Kengeya-Kayondo, S.S. Malamba, J.A. Seeley, and D.W. Mulder. 1994. Risk factors for HIV-1 infection in adults in a rural Ugandan community: a population study. *AIDS* 8 (1):81-86.

Odimegwu, Clifford. 2005. Influence of religion on adolescent sexual attitudes and behaviour among Nigerian university students: affiliation or
commitment? *African Journal of Reproductive Health* 9 (2):125-140.

Oppong, Joseph R., and Samuel Agyei-Mensah. 2004. HIV/AIDS in West
Africa: The Case of Senegal, Ghana, and Nigeria. In *HIV/AIDS in
Africa: Beyond Epidemiology*, edited by E. Kalipeni, S. Craddock, J. R.
Oppong and J. Ghosh. Malden, MA: Blackwell Publishing Ltd.

Parrado, Emilio A., Chenoa A. Flippen, and Chris McQuiston. 2004. Use of
Commercial Sex Workers Among Hispanic Migrants in North Caro-
lina: Implications for the Spread of HIV. *Perspectives on Sexual and
Reproductive Health* 36 (4):150-156.

Paul, Charlotte, Julie Fitzjohn, Jason Eberhart-Phillips, Peter Herbison, and
Nigel Dickson. 2000. Sexual abstinence at age 21 in New Zealand: the
importance of religion. *Social Science & Medicine* 51 (1):1-10.

Pearce, Tola Olu. 2002. Cultural Production and Reproductive Issues: The
Significance of the Charismatic Movement in Nigeria. In *Religion and
Sexuality in Cross-Cultural Perspective*, edited by S. Ellingson and M. C.
Green. New York and London: Routledge.

Pfeiffer, James. 2004. Condom Social Marketing, Pentecostalism, and Structural Adjustment in Mozambique: A Clash of AIDS Prevention Messages. *Medical Anthropology Quarterly* 18:77-103.

Pool, Robert, Mary Maswe, J. Ties Boerma, and Soori Nnko. 1996. The Price
of Promiscuity: Why Urban Males in Tanzania are Changing Their
Sexual Behavior. *Health Transition Review* 6:203-222.

Power, R., L. Langhaug, and F. Cowan. 2007. "But there are no snakes in the
wood": risk mapping as an outcome measure in evaluating complex
interventions. *Sexually Transmitted Infections* 83 (3):232-236.

Quigley, M., K. Munguti, H. Grosskurth, J. Todd, F. Mosha, K. Senkoro, J.
Newell, P. Mayaud, G. ka-Gina, A. Klokke, D. Mabey, A. Gavyole, and
R. Hayes. 1997. Sexual Behaviour Patterns and Other Risk Factors for
HIV Infection in rural Tanzania: A Case Control Study. *AIDS* 11:237-
248.

Rakwar, Joel, Ludo Lavreys, Mary Lou Thompson, Denis Jackson, Job Bwayo,
Salim Hassanali, Kishorchandra Mandaliya, Jeckoniah Ndinya-Achola,
and Joan Kreiss. 1999. Cofactors for the acquisition of HIV-1 among
heterosexual men: Prospective cohort study of trucking company
workers in Kenya. *AIDS* 13 (5):607–614.

Rankin, Sally H., Teri Lindgren, William W. Rankin, and Joyce Ng'Oma. 2005. Donkey work: women, religion, and HIV/AIDS in Malawi. *Health Care For Women International* 26 (1):4-16.

Regnerus, Mark D., and Jenny Trinitapoli. 2006. Village Sexual Norms and Links between Religion and HIV Infection Risk in Rural Malawi. Paper presented at the annual meeting of the Population Association of America, Los Angeles, March 31, 2006.

Regnerus, Mark D., and Jeremy E. Uecker. 2007. Religious Influences on Sensitive Self-Reported Behaviors: The Product of Social Desirability, Deceit, or Embarrassment? *Sociology of Religion* 68 (2):145-166.

Reniers, Georges. 2008. Marital Strategies for Regulating Exposure to HIV. *Demography* 45 (2):417-438.

Rostosky, Sharon Scales, Mark D. Regnerus, and Margaret Laurie Comer Wright. 2003. Coital Debut: The Role of Religiosity and Sex Attitudes in the Add Health Survey. *Journal of Sex Research* 40 (4):358-367.

Rwenge, Mburano. 2000. Sexual Risk Behaviors Among Young People in Bamenda, Cameroon. *International Family Planning Perspectives* 26 (3):118-123.

Sa, Zhihong, and Ulla Larsen. 2008. Gender Inequality Increases Women's Risk of HIV Infection in Moshi, Tanzania. *Journal of Biosocial Science* 40 (4):505-525.

Sadgrove, Jo. 2007. 'Keeping Up Appearances': Sex and Religion amongst University Students in Uganda. *Journal of Religion in Africa* 37 (1):116-144.

Sagay, A.S., S.H. Kapiga, G.E. Imade, J.L. Sankale, J. Idoko, and P. Kanki. 2005. HIV infection among pregnant women in Nigeria. *International Journal of Gynaecology and Obstetrics* 90 (1):61-67.

Slap, Gail B., Lucy Lot, Bin Huang, Comfort A. Daniyam, Therese M. Zink, and Paul A. Succop. 2003. Sexual Behaviour of Adolescents in Nigeria: Cross Sectional Survey of Secondary School Students. *British Medical Journal* 326 (7375):15-18.

Smith, Daniel Jordan. 2003. Imagining HIV/AIDS: Morality and Perceptions of Personal Risk in Nigeria. *Medical Anthropology* 22:343-372.

———. 2004. Youth, Sin and Sex in Nigeria: Christianity and HIV/AIDS-Related Beliefs and Behaviour Among Rural-Urban Migrants. *Culture, Health and Sexuality* 6 (5):425-437.

———. 2007. Modern marriage, men's extramarital sex, and HIV risk in Nigeria. *American Journal of Public Health* 97 (6):997-1005.

Smith, Kirsten P., and Susan Cotts Watkins. 2005. Perceptions of Risk and Strategies for Prevention: Responses to HIV/AIDS in Rural Malawi. *Social Science & Medicine* 60 (3):649-660.

Snelling, Dana, D. Walter Rasugu Omariba, Sungjin Hong, Katholiki Georgiades, Yvonne Racine, and Michael H. Boyle. 2007. HIV/AIDS knowledge, women's education, epidemic severity and protective sexual behaviour in low and middle income countries. *Journal of Biosocial Science* 39 (3):421-442.

Takyi, Baffour K. 2001. Correlates of HIV/AIDS-related knowledge and preventive behavior of men in Africa. *Journal of Health and Human Services Administration* 24 (2):234-257.

———. 2003. Religion and Women's Health in Ghana: Insights into HIV/ AIDs Preventive and Protective Behavior. *Social Science & Medicine* 56 (6):1221-1234.

Trinitapoli, Jenny. 2006. Religious Responses to AIDS in Sub-Saharan Africa: An Examination of Religious Congregations in Rural Malawi. *Review of Religious Research* 47 (3):253–270.

Trinitapoli, Jenny, and Mark D. Regnerus. 2006. Religion and HIV Risk Behaviors among Married Men: Initial Results from a Study in Rural Sub-Saharan Africa. *Journal for the Scientific Study of Religion* 45 (4):505-528.

UNAIDS. 2000. Report on the Global HIV/AIDS Epidemic.

Watkins, Susan C. 2004. Navigating AIDS in Rural Malawi. *Population and Development Review* 30 (4):673–705.

Watkins, Susan C., and Chiweni Chimbwete. 2004. Repentence and Hope Among Christians and Muslims in Rural Malawi. *Religion in Malawi* 11:1-13.

White, Richard, John Cleland, and Michel Caraël. 2000. Links between premarital sexual behavior and extramarital intercourse: a multi-site analysis. *AIDS* 14 (15):2323-2331.

Notes on Contributors

Erdmute Alber holds a chair in Social Anthropology at the University of Bayreuth, Germany. She currently serves as vice-dean of the Bayreuth International Graduate School of African Studies (BIGSAS). She has carried out research in Latin America and Africa. Originally specialized in political anthropology, she has worked on childhood and child fosterage in northern Benin since 1998. In Bayreuth, she headed a research project on changing family structures in Ghana, Togo and Benin. She is a member of the Collaborative Research Center 'Local action in Africa' at the University of Bayreuth and the editor of the journal *Sociologus*.

Leslie Bank is Director of the Fort Hare Institute for Social and Economic Research at the University of Fort Hare in Alice, South Africa. A social anthropologist by training, his main research interests are in the field of urban studies, although he is currently managing a large research project investigating land tenure and land reform in the Eastern Cape. He received his doctorate from the University of Cape Town in 2002. He has served as a research fellow at the University of Cambridge's Centre for African Studies and as the Sir Harry Oppenheimer senior research fellow at St Antony's College at Oxford University.

Astrid Bochow is a Ph.D. candidate in social anthropology at the University of Bayreuth, Germany. Since 2004, she has been doing research in Kumasi and Assin Endwa, Ghana, within the framework of the research project, 'Family change in West Africa'. Her research interests are marriage and premarital relationships, concepts of romantic love, sexuality, changes in life courses and youth culture. Her regional interests are Ghana (West Africa) and South Africa.

Abena P. A. Busia is Associate Professor of English at Rutgers University. Her research interests include African American and African literature and cultural studies. Her major works include: *Beyond Survival: African Literature and the Search for New Life*, co-edited with Kofi Anyidoho and Anne Adams (1999), *Theorizing Black Feminisms: the Visionary Pragmatism of Black Women*, co-edited with Stanlie James (1993), and a book of poems, *Testimonies of Exile*. Recent essays include: "In Search of Home" in *Beyond Survival*; "Relocations—Rethinking Britain from Accra, New York and the Map Room of the British Museum" in *Culture and Difference*, edited by David Bennett (1998); "On Cultures of Communication: Notes from Beijing" in Signs 22.1 (1996). She is currently editing a series, Women Writing Africa.

Laurie F. DeRose is a research associate with the Maryland Population Research Center. Her research centers on the demography of underdevelopment: demographic outcomes and decision-making processes in disadvantaged contexts, particularly in sub-Saharan Africa. She is currently the director of research for the *World Family Map Project*, which is assembling comparable cross-national data on causes and outcomes of family strength. She received her PhD in Sociology from Brown University in 1995.

Paloma Durán y Lalaguna earned a PhD on the Jurisprudence of the European Court on Human Rights and has since written many books and articles on Human Rights and Social Rights. She participated in many UN and European meetings, as academic, expert and adviser. She was Counselor for Human Rights and Social Affairs in the Permanent Mission of Spain to the UN during 2001/2004. During that time she was the main negotiator for many resolutions of the UN on Human Rights and Social issues, and she also was the main negotiator on those themes in UN-New York, during the Spanish Presidency of the European Union (2002). She was one of the six experts of the Working Group of the Council of Europe on Affirmative Actions and one of the authors of the report approved by the Council. Currently, she is

Profesora Titular in the Law School of the University Complutense (Madrid, Spain).

Ana Marta González is professor of Ethics and Social Anthropology at the University of Navarra in Pamplona, Spain. She was a Fulbright Scholar at Harvard in 2002-2003 where she worked on the relationship between nature, culture, and morality in Kant's practical philosophy. She has led several research projects, exploring intersections between moral philosophy and social sciences, and is currently leading an interdisciplinary project on "Emotional Culture and Identity." Professor González is the author and editor of several books, including: *Practical Rationality. Scope and Structures of Human Agency* (with Alejandro G. Vigo), *Contemporary Perspectives on Natural Law: Natural Law as a Limiting Concept, Gender Identities in a Globalized World* (with Victor Seidler), *Fashion and Identity: A Multidisciplinary Approach* (with Laura Bovone), *Distinción social y moda* (with Alejandro García), and *Moral, Razon y Naturaleza: Una Investigacion Sobre Tomas de Aquino.*

Florence Oloo is Deputy Vice Chancellor of Strathmore University in Nairobi, Kenya. Dr. Oloo leads the University's development, administration and implementation of Academic Policies and supervision of academic staff and programs. Prior to her appointment at Strathmore, Dr. Oloo served for several years on the faculty of Jomo Kenyatta University of Agriculture and Technology. Her various responsibilities there include teaching chemistry, supervising projects of fourth year students, and helping organize the Kenya Chemical Society Conference. Dr. Oloo received her Bachelor of Science degree in Chemistry from the University of Nairobi, followed by a Masters of Science degree in Chemistry from the University of Ibadan in Nigeria. She received her doctorate in Chemistry from Jomo Kenyatta University of Agriculture and Technology.

Victor J. Seidler is Professor of Social Theory in the Department of Sociology, Goldsmiths, University of London, UK. He has written in the areas of social theory, ethics and gender, particularly in relation to men and masculinities. His most recent book is *Recreating Sexual Politics: Men, Feminism and Politics* (Routledge, 2009).

Daniel Jordan Smith is Associate Professor of Anthropology at Brown University. Smith conducts research in Nigeria focusing on a range of issues, including social change, political culture, kinship, and health. He won the 2008 Margaret Mead Award for his book, *A Culture of Corruption: Everyday Deception and Popular Discontent in Nigeria* (Princeton University Press, 2007). He has completed several research projects with grants awarded by NSF and NIH, with a major focus in the HIV epidemic in Nigeria. Smith is the recipient of the 2007-9 William C. McGloughlin Award for Teaching Excellence in the Social Sciences. Since 2006 he has been Associate Director of the Population Studies and Training Center at Brown University. He received his PhD in Anthropology from Emory University in 1999.

Susanna D. Wing is Assistant Professor of Political Science at Haverford College. She received her PhD in Political Science from UCLA in 2000. Her book, *Constructing Democracy in Transitioning Societies of Africa*, received the 2009 Best Book Award from the African Politics Conference Group. Her research and teaching interests include comparative politics, development, women's rights and Africa. She has conducted fieldwork in Mali, Niger, Benin and Nigeria. Her current project is on legal pluralism and democracy in francophone Africa. In 2007-08 she was on leave and a visiting researcher at the Centre d'etudes des mondes africains in Paris, France. Before coming to Haverford, Susanna taught at UCLA. She was awarded a Chateaubriand Post-doctoral Fellowship and conducted research at the Centre d'étude d'afrique noir (CEAN) at the University of Bordeaux. She has worked as a consultant for USAID and the World Bank.

Index